T0300195

The Internationalisation of Corruption

Scale, Impact and Countermeasures

CLARE FLETCHER
AND
DANIELA HERRMANN

Routledge
Taylor & Francis Group

LONDON AND NEW YORK

First published 2012 by Gower Publishing

2 Park Square, Milton Park, Abingdon, Oxon OX14 4RN
711 Third Avenue, New York, NY 10017, USA

Routledge is an imprint of the Taylor & Francis Group, an informa business

First issued in paperback 2017

Gower Applied Business Research
Our programme provides leaders, practitioners, scholars and researchers with thought provoking, cutting edge books that combine conceptual insights, interdisciplinary rigour and practical relevance in key areas of business and management.

British Library Cataloguing in Publication Data
Fletcher, Clare.
  The internationalisation of corruption : scale, impact and
  countermeasures.
  1. Corruption. 2. Corporations--Corrupt practices.
  3. Financial institutions--Corrupt practices.
  4. Corruption investigation. 5. Corruption--Prevention.
  6. Transnational crime.
  I. Title II. Herrmann, Daniela.
  364.1'323-dc23

Library of Congress Cataloging-in-Publication Data
Fletcher, Clare.
  The internationalisation of corruption : scale, impact and countermeasures
  / by Clare Fletcher and Daniela Herrmann.
    p. cm.
  Includes bibliographical references and index.
  ISBN 978-1-4094-1129-1 (hardback) -- ISBN 978-1-4094-1130-7 (ebook) 1. Transnational crime. 2. Organized crime. 3. Business--Corrupt practices. 4. Political corruption. 5. Economic assistance--Corrupt practices. 6. Corruption. I. Herrmann, Daniela. II. Title.
  HV6252.F54 2012
  364.1'323--dc23   2011031230

ISBN 13: 978-1-4094-1129-1 (hbk)
ISBN 13: 978-1-138-11069-4 (pbk)

Contents

List of Figures, Tables and Lists

Figures

Tables

Lists

List of Abbreviations

ADB	Asian Development Bank
AFDB	African Development Bank
AML	Anti-Money Laundering
ARD	Anti-Retroviral Drugs
AusAID	Australian Government Overseas Aid Program
BAE	BAE Systems PLC
BP	British Petroleum
BPI	Bribe Payers Index
BRIBEline	Business Registry for International Bribery and Extortion
BTI	Bertelsmann Transformation Index
CAP	Common Agricultural Policy
CFE	Certified Fraud Examiners
CFT	Counter Financing of Terrorism
COE	Council of Europe
CPI	Corruption Perceptions Index
CPIA	Country Policy and Institutional Assessment
DAC	Development Assistance Committee
DFID	Department for International Development
DLH	Dalhogg Larsen Horneman
DRC	Democratic Republic of Congo
EC	European Commission
EITI	Extractive Industries Transparency Initiative
EIU	Economist Intelligence Unit
EU	European Union
FATF	Financial Action Task Force
FCPA	Foreign Corrupt Practices Act
FH	Freedom House
FIUs	Financial Intelligence Units
FSA	Financial Services Authority
GCB	Global Corruption Barometer

GI	Global Insight
GOPAC	Global Organisation of Parliamentarians Against Corruption
GPAC	UN Global Programme Against Corruption
GRECO	Group of States Against Corruption
GSK	GlaxoSmithKline
GTI	Global Transparency Initiative
IACC	International Anti-Corruption Conference
IACA	International Anti-Corruption Academy
IACO	Interpol Anti-Corruption Office
IAFCI	International Association of Financial Crimes Investigators
IBRD	International Bank for Reconstruction and Development
ICAR	International Centre for Asset Recovery
ICC	International Chamber of Commerce
IDA	International Development Association
IFI	International Financial Institution
IGAC	International Group for Anti-Corruption Coordination
IGEC	Interpol Group of Experts on Corruption
IMD	International Institute for Management Development
IMF	International Monetary Fund
IMPACT	International Medical Products Anti-Counterfeiting Taskforce
IR	International Relations
ITRI	International Tin Research Institute
IWC	International Whaling Commission
KYC	'Know Your Customer'
LHWP	Lesotho Highlands Water Project
MDG	Millennium Development Goals
MEP	Member of the European Parliament
MLA	Mutual Legal Assistance
NAFDAC	National Agency for Food and Drug Administration and Control
NAO	National Audit Office
NGO	Non-Governmental Organisation
NHS CFSMS	NHS Counter Fraud and Security Management Service
NIS	National Integrity Systems
OAS	Organisation of American States
OCC	Office of the Controller of the Currency
OECD	Organisation for Economic Cooperation and Development
OFF	Oil-For-Food
OLAF	European Anti-Fraud Office
PACI	Partnering Against Corruption Initiative

PEPs	Politically Exposed Persons
PETS	Public Expenditure Tracking Surveys
PTF	Partnership Transparency Fund
SEC	US Securities and Exchange Commission
SFO	Serious Fraud Office
SIDA	Swedish International Development Cooperation Agency
SocGen	Société Générale
SPAI	Stability Pact Anti-Corruption Initiative
TI	Transparency International
TRaCC	Transnational Crime and Corruption Centre
UN	United Nations
UNDP	United Nations Development Programme
UNCAC	United Nations Convention Against Corruption
UNESCO	United Nations Educational, Scientific and Cultural Organisation
UNHCR	United Nations High Commissioner for Refugees
UNICEF	United Nations Children's Fund
UNOCHA	United Nations Office for the Coordination of Humanitarian Affairs
UNODC	United Nations Office on Drugs and Crime
UNTOC	United Nations Convention against Transnational Organised Crime
USAID	United States Agency for International Development
WEF	World Economic Forum
WHO	World Health Organisation

About the Authors

Clare Fletcher and Daniela Herrmann are Senior Researchers at NHS Protect (responsible for countering corruption in the UK health service), and work with the University of Portsmouth to deliver a bespoke postgraduate degree: MSc in Counter Fraud and Counter Corruption Studies. Together, they make up NHS Protect's Research Unit, which carries out research to support evidence-based policy-making on a wide range of counter fraud and corruption issues.

Daniela Herrmann has a keen interest in international anti-corruption research, coupled with skills and experience in policy analysis, evaluation and advocacy. Before joining NHS Protect, Daniela has worked with the UN Development Fund for Women in Beijing and with parliamentarians in Westminster and Brussels. She graduated with an MSc in International Relations from the London School of Economics and a BSc in Social Sciences from Heinrich-Heine University, Düsseldorf. Daniela is also an Accredited Counter Fraud Specialist.

Clare Fletcher has a keen interest in transparency and accountability issues, particularly in relation to the management of public services. She has skills and experience in policy research, analysis and evaluation, having worked for a number of organisations in the public, private and voluntary sectors in the UK, across a broad range of multidisciplinary policy areas. Clare graduated from the University of Birmingham with an MA in Political Science Research Methods and a BSocSc in Political Science and International Studies.

About the authors

Foreword

By Dr Mark Button

It is an enormous pleasure to be asked to write the Foreword for this book. Corruption is a problem across the globe and in some countries it is a devastating blight undermining every aspect of society. It is a problem that arises in political institutions, corporations, industry bodies as well as development agencies in the international community. Corruption is also a problem which varies significantly in its characteristics from country to country, corporation to corporation and industry to industry. There is a growing academic literature on it, but still not enough given the size of the problem and the comparable research output on other problems such as terrorism and drugs.

International corruption is a very important aspect of corruption which deserves much more consideration and this book is a welcome and authoritative addition to the literature on this subject. It illustrates the challenges of measuring corruption and assesses the strengths and weaknesses of some of the measures which are commonly used. The book also reviews the literature to get to grips with the many causes of corruption. There are a diverse range of international, state and non-state bodies combating corruption and the book investigates these.

The best part of the book examines some case studies of corruption by sector. World politics, international business, global finance, transnational organised crime, international aid and world health are all considered in depth. One is struck by the diversity of corruption, the variation in success in challenging it but also the commonness of the damage it does.

The book provides a solid grounding for students at undergraduate and postgraduate level interested in corruption and the comparative nature of it at a global and sector level. It will also be of use to the practitioner working in counter corruption eager to learn of the experience of other sectors.

2011 has already been a good year for the fight against corruption with the International Anti-Corruption Academy acquiring the status of an international organisation. With the good work the academy does in educating the anti-corruption staff from around the globe and the growth in research to develop best practice, that this book will play a small but important part in, there is hope the fight against corruption will become ever more successful.

Dr Mark Button
Reader in Criminology and Director of the Centre for Counter Fraud Studies, University of Portsmouth

1

Introduction

1 Background

In recent years, corruption scandals have hit the headlines all around the world, across a diverse range of institutional, organisational and cultural settings. These series of events have exploded the myth that corruption is a problem which is confined to a specific sector or to the developing world.

The costs of corruption are significant and affect people worldwide. Analysts have linked corruption with political instability, human rights violations, the exacerbation of poverty, the erosion of public confidence in institutions and many other negative outcomes. It has also been identified as a major obstacle to political, social and economic development in many parts of the world.

The increasing complexity of corrupt transactions presents significant challenges for those working in the field of counter corruption. In a globalised world characterised by increasing flows of goods, capital, people and knowledge, corrupt activity not only takes place within national boundaries but also across them. Furthermore, the broadening and deepening of political and economic integration means that events in one part of the world polity can often have knock-on effects elsewhere; even when corruption occurs at either local or national level, its consequences can resonate globally.

The 'internationalisation' of corruption has profound implications for counter corruption efforts, which have traditionally fallen within the remit of national politics and law-making. The proliferation of corruption transnationally has destroyed the notion that corruption is a domestic political issue which can be dealt with by individual countries alone, and is increasingly perceived as a problem which can only be addressed collectively by a collaborative approach between international actors.

Indeed, as the international community strives to meet its Millennium Development Goals (MDGs), tackling corruption has been placed firmly on its agenda. Over the past decade, therefore, visible attempts have been made to collectively counter this threat, including the creation of several international conventions and treaties in this policy area.

It is in this context that there has been a growing interest in the subject of corruption, internationally, as well as a burgeoning workforce of professionals tasked with fighting corruption in their respective fields. This includes, for example, counter corruption specialists in public and private sector organisations, investigative and policing personnel with roles in counter corruption and policy/law makers with responsibilities for countering corruption.

Correspondingly, governments and other organisations are investing more and more in the expansion of 'knowledge' in this important area of study. The creation of the International Anti-Corruption Academy – the world's first educational institute dedicated to fighting corruption – is indicative of this trend, as is the emergence of several bespoke degree programmes on the subject and numerous initiatives to professionalise the investigation of corruption.

Despite the growing interest of governments, organisations and academic institutions in addressing this worldwide problem, literature on corruption is relatively sparse. As Lambsdorff (2007: 1) notes: 'Corruption, the misuse of public power for private benefit, turns out to be a relatively new challenge for social sciences. It has been an issue for politics and society for many centuries, but its systematic scientific treatment is rather novel.'

This text is therefore intended to offer a timely contribution to literature in this field, by providing an accessible, entry-level introduction to this area of study.

The complex nature of corruption and the multiple levels at which it pervades international society means that the subject can be approached from a wide range of academic disciplines; by its very nature, the subject is interdisciplinary. The text will develop an inclusive and broad-based understanding of corruption from the perspective of international studies as an interdisciplinary space in the social sciences. The book is written from a social science perspective, making it accessible to anyone approaching the study of corruption from any one of the different disciplinary traditions.

2 Defining Corruption

One of the difficulties of examining corruption from an international perspective is the challenge of achieving a common definition of the term. Indeed, definitions employed by different nations, legal systems, organisations and cultures can vary. As Iyer and Samociuk (2006: 2) note, 'there are dozens of definitions of … corruption in use around the world'. For example, Table 1.1 demonstrates the range of definitions which are currently employed internationally. This is by no means an exhaustive list but indicates the nuances created by the existence of different definitions.

Table 1.1   Definitions of corruption from around the world

Jurisdiction	Definition
International	'The misuse of public powers, office and authority for private gain through briber, extortion, influence, peddling, nepotism, fraud, speed money or embezzlement' (United Nations Development Programme 1999: 7)
Europe	'Requesting, offering, giving or accepting, directly or indirectly, a bribe or any undue advantage or prospect thereof, which distorts the proper performance of any duty of behaviour required of the recipient of the bribe, the undue advantage or the prospect thereof' (Council of Europe 1999)
Africa	'The Soliciting, accepting, obtaining, giving, promising or offering of gratification by way of a bribe or other personal temptations of inducement or the misuse or abuse of a public office for private advantage or benefit' (Zambia Anti-Corruption Commission 1996, s.3)
Asia	'Corruption is the asking, receiving or agreeing to receive, giving, promising or offering any gratification as an inducement or reward to a person to do or not to do any act, with a corrupt intention' (Corruption Prevention Investigation Bureau, Singapore 2001)
Middle East	'Corruption is the behaviour of private individuals or public officials who deviate from set responsibilities and use their position of power in order to serve private ends and secure private gains' (Lebanon Anti-Corruption Initiative Report 1999)
North America	'The misuse of public office for private gain' (United States Agency for International Development 2003)
Academic	'The use of public office for private advantage, the latter term understood not only in the pecuniary sense but also in terms of status and influence' (Palmier 1983: 207)

Source: Gilligan and Bowman (2007: 172).

Tanzi argues that an increasingly common definition of corruption is the 'abuse of public power for private benefit' (Tanzi 1998: 564). It has been suggested by some that this definition should be extended, since it cannot be applied to all types of corruption. Corruption can also be committed not only for private gain but, as Tanzi points out, 'for the benefit of one's party, class, tribe, friends, family, and so on' (Tanzi 1998: 564). Furthermore, this definition does not address the problem of corruption in the private sector, or the links between private and public sector corruption, such as the role of the private sector in fostering corruption in the public sector. Not only public officials may be tempted by bribes, but also those in positions of trust or authority in private corporations, NGOs or charities. The Asian Development Bank (2008), for example, has addressed some of the above issues by defining corruption as 'the abuse of public or private office for personal gain'. The Bank also provides a more comprehensive definition: 'Corruption involves behavior on the part of officials in the public and private sectors, in which they improperly and unlawfully enrich themselves and/or those close to them, or induce others to do so, by misusing the position in which they are placed' (Asian Development Bank 2008).

As the above discussion demonstrates, while it is possible to identify commonalities in terms of respective definitions, there remain tensions between competing classifications. Table 1.2 demonstrates some of these commonalities and tensions.

Table 1.2   Common threads and tensions in defining corruption

Threads	Tensions
The misuse of discretionary power	Generally a much greater focus on the public sector, and less on the private
Active	
	Generally economic in motivation with less
Gain/benefit may be for the individual or for others	consideration given to alternative motivations of the actions
Violation, e.g. of trust, position	Must the gain/benefit be pecuniary? Or may the advantage be social/hierarchical?
Positive result for one or more parties, with generally a negative consequence for society	Can corruption ever be seen as advantageous – even if only in the short term?
Socially aggregated phenomenon	

Source: Gilligan and Bowman (2007: 173).

In addition to defining the term itself, analysts have sought to provide typologies of corruption; in other words, defining which types of behaviour can be classified as 'corrupt'. In this sense, corruption is often used as an umbrella term to refer to a range of specific illicit activities. For example, Langseth (2006) lists different types of corruption:

- 'grand' corruption

- 'petty' corruption

- 'active' corruption

- 'passive' corruption

- bribery

- embezzlement

- theft

- fraud

- extortion

- abuse of discretion

- favouritism

- nepotism, and

- improper political contributions.

 For a more detailed consideration of these terms, refer to Langseth (2006: 9–14). Also see Brown (2006).

Even within the above categories, definitional variations abound. Taking fraud, for example, a report published by the NHS Counter Fraud and Security Management Service (NHS CFSMS 2006) identified a range of different national definitions for fraud. These are highlighted in Table 1.3.

Table 1.3   National definitions of fraud

Country	Definition
Australia	The criminal definition of fraud is 'dishonestly obtaining a benefit by deception or other means' (Australian Attorney General's Department, cited by NHS CFSMS 2006: 11).
Canada	A fraudster is defined under Section 380 of the Canadian Criminal Code as someone 'who, by deceit, falsehood or other fraudulent means, whether or not it is a false pretence within the meaning of this Act, defrauds the public or any person, whether ascertained or not, of any property, money or valuable security of any service' (Canadian Public Works and Government Services, cited ibid.: 30).
France	There is no legal definition of fraud under French law. However, the following activities have been defined as illegal (ibid.: 46–47): • breach of trust; • counterfeiting; • deceit; • forgery of means of payment; • intentional use of or attempt to use counterfeit or forged payment cards, and so on; • theft; and • violation of an automated data system.
Germany	The German Criminal Code (Strafgesetzbuch, StGB) defines fraud in Section 263 as an act committed by someone with the intent of obtaining for themselves or another an unlawful material benefit and which damages the assets of another by (ibid.: 62): • provoking or affirming a mistake; • pretending that false facts exist; or • distorting or suppressing true facts.
Ireland	There is no legal definition of fraud *per se*; however, the following behaviours together are classed as being fraudulent (ibid.: 79): • deception; • dishonesty; and • intention.
United States	The criminal definition of fraud is 'a false representation of a matter of fact – whether by words or by conduct, by false or misleading allegations, or by concealment of what should have been disclosed – that deceives and is intended to deceive another so that the individual will act upon it to her or his legal injury' (E-notes: Fraud, cited ibid.: 90).

Differences notwithstanding, there is a degree of convergence between these definitions. For example, as the NHS Counter Fraud and Security Management Service report points out, 'the main common elements that constitute an offence of fraud are dishonesty, deceit, deception and intent' (NHS CFSMS: 6).

Due to the different interpretations of corruption, operationalising the concept 'corruption' is often deemed to be challenging. For example, some question whether it is possible to be compare incidences of corruption in different countries if their conceptions of what constitutes corrupt acts differ. These issues will be considered in greater detail throughout the text. However, the purpose of this introduction is not to resolve these issues of definition, but to offer some conceptual caveats. It is perhaps worth noting the sentiments of a prominent anti-corruption scholar, Johann Graf Lambsdorff (2007: 15):

> *Definitions of corruption can be discussed at length without necessarily providing an actual value to the reader. Still some researchers display their endeavours in this area. They are willing to go into time-consuming debate and are fierce in preferring one approach to another. Such debate, however, tends to absorb much of the energy that is desperately needed elsewhere. Recognising this, some colleagues have started to avoid definitions of corruption, claiming that most cases of corruption are unambiguously perceived by most observers.*

For a detailed consideration of the definitional issues relating to corruption, read Chapter 2 of Holmes (2006), De Sousa, Larmour and Hindess (2009) and Gambetta (2002).

3 The Study of Corruption in an International Context

Analysts engaged with the study of corruption in an international context have sought to answer a number of different questions. For example:

- Is it possible to measure the scale of corruption globally?

- Is it possible to identify the causes of corruption?

- What is the impact of corruption?

- To what extent does corruption exist in different parts of the world?

- How can the international community effectively counter corruption?

- Who are the actors involved and what progress is being made?

- Which sectors are most affected by corruption, internationally?

- Which international transactions are vulnerable to corruption, and which actors are involved?

This text will give an introduction to the above themes.

4 Structure of the Book

PART I – SCOPE AND IMPACT OF CORRUPTION

Part I introduces perspectives on the scale and impact of international corruption. It considers the various surveys and measurement methods employed, and the impact of these levels of corruption around the world.

CHAPTER 2 – SCALE AND MEASUREMENT

This chapter considers the importance of measuring corruption, internationally. It introduces some measurement methods and discusses the relative merits of these approaches, while also looking at the costs of corruption.

CHAPTER 3 – CAUSES AND CONSEQUENCES

This chapter introduces perspectives on the causes and consequences of international corruption. It concludes by highlighting some of the particularly grave effects that these illicit activities have on economic, social and political development in the developing world.

PART II – CHALLENGING CORRUPTION

Part II introduces the response of the international community to corruption. It considers the roles of state and non-state actors and their interaction, and the counter measures that have been used to combat international corruption.

CHAPTER 4 – COUNTERING CORRUPTION: THE ROLE OF STATE ACTORS

This chapter considers the role of state actors in challenging corruption. It examines the nature and evolution of international regimes and international law, including developments in this field in terms of international conventions tackling international corruption, and introduces some of the critical assessments which have been made in relation to these approaches.

CHAPTER 5 – COUNTERING CORRUPTION: THE ROLE OF NON-STATE ACTORS

This chapter focuses on the role of non-state actors, or Non-Governmental Organisations (NGOs), and their efforts to counter international corruption. It also considers how these organisations interact with the international regimes and regulatory frameworks outlined in Chapter 4.

PART III – SECTOR ANALYSES AND CASE STUDIES

Part III introduces some of the sectors affected by international corruption, including politics, business, finance, transnational organised crime, international aid and world health. Each chapter includes detailed case studies and examples to highlight some of the issues identified in relation to each sector.

CHAPTER 6 – CORRUPTION AND WORLD POLITICS

This chapter considers corruption in the context of world politics. It examines both the governmental and intergovernmental level of international politics by examining corrupt political leaders, and corruption specific to the European Union and the United Nations. The chapter concludes with a case study on vote-buying in the International Whaling Commission.

CHAPTER 7– CORRUPTION AND INTERNATIONAL BUSINESS

This chapter considers corruption in international business. It examines corporate bribery in emerging markets, and explores corporate governance and business ethics. It also introduces various international anti-bribery laws and concludes with a case study on BAE Systems' controversial arms deals with Saudi Arabia.

CHAPTER 8 – CORRUPTION AND GLOBAL FINANCE

This chapter introduces the problem of corruption in global finance and focuses on the problem of rogue trading, the role of auditing firms and financial regulation in both the EU and the US. The chapter also provides an overview of the US Sarbanes-Oxley Act and concludes with a case study of Bernard Madoff and his 'Ponzi' scheme.

CHAPTER 9 – CORRUPTION AND TRANSNATIONAL ORGANISED CRIME

This chapter considers the links between corruption and transnational organised crime. In particular, it examines the role of money laundering, offshore havens and Anti-Money Laundering regimes. The chapter also briefly visits other forms of transnational organised crime which are linked to corruption, such as the illegal drug trade, human trafficking and illicit arms trade. The chapter introduces the concept of 'politically exposed persons' and concludes with a case study on Pinochet and Riggs Bank.

CHAPTER 10 – CORRUPTION AND INTERNATIONAL AID

This chapter introduces the problem of corruption in the field of international aid and examines the vulnerabilities evident in both humanitarian and development aid. It explores the problem of accountability and the efforts by aid agencies to minimise the risk of corruption. The chapter considers the role of the World Bank and its anti-corruption initiatives and concludes with a case study on public expenditure-tracking surveys in the Ugandan-education sector.

CHAPTER 11 – CORRUPTION AND WORLD HEALTH

This chapter looks at corruption in world health and considers why this sector is particularly vulnerable and how corruption is affecting health in the developing world. It analyses the impact of the proliferation of counterfeit medicines into the global health market and the effects of corruption on the HIV/AIDS epidemic. The chapter concludes with a case study on the global fight against fake malaria drugs.

CHAPTER 12 – SUMMARY

This chapter summarises the key points and themes visited in this book and offers suggestions for further study.

PART I

Scope and Impact of Corruption

2

Scale and Measurement

1 Introduction

This chapter considers the importance of measuring corruption, introduces some of the indices and surveys that have been used to quantify the scale and extent of international corruption, and considers the relative merits of these approaches.

2 Why Measure International Corruption?

The measurement of corruption is deemed important for several reasons. Gorta (2006: 205) summarises: 'not only does it draw attention to the extent of the issue, thus promoting the need to take action, but it also helps us identify how and where to focus these practical interventions'. In other words, without knowing what types of corruption are most widespread in different systems, sectors or countries, or where corruption is most likely to occur, it is difficult to know where to direct efforts to counter the phenomenon.

Furthermore, by attempting to measure corruption levels across time, policy-makers and anti-corruption advocates are better able to measure the relative successes of anti-corruption strategies. As Gorta (2006: 205) points out, to evaluate the success of different corruption minimisation strategies, or measure the performance of an anti-corruption strategy, it is necessary to: 'compare the amount (and type) of corruption that was occurring before an intervention with the amount that occurred after the intervention and to see how any changes in the amount or nature of the corruption compare to "before" and "after" measures with similar systems where there was no intervention'.

However, while most commentators agree on the value of attempting to measure international corruption, this is by no means a simple task. As Huberts, Lasthuizen and Peeters (2006: 265) note:

> We all agree that corruption is an important and complex phenomenon and we agree that we disagree about its content. There are many different theories and conceptual frameworks, which lead to a multitude of descriptions, explanations and evaluations. As a consequence, to attempt to measure 'corruption' is, by definition, a risky and much disputed endeavour.

Measurement issues that are most frequently cited as problematic are the lack of consensus about the definition of corruption, the hidden nature of corruption, and disagreements over which types of data can be used reliably as indicators.

3 Measurement Issues

3.1 LACK OF CONSENSUS ON THE DEFINITION OF CORRUPTION

Any meaningful attempt to measure the incidence of corruption on a cross-country basis requires that data is compiled using a common definition or understanding of corruption. Without a consensus on the definition, it is almost impossible to reconcile different data sets and they become incommensurable.

As Chapter 1 demonstrated, arriving at a definition of corruption is far from easy. Some analysts would argue, therefore, that it is almost impossible to measure the incidence of corruption across nations because legal definitions and cultural understandings of fraudulent and corrupt acts vary so much from nation to nation. As Xin and Rudel (2004: 300) comment, 'what people call corruption in one place may be regarded as a legal exercise to influence in another place'. For example, Furnivall suggests that cultural differences between the British and Burmese can explain why Burma was viewed as corrupt by British standards. In many cases, he argues, where the British perceived the Burmese to be engaging in corrupt activity, 'the Burmese were simply following their customary norms of correct conduct' (cited by Klitgaard 1998: 3).

Refer to Chapter 6 of Klitgaard (1998) for a more detailed consideration of culturally specific interpretations of corruption.

This difficulty is compounded by the fact that, as Gorta notes, commentators often write about corruption as if it were a single, unitary phenomena. The reality is, as Chapter 1 demonstrates, that the term 'corruption' encompasses many different forms of activity – from grand corruption that pervades the highest levels of government to the bribery of payroll officials, embezzlement, extortion, nepotism and many more (Langseth 2006). Gorta (2006: 204–5) suggests, therefore, that the multi-faceted nature of corruption raises several problematic questions about what a measure of corruption could possibly look like and, in particular, whether all these different facets can be combined into a single measure.

To counter these criticisms, some would argue that recent years have in fact witnessed a growing international consensus on the definition. Certainly, the growing number of international conventions that seek to regulate international corruption would indicate a degree of consensus among signatories. As Xin and Rudel (2004: 300) noted: 'The international trends in the contexts and meanings of corruption suggest that it may be possible to construct a valid and reliable index of corruption from cross-national surveys that ask people questions about the local incidence of corruption.'

Furthermore, in terms of the multi-faceted nature of corruption, commentators point to the fact that survey questions have become increasingly specific and focused in order to address this ambiguity (Kaufmann, Kraay and Mastruzzi 2006).

3.2 THE HIDDEN NATURE OF CORRUPTION

Measuring the incidence of any kind of crime tends to be problematic because crime often goes unreported. But since crimes such as theft or assault have direct victims, criminologists can attempt to quantify their prevalence by, for example, conducting victimisation surveys, which entail 'interviewing a representative sample of the population to find out what, if any, crimes they have been subject to in a given period of time' (Gorta 2006: 204). This is far more difficult in the case of corruption. Unlike crimes such as theft and assault, corruption has no direct victims. It tends to be the community at large that ultimately bears the brunt of corruption – indirectly, through the diversion of funds from public goods and services. This means corruption often goes unnoticed.

This is compounded by the fact that most fraudulent or corrupt activities tend to be carried out in secret, with few or no witnesses. As Sandholtz and Gray (2003: 775) point out: 'By their very nature, corrupt acts are intended to be secretive.' Corruption is therefore even less likely to be reported than other crimes because 'that which is not witnessed cannot be reported' (Gorta 2006: 204).

The picture may be complicated further still as corrupt individuals modify their behaviour and activities in the face of increasingly sophisticated methods of detection and measurement. This difficulty is summarised in a World Bank publication (2004: 6):

> *Corruption is a dynamic phenomenon; it develops and mutates, reacts and transforms to changing circumstances. We need to be aware of the limits of measurement. Measurements that focus in on one dimension might miss relevant and even contradictory changes in other dimensions. The more effective that existing measurement efforts are at shedding light on corrupt practices in a society, the more efforts will be made by corrupt members of that society to transform those practices into less visible and measurable forms.*

3.3 THE USE OF DIFFERENT TYPES OF DATA

A third issue relates to the types of data used to measure corruption. This debate can be seen as part of a wider dialogue in the social sciences about the extent to which we can construct knowledge about the social world and, correspondingly, *how* we can construct this knowledge in terms of research methods and types of data used. In social science research terms, this is often expressed using the following concepts:

Ontology

Ontology is best described as someone's image of social reality – in other words, what they believe exists in that reality (Grix 2002: 177). Ontology is the starting point of all research, since it determines what we think there is to know – or, what phenomena exist that can be researched. It can be said that those seeking to measure corruption have a common ontological position, in so far as they see corruption as something which exists in social reality.

Epistemology

Epistemology is concerned with the theory of knowledge and *how* knowledge can be constructed in terms of its methods, validation and 'the possible ways of gaining knowledge of social reality, whatever it is understood to be. In short, claims about how what is assumed to exist can be known' (Blaikie, cited in Grix 2002: 177). As will be demonstrated, analysts seeking to measure corruption differ in their epistemological positions. In other words, they disagree about how to acquire this knowledge, and use a range of different methods and data sources.

Methodology

Methodology is intrinsically linked to epistemology; a chosen methodology determines how researchers go about acquiring knowledge. Choosing a methodology invariably involves making decisions about what types of data will be used, from what source, and what methods will be used to capture this information. Researchers have employed a number of different methodologies in an attempt to capture the incidence of corruption.

For a good overview of these concepts and their applicability to social science research, see Grix (2002).

In terms of the study of corruption, analysts represent a range of epistemological and methodological positions. Some analysts prefer the use of 'objective' data and seek to provide 'quantitative assessments of the extent of corruption in a country or within specific sectors of a country' (Langseth 2006: 14). Others have relied on 'subjective', qualitative data, providing analyses based on perceptions about the types of corruption that are prevalent in a given sector/country/transaction or the likelihood of certain acts taking place in different contexts.

'Objective' data

Kaufmann, Kraay and Mastruzzi (2006) argue that it is possible to provide objective indicators of opportunities and/or incentives for corruption, by tracking countries' institutional features, such as procurement practices and budget transparency. Certainly, surveys of this kind are already underway . But, as Kaufmann, Kraay and Mastruzzi. also point out, these indicators do not measure corruption *per se*, but the possibility of corruption. Furthermore, these surveys 'as yet have relatively limited country coverage, especially among developing countries' (2006: 2).

Sandholtz and Gray (2003: 775) suggest that the possibility of constructing an objective indicator by surveying and coding newspaper reports of the incidence of corruption. However, as they themselves point out, this approach has its own limitations because it relies on the quality of press coverage, which in turn rests on the effectiveness of the legal system in question in exposing corrupt acts and on the freedom of the press in that country, neither of which can be assumed, particularly in less developed countries.

We might conclude, therefore, that while it would be desirable to gather 'hard', objective data about the scale of corruption, it is extremely difficult to obtain such observations and measurements in practice.

'Subjective' data

Researchers have attempted to overcome this stumbling block by turning to the use of subjective rather than objective data. This type of data is typically assembled by surveying the perceptions or views of relevant stakeholders, whether firms, public officials, NGOs, multilateral donors, private sector representatives or the general public. These data sources can be used in a variety of ways, whether individually, relating specifically to a particular sector or industry, or in aggregate, by combining data from several sources.

Critics of these types of approach claim that subjective data is unreliable in measuring corruption because it merely reflects the vague perceptions of corruption as opposed to objective realities. Furthermore, as Dahl (2009: 164) argues:

> *Measuring perceptions of corruption can have an endogenous effect:*
> *if people read in the newspaper that Lithuania is perceived as a highly*

corrupt country, this will influence their own perception of corruption in Lithuania, which then is measured in another type of, or later, survey. The results of such measurements are thus being reproduced and reinforced.

However, as Kaufmann *et al.* (2006) point out, 'since corruption usually leaves no paper trail, responses about corruption based on individuals' actual experiences are sometimes the best available, and the only information we have'. They would also contend that the measurement of perceptions of corruption is important in itself, because if citizens believe their courts and police force, for example, to be corrupt, 'they will not want to use their services regardless of what the objective reality is' (ibid. 2006: 1). Furthermore, perceptions of corruption in specific countries, drawn from different surveys, have tended to be consistent:

It is telling ... that the correlation of perceptions of corruption from cross-country surveys of domestic firms tend to be very highly correlated with perceptions of corruption from commercial risk rating agencies or multilateral development banks (Kaufmann, et al. 2006: 2).

For a more detailed discussion of the relative merits of objective and subjective data in measuring corruption, and direct/indirect approaches to measurement, refer to Kaufmann *et al.* (2006) and Kalnins (2005).

For further discussion of the difficulties in measuring corruption, see Sik (2002).

4 Surveys and Indices

As the discussion above indicates, measuring corruption on an international scale is no simple task. Despite this, several attempts have been made to quantify the scale of international corruption, using a range of survey methods. Among these are public polls, private sector surveys, surveys of perceptions of risk-taking agencies and consultancies, and reports published by international financial institutions. Overall, the use of these indices is believed to have 'helped bring corruption into the spotlight as an economic and institutional issue, increasingly divorced from its local context' (Ivanov 2007: 34).

4.1 TRANSPARENCY INTERNATIONAL

Transparency International (TI) has pioneered several quantitative diagnostic tools intended to measure levels of transparency and corruption at local and global levels. Arguably the most comprehensive, the Corruptions Perceptions Index (CPI) was released in 1995 but has since been complemented by the development of additional measurement tools: the Bribe Payers Index (BPI) and Global Corruption Barometer (GCB). In addition to these indices, TI's national chapters have developed their own corruption measurement tools (TI n.d.a.).

4.1.1 Corruption Perceptions Index

The Corruption Perceptions Index (CPI) is the best known of TI's various tools for measuring fraud and corruption and it has become a widely-used measure for the purposes of social science research (Sandholtz and Gray 2003). It ranks countries in terms of the degree to which corruption is perceived to exist among public officials and politicians. TI (TI n.d.b.) describes it as follows:

> The CPI is an aggregate indicator that combines different sources of information about corruption, making it possible to compare countries. ... It captures information about the administrative and political aspects of corruption. Broadly speaking, the surveys and assessments used to compile the index include questions relating to bribery of public officials, kickbacks in public procurement, embezzlement of public funds, and questions that probe the strength and effectiveness of public sector anti-corruption efforts.

TI works with the definition of corruption as 'the abuse of entrusted power for private gain (TI 2010: 4) and assigns a score to each country, ranging from 0 (most corrupt) to 10 (least corrupt) each year the survey is carried out. It draws on different assessments and business opinion surveys carried out by 'independent and reputable institutions' (TI 2010: 4). The 2010 CPI was compiled using data from the following surveys and assessments which were published between January 2009 and September 2010:

1. Asian Development Bank (ADB) – Country Performance Assessment Ratings

2. African Development Bank (AFDB) – Country Policy and Institutional Assessments

3.   Bertelsmann Foundation (BTI) – Bertelsmann Transformation Index

4.   World Bank (CPIA) – Country Policy and Institutional Assessment

5.   Economist Intelligence Unit (EIU) – Country Risk Service and Country Forecast

6.   Freedom House (FH) – Nations in Transit

7.   Global Insight (GI) – Country Risk Ratings

8.   IMD International (IMD) – IMD World Competitiveness Yearbooks 2009 and 2010

9.   World Economic Forum (WED) – Global Competitiveness Report, 2009 and 2010

10.   Political and Economic Risk Consultancy (PERC) – Asian Intelligence Newsletters, 2009 and 2010.

For a more detailed overview of these data sources, coverage, the nature of the survey questions and respondents, and methodology used for compiling the data, see TI (2010: 15–19).

For an overview of additional tools and surveys used in assessing country governance, country counter-corruption initiatives and global comparisons of these national assessments, see Governance Assessment Portal (n.d.).

The CPI is often regarded as the most comprehensive measurement tool of international corruption. However, it is not unproblematic and critics are quick to point to its limitations. Lambsdorff, for example, points out that the index only really provides a 'snapshot' of the views of business people, with less focus on year-on-year analysis. Furthermore, since different data sources are used from one year to the next, Sandholtz and Gray (2003: 775) argue, 'the CPI does not yet lend itself to a time-series estimation that would allow one to answer more adeptly some questions of causation'. They also point out (2003: 776) that 'the

CPI has not been calculated for every year for every country. Some countries are added in one year and dropped in another, depending on the availability of survey data'. This poses limitations in terms of methodological consistency. As the index designers themselves acknowledge: 'One of the drawbacks to this approach is that year-to-year comparisons of a country's score do not only result from a changing perception of a country's performance but also from a changing sample and methodology' (TI n.d.b).

However, the index designers maintain that 'in practice, the sources continue to show a high degree of correlation. So, the impact of differing samples and methodologies on the outcome appears to be rather small' (ibid.).

Table 2.1 was compiled using CPI data, and indicates scores and rankings for countries in 2001, 2004, 2007 and 2010. For some countries the data appears to highlight major differences in the ranking positions, inferring great improvements in tackling corruption. However, it is important to note that this may not necessarily be the result of real changes but instead reflect changing methodology. For example, in 2001 only 91 countries were surveyed, compared with 180 in 2007.

Table 2.1   Corruption Perceptions Index

Country	Year							
	2010		2007		2004		2001	
	Score	Rank	Score	Rank	Score	Rank	Score	Rank
Denmark	9.3	1	9.4	1	9.5	3	9.5	2
New Zealand	9.3	1	9.4	1	9.6	2	9.4	3
Singapore	9.3	1	9.3	4	9.3	5	9.2	4
Finland	9.2	4	9.4	1	9.7	1	9.9	1
Sweden	9.2	4	9.3	4	9.2	6	9.0	6
Canada	8.9	6	8.7	9	8.5	12	8.9	7
Netherlands	8.8	7	9.0	7	8.7	10	8.8	8
Australia	8.7	8	8.6	11	8.8	9	8.5	11
Switzerland	8.7	8	9.0	7	9.1	7	8.4	12
Norway	8.6	10	8.7	9	8.9	8	8.6	10
Iceland	8.5	11	9.2	6	9.5	3	9.2	4
Luxembourg	8.5	11	8.4	12	8.4	13	8.7	9
Hong Kong	8.4	13	8.3	14	8.0	16	7.9	14

Table 2.1   *Continued*

Ireland	8	14	7.5	17	7.5	17	7.5	18
Austria	7.9	15	8.1	15	8.4	13	7.8	15
Germany	7.9	15	7.8	16	8.2	15	7.4	20
Barbados	7.8	17	6.9	23	7.3	21	–	–
Japan	7.8	17	7.5	17	6.9	24	7.1	21
Qatar	7.7	19	6.0	32	5.2	38	–	–
United Kingdom	7.6	20	8.4	12	8.6	11	8.3	13
Chile	7.2	21	7.0	22	7.4	20	7.5	18
Belgium	7.1	22	7.1	21	7.5	17	6.6	24
United States	7.1	22	7.2	20	7.5	17	7.6	16
Uruguay	6.9	24	6.7	25	6.2	28	5.1	35
France	6.8	25	7.3	19	7.1	22	6.7	23
Estonia	6.5	26	6.5	28	6.0	31	5.6	28
Slovenia	6.4	27	6.6	27	6.0	31	5.2	34
Cyprus	6.3	28	5.3	39	5.4	36	–	–
United Arab Emirates	6.3	28	5.7	34	6.1	29	–	–
Israel	6.1	30	6.1	30	6.4	26	7.6	16
Spain	6.1	30	6.7	25	7.1	22	7.0	22
Portugal	6	32	6.5	28	6.3	27	6.3	25
Botswana	5.8	33	5.4	38	6.0	31	6.0	26
Puerto Rico	5.8	33	–	–	–	–	–	–
Taiwan	5.8	33	5.7	34	5.6	35	5.9	27
Bhutan	5.7	36	5.0	46	–	–	–	–
Malta	5.6	37	5.8	33	6.8	25	–	–
Brunei	5.5	38	–	–	–	–	–	–
Korea (South)	5.4	39	5.1	43	4.5	47	–	–
Mauritius	5.4	39	4.7	53	4.1	54	4.5	40
Costa Rica	5.3	41	5.0	46	4.9	41	4.5	40
Oman	5.3	41	4.7	53	6.1	29	–	–
Poland	5.3	41	4.2	61	3.5	67	4.1	44
Dominica	5.2	44	5.6	37	–	–	–	–
Cape Verde	5.1	45	4.9	49	–	–	–	–
Lithuania	5	46	4.8	51	4.6	44	4.8	38
Macau	5	46	5.7	34	–	–	–	–
Bahrain	4.9	48	5.0	46	5.8	34	–	–
Seychelles	4.8	49	4.5	57	4.4	48	–	–

Table 2.1   *Continued*

Hungary	4.7	50	5.3	39	4.8	32	5.3	31
Jordan	4.7	50	4.7	53	5.3	37	4.9	37
Saudi Arabia	4.7	50	3.4	79	3.4	71	–	–
Czech Republic	4.6	53	5.2	41	4.2	51	3.9	47
Kuwait	4.5	54	4.3	60	4.6	44	–	–
South Africa	4.5	54	5.1	43	4.6	44	4.8	38
Malaysia	4.4	56	5.1	43	5.0	39	5.0	36
Namibia	4.4	56	4.5	57	4.1	54	5.4	30
Turkey	4.4	56	4.1	64	3.2	77	3.6	54
Latvia	4.3	59	4.8	51	4.0	57	3.4	59
Slovakia	4.3	59	4.9	49	4.0	57	3.7	51
Tunisia	4.3	59	4.2	61	5.0	39	5.3	31
Croatia	4.1	62	4.1	64	3.5	67	3.9	47
Macedonia, FYR	4.1	62	3.3	84	2.7	97	–	–
Ghana	4.1	62	3.7	69	3.6	64	3.4	59
Samoa	4.1	62	4.5	57	–	–	–	–
Rwanda	4	66	2.8	111	–	–	–	–
Italy	3.9	67	5.2	41	4.8	42	5.5	29
Georgia	3.8	68	3.4	79	2.0	133	–	–
Brazil	3.7	69	3.5	72	3.9	59	4.0	46
Cuba	3.7	69	4.2	61	3.7	62	–	–
Montenegro	3.7	69	3.3	84	2.7	97	–	–
Romania	3.7	69	3.7	69	2.9	87	2.8	69
Bulgaria	3.6	73	4.1	64	4.1	54	3.9	47
El Salvador	3.6	73	4.0	67	4.2	51	3.6	54
Panama	3.6	73	3.2	94	3.7	62	3.7	51
Trinidad and Tobago	3.6	73	3.4	79	4.2	51	5.3	31
Vanuatu	3.6	73	3.1	98	–	–	–	–
China	3.5	78	3.5	72	3.4	71	3.5	57
Colombia	3.5	78	3.8	68	3.8	60	3.8	50
Greece	3.5	78	4.6	56	4.3	49	4.2	42
Lesotho	3.5	78	3.3	84	–	–	–	–
Peru	3.5	78	3.5	72	3.5	67	4.1	44
Serbia	3.5	78	3.4	79	2.7	97	–	–
Thailand	3.5	78	3.3	84	3.6	64	3.2	61
Malawi	3.4	85	2.7	118	2.8	90	3.2	61

Table 2.1   *Continued*

Morocco	3.4	85	3.5	72	3.2	77	–	–
Albania	3.3	87	2.9	105	2.5	108	–	–
India	3.3	87	3.5	72	2.8	90	2.7	71
Jamaica	3.3	87	3.3	84	3.3	74	–	–
Liberia	3.3	87	2.1	150	–	–	–	–
Bosnia and Herzegovina	3.2	91	3.3	84	3.1	82	–	–
Djibouti	3.2	91	2.9	105	–	–	–	–
Gambia	3.2	91	2.3	143	2.8	90	–	–
Guatemala	3.2	91	2.8	111	2.2	122	2.9	65
Kiribati	3.2	91	3.3	84	–	–	–	–
Sri Lanka	3.2	91	3.2	94	3.5	67	–	–
Swaziland	3.2	91	3.3	84	–	–	–	–
Burkina Faso	3.1	98	2.9	105	–	–	–	–
Egypt	3.1	98	2.9	105	3.2	77	3.6	54
Mexico	3.1	98	3.5	72	3.6	64	3.7	51
Dominican Republic	3	101	3.0	99	2.9	87	3.1	63
Sao Tome and Principe	3	101	2.7	118	–	–	–	–
Tonga	3	101	1.7	175	–	–	–	–
Zambia	3	101	2.6	123	2.6	102	2.6	75
Algeria	2.9	105	3.0	99	2.7	97	–	–
Argentina	2.9	105	2.9	105	2.5	108	3.5	57
Kazakhstan	2.9	105	2.1	150	2.2	122	2.7	71
Moldova	2.9	105	2.8	111	2.3	114	3.1	63
Senegal	2.9	105	3.6	71	3.0	85	2.9	65
Benin	2.8	110	2.7	118	3.2	77	–	–
Bolivia	2.8	110	2.9	105	2.2	122	2.0	84
Gabon	2.8	110	3.3	84	3.3	74	–	–
Indonesia	2.8	110	2.3	143	2.0	133	1.9	88
Kosovo	2.8	110	–	–	–	–	–	–
Solomon Islands	2.8	110	2.8	111	–	–	–	–
Ethiopia	2.7	116	2.4	138	2.3	114	–	–
Guyana	2.7	116	2.6	123	–	–	–	–
Mali	2.7	116	2.7	118	3.2	77	–	–
Mongolia	2.7	116	3.0	99	3.0	85	–	–
Mozambique	2.7	116	2.8	111	2.8	90	–	–

Table 2.1   *Continued*

Tanzania	2.7	116	3.2	94	2.8	90	2.2	82
Vietnam	2.7	116	2.6	123	2.6	102	2.6	75
Armenia	2.6	123	3.0	99	3.1	82	–	–
Eritrea	2.6	123	2.8	111	2.6	102	–	–
Madagascar	2.6	123	3.2	94	3.1	82	–	–
Niger	2.6	123	2.6	123	2.2	122	–	–
Belarus	2.5	127	2.1	150	3.3	74	–	–
Ecuador	2.5	127	2.1	150	2.4	112	2.3	79
Lebanon	2.5	127	3.0	99	2.7	97	–	–
Nicaragua	2.5	127	2.6	123	2.7	97	2.4	77
Syria	2.5	127	2.4	138	3.4	71	–	–
Timor–Leste	2.5	127	2.6	123	–	–	–	–
Uganda	2.5	127	2.8	111	2.6	102	1.9	88
Azerbaijan	2.4	134	2.1	150	1.9	140	2.0	84
Bangladesh	2.4	134	2.0	162	1.5	145	0.4	91
Honduras	2.4	134	2.5	131	2.3	114	2.7	71
Nigeria	2.4	134	2.2	147	1.6	144	1.0	90
Philippines	2.4	134	2.5	131	–	–	2.9	65
Sierra Leone	2.4	134	2.1	150	2.3	114	–	–
Togo	2.4	134	2.3	143	–	–	–	–
Ukraine	2.4	134	2.7	118	2.2	122	2.1	83
Zimbabwe	2.4	134	2.1	150	2.3	114	2.9	65
Maldives	2.3	143	3.3	84	–	–	–	–
Mauritania	2.3	143	2.6	123	–	–	–	–
Pakistan	2.3	143	2.4	138	2.1	129	2.3	79
Cameroon	2.2	146	2.4	138	2.1	129	2.0	84
Côte d'Ivoire	2.2	146	2.1	150	2.0	133	2.4	77
Haiti	2.2	146	1.6	177	1.5	145	–	–
Iran	2.2	146	2.5	131	2.9	87	–	–
Libya	2.2	146	2.5	131	2.5	108	–	–
Nepal	2.2	146	2.5	131	2.8	90	–	–
Paraguay	2.2	146	2.4	138	1.9	140	–	–
Yemen	2.2	146	2.5	131	2.4	112	–	–
Cambodia	2.1	154	2.0	162	–	–	–	–
Central African Republic	2.1	154	2.0	162	–	–	–	–
Comoros	2.1	154	2.6	123	–	–	–	–

Table 2.1   *Concluded*

Congo	2.1	154	2.1	150	2.3	114	–	–
Guinea–Bissau	2.1	154	2.2	147	–	–	–	–
Kenya	2.1	154	2.1	150	2.1	129	2.0	84
Laos	2.1	154	1.9	168	–	–	–	–
Papua New Guinea	2.1	154	2.0	162	2.6	102	–	–
Russia	2.1	154	2.3	143	2.8	90	2.3	79
Tajikistan	2.1	154	2.1	150	2.0	133	–	–
Congo, Dem Rep	2	164	1.9	168	2.0	133	–	–
Guinea	2	164	1.9	168	–	–	–	–
Kyrgyzstan	2	164	2.1	150	2.2	122	–	–
Venezuela	2	164	2.0	162	2.3	114	2.8	69
Angola	1.9	168	2.2	147	2.0	133	–	–
Equatorial Guinea	1.9	168	1.9	168	–	–	–	–
Burundi	1.8	170	2.5	131	–	–	–	–
Chad	1.7	171	1.8	172	1.7	142	–	–
Sudan	1.6	172	1.8	172	2.2	122	–	–
Turkmenistan	1.6	172	2.0	162	2.0	133	–	–
Uzbekistan	1.6	172	1.7	175	2.3	114	2.7	71
Iraq	1.5	175	1.5	178	2.1	129	–	–
Afghanistan	1.4	176	1.8	172	–	–	–	–
Burma	1.4	176	–	–	–	–	–	–
Somalia	1.1	178	1.4	179	–	–	–	–

 For a critical appraisal of the CPI methodology, see Lambsdorff (2006a) and Sandholtz and Gray (2003).

4.1.2 Global Corruption Barometer

The Global Corruption Barometer (GCB) assesses the general public's perception and experience of corruption. In 2010 the Barometer surveyed more than 91,500 people in 86 countries, making it the largest cross-country survey to collect the general public's views on corruption. The 2010 GCB reported the following findings:

- Over the preceding three-year period, corruptions levels were perceived to have increased: almost six out of ten people reported that corruption levels in their country had increased, with the biggest increases being reported in North America and the EU;

- The most corrupt institution in the world was identified as being political parties;

- Petty bribery remained widespread, seeing no decline since 2006;

- Government attempts to counter corruption were often seen as ineffective;

- Respondents displayed little trust in formal institutions in terms of fighting corruption; and

- A significant number of respondents believed that the public has a role to play in the fight against corruption, and demonstrated a willingness to report corruption when it presents itself

(TI n.d.c.).

4.1.3 Bribe Payers Index

The Bribe Payers Index (BPI) ranks leading exporting countries 'in terms of the degree to which international companies with their headquarters in those countries are likely to pay bribes to senior public officials in key emerging market economies' (TI n.d.d.). In that sense, it assesses the supply side of corruption by ranking corruption by source country and industry sector.

The most recent BPI, carried out in 2011, covered 28 countries and consisted of 3,016 interviews with senior business executives conducted between 5 May 2011 and 8 July 2011 (TI 2011: 24). Surveys were conducted in: Argentina, Austria, Brazil, Chile, China, Czech Republic, Egypt, France, Germany, Ghana, Hong Kong, Hungary, India, Indonesia, Japan, Malaysia, Mexico, Morocco, Nigeria, Pakistan, Philippines, Poland, Russia, Senegal, Singapore, South Africa, South Korea, Turkey, United Kingdom and United States (TI 2011: 25).

Findings from the 2011 exercise showed that bribery between companies across different sectors is viewed as equally prevalent as that between firms and public officials (TI 2011: 3). Companies from Russia and China were ranked by respondents as being most likely to engage in bribery (TI 2011: 3), with the Netherlands, Switzerland and Belgium being ranked the least likely. While bribery was perceived to exist in all sectors, it was seen as most common in the public works contracts and construction sector (TI 2011: 3). The exercise also found no improvement in the perceptions of bribery since the previous report in 2008.

For more information about the methodology and survey protocol of BPI and results from the 2011 exercise, see TI (2011).

4.2 WORLD ECONOMIC FORUM'S 'GLOBAL COMPETITIVENESS REPORT' AND 'EXECUTIVE OPINION SURVEY'

The World Economic Forum, incorporated in 1971, is an independent international organisation whose aim is to improve world development by shaping global, regional and industry agendas and facilitating partnership work (World Economic Forum n.d.).

One of its key activities is monitoring the 'competitiveness' of nations. It defines competitiveness as 'the set of institutions, policies, and factors that determine the level of productivity of a country' (World Economic Forum n.d.: 4). This includes consideration of the prevalence of corruption, degree of transparency and relationships between political and judicial systems.

Every year, the forum publishes a 'Global Competitiveness Report', which polls over 11,000 business executives worldwide in an 'Executive Opinion Survey'.

For more information, see the 2010/11 report: World Economic Forum (n.d).

4.3 ERNST & YOUNG'S GLOBAL FRAUD SURVEY

Ernst & Young's *Global Fraud Survey* is a biennial survey designed to provide information on 'trends in the nature and incidence of fraud, both over time and across national borders' (Ernst & Young 2008: 2). It is a global survey conducted by professionals who have experience in dealing with fraud. Questionnaires are sent out to directors and managers in major organisations, internationally, from across the following sectors: energy, chemicals and utilities; financial services; health; industrial products; government; retail and consumer products; and technology, communications and entertainment.

The eleventh survey, coordinated in 2010, reported the following key findings:

- There were a significant number of respondents who reported to have suffered a significant fraud over the past two years;

- Corporate entities' responses to fraud appear insufficient, despite fraud levels increasing;

- Proactive approaches to minimising the risk of fraud were not universally contemplated by corporate entities; and

- Companies had still not incorporated measures to mitigate corruption and bribery as standard practice.

For the full report and detailed findings, see Ernst & Young (2010).

For a comprehensive overview of debates on measuring corruption, see Sampford *et al.* (2006).

Study Questions

- What are the main obstacles to measuring the scale of international corruption? Given the inherent difficulty in measuring international corruption, do you think it is a worthwhile project?

- What methods have been used to measure international corruption? What are the main indices?

- What are the relative merits of using subjective/objective data to measure international corruption?

3

Causes and Consequences

1 Introduction

As the indices introduced in Chapter 2 indicate, different parts of the world experience different levels of corruption. These cross-country comparisons have raised further questions about whether it might be possible to construct a theory of the causes and consequences of corruption. By identifying commonalities and divergences between various countries and their experiences of corruption, theorists have sought to answer the following questions:

- What can we learn by comparing the incidence of corruption in different countries?

- Why is the incidence of corruption high in some countries but low in others? Is it possible to generalise about necessary pre-conditions for high levels of corruption? Can we identify the root causes of corruption, or dynamics that facilitate corrupt activities?

- What are the effects of corruption? How and why do countries experience their effects differently?

In attempting to answer some of these questions, analysts have generated a substantial body of theoretical literature. This chapter considers some of these perspectives.

2 Perspectives on the Causes of International Corruption

Determining the causes and consequences of corruption is not an easy task because it is likely to involve the complex interplay of several factors. For example, it may occur within particular institutional arrangements which have other weaknesses. In this instance, therefore, it would be difficult to isolate corruption as an independent variable and determine links between cause and effect. Difficulties notwithstanding, it is generally agreed that the incidence of corruption is 'a result of the strength of incentives, the range and scale of opportunities, the availability of means and the risks of punishment' (U4, n.d.a.). However, which particular economic, political and/or social dynamics provide the necessary conditions of incentive and opportunity? In seeking to answer this question, theorists have identified a number of variables as drivers of corruption.

 For background information on the theoretical causes and consequences of corruption, read Tanzi (1998).

2.1 ECONOMIC VARIABLES

Several economic variables are thought to be related to corruption: the level of economic development, the openness of the economy and individual poverty.

2.1.1 Level of economic development

It has been suggested that low levels of economic development provide an environment in which corruption can thrive. Early analyses of the relationship between levels of economic development and the incidence of corruption, which took place during the 1960s and 1970s, argued that corruption was best viewed as a phase of development (U4, n.d.a.). At that time, experts argued that corruption would be rife during early phases of development, but would decline as national economies became more prosperous and it was able to 'wither away' (ibid.).

This analysis is now seen as flawed because it was based on the development models of Western Europe and North America and therefore is not universally applicable. History has shown that not all economies develop at the same pace or in the same manner. As U4 (ibid.) documents:

> *The development process in many parts of the developing world (and especially in Africa) appears stalled and those countries experience high levels of corruption. Elsewhere, as in the 'Asian Tigers', rapid economic*

*growth and development have occurred but usually accompanied by
high levels of corruption. Yet remarkably low levels of corruption
accompany Singapore's economic development.*

At the macroeconomic level, therefore, it cannot be said that there is a firm
correlation between the overall level of economic development and the incidence
of corruption. As stated by U4 (ibid.), 'according to the 2002 CPI, there is more
corruption in Italy than there is in Botswana and there is more corruption in
Germany than there is in Chile'. High levels of economic development do
not necessarily equate with low levels of corruption. As Heimann comments,
'scandals in Europe, Japan, and South Korea have demolished the notion that
corruption is primarily a disease of the developing world' (Heimann 1997: 147).

2.1.2 Openness of economy

It has been argued that corrupt practices can exist more easily in closed
economies, which are cut off from the competitive pressures of an open market.
As Sandholtz and Gray (2003: 765–6) explain:

> *If we think of bribes, kickbacks, extortion payments, and speed money
> as a sort of (illegitimate) tax, then that tax adds to the costs of local
> producers who have to pay it. Under conditions of international
> economic competition, companies so taxed will experience returns
> lower than those prevailing elsewhere, resulting in lower profits and
> possibly extinction. Domestic firms seeking foreign capital may not
> be able to secure it, or they will have to pay, at least, a premium for
> foreign capital. Finally, corrupt officials would also feel the pinch of
> international openness. Because bribe-paying companies suffer under
> international competition, they will have less money to offer, and
> bureaucrats will find that their corruption-related income declines.
> Greater exposure to international trade thus penalises corruption.*

Sandholtz and Gray argue, therefore, that liberalisation and greater
economic integration can hinder corrupt transactions by increasing their costs.
They report that 'existing research finds a significant inverse relationship
between international trade and corruption levels' (ibid.). In other words, they
contend, greater exposure to global trade and deeper international economic
integration lead to lower levels of corruption. Lambsdorff (2006b: 8) endorses
this view, by stating that 'corruption simply mirrors the absence of economic
competition'.

While greater economic liberalisation has been identified as a means of reducing corruption, it has also been seen by some as having the opposite effect. Indeed, international trade is often cited as a major source of large-scale corruption because, by increasing the number of international transactions made between growing numbers of diverse actors, it increases the opportunity for corrupt activities to take place (U4 n.d.a.).

Furthermore, as Hawley (2000: 13) notes: 'regulatory mechanisms have been weakened; there is no longer any need to provide economic justification for money transfers, and it has become far easier to exchange and transfer monies and capital'. Hawley points to some of the problems that have accompanied political and economic liberalisation in Russia. While Russia was expected to make a swift transition to a market economy, Hawley argues that the existence of open capital accounts made it easy for state assets to be mismanaged and wealth shipped abroad.

Similarly, Robinson (2002: 7) writes: 'Rather than curbing corruption, economic and political liberalisation in South Korea has strengthened the bargaining power of the business sector in relation to the government, a situation which could lead to the persistence of the institutional foundations of corruption.'

Furthermore, Glynn, Kobrin and Naim (1997: 12) observe that the broadening and deepening of global economic integration increases the possibility that the effects of corruption in one part of the world will resonate in other parts of the world economy. They recall that 'when the corrupt Bank of Credit and Commerce International went belly-up in 1991, for example, the entire social security fund of Gabon was wiped out'.

2.1.3 Individual poverty

While corruption is not confined to poorer countries, evidence does suggest that it is linked to poverty and inequality (Budima 2006). Whether in the developed or developing world, poverty at the micro level – that is, low income at the individual level – is thought to contribute to corruption. As Mauro (1998: 13) comments, 'poverty itself might cause corruption, perhaps because ... people in need are more likely to abandon their moral principles'.

For example, some researchers have analysed the link between civil servant salaries and levels of corruption, on a cross-country basis. It is suggested that there is positive correlation between low incomes and high levels of corruption, and that providing good wages and a reasonable standard of living is necessary in order to prevent fraud and corruption. In the case of Africa, for example, Riley (2002) argues that when poorly paid or unpaid public officials demand and receive corrupt payments, they typically do so out of necessity. In other words, because of their own poverty and low living standards they are forced to 'sell' what would otherwise be free services such as health care and drug supplies.

It is worth bearing in mind, however, the broader context in which corrupt acts take place. As U4 (n.d.a.) states: 'Low salaries can provide a powerful incentive for officials to become corrupt but they only form part of the environment in which corruption flourishes. The incidence of corruption depends more crucially on the wider economic, political and social context.'

2.2 POLITICAL VARIABLES

Several political variables are thought to be related to corruption: type of governance, the legacy of colonial rule and the degree of international political integration.

2.2.1 Type of governance

It is reasonable to assume that corruption thrives on bad governance, where controls are weak and decision-making lacks accountability controls and checks – but are there any particular types of institutional or governmental arrangement that lend themselves to corrupt activity?

Certainly, history demonstrates that corruption affects all types of regime. As Heimann (1997) notes, it has been found to be present in advanced industrialised economies as well as in developing economies, market economies, government-controlled economies, states with long democratic traditions, states with authoritarian regimes, and states in transition to democracy. Nonetheless, Transparency International's Corruption Perceptions Index (CPI) consistently shows long-established democracies to be the least corrupt. As Glynn *et al.* (1997: 11) state: 'A regime that has frequent elections, political competition, active and well-organised opposition forces, an independent legislature and judiciary, free media, and liberty of expression is bound to generate more limits on the scope and frequency of corruption than one that does not have them.'

Unfortunately, as Gerring and Thacker point out (2004: 298), 'there have been few attempts to study the relationships between basic-level institutions and political corruption in an empirical, cross-national setting'. The research that has been carried out, however, tends to support the theory that more democratised states experience lower levels of corruption. For example, by conducting a cross-country analysis of Israel, the US, India and Russia, Johnson (2004: 155) found that the presence of independent, fair, strong and effective laws and law enforcement agencies correlated with lower levels of corruption. Similarly, empirical research has indicated that countries with improved civil liberties are more successful in addressing corruption (Gray and Kaufmann 1998).

Is there, however, a simple correlation between democracy and levels of corruption? Most would argue not. Scandals in industrial and developing democratic countries indicate that democracy 'bestows no automatic immunisation against public malfeasance' (Glynn et al. 1997: 11). Indeed, the perceived increase in corrupt activity in the former Soviet bloc countries during the early 1990s is a case in point – these increases occurred as the countries were becoming more democratic (Xin and Rudel 2004).

It is perhaps useful to distinguish between established and transitional democracies. As Glynn et al. (1997: 11) point out, the transition from authoritarian rule to democracy is complex, and during this transition many opportunities for corruption may present themselves:

> ... the sudden deregulation of entire new arenas of economic activity that were once under the exclusive control of the state can vastly expand room for misconduct, opening the door to fraud and all sorts of abuses by firms trying to take advantage of the opportunities created by capitalism.

In the long run, however, a less centralised and more democratic political system is believed to offer less opportunity for corruption, by redefining the public–private balance of power and making institutions more accountable (Glynn et al. 1997: 11). A democratic society can provide a number of tools to limit corruptive behaviour. Among the most important of these are free elections, political competition, freedom of speech and press, and the rule of law. In democratic states, the chances of corrupt acts being discovered, publicised and sanctioned are much higher than in countries with other types of governance due to democratic freedoms such as investigative journalism, public hearings, parliamentary inquiries and public opinion sensitivity of elected officials. In other words, democracy is believed to empower people: in politics this power can assist citizens to 'vote out of office politicians who are tainted' (Sandholtz and Gray 2003: 10).

For a more detailed consideration of the relationship between democracy and corruption, refer to Johnston (1997).

2.2.2 Legacy of colonial rule

Some analysts believe that the legacy of colonial rule is a significant explanatory factor in the presence and intensity of some forms of corruption in Africa, Asia and Latin America. For example, some have argued that corruption in Latin America became widespread during the period of colonial rule, and has subsequently become entrenched in socio-cultural traditions. This, it is argued, has made these countries resistant to change (Robinson 2002).

Of course, corruption is present in countries that have not experienced colonial rule. However, theorists contend that differences in colonial rule have rendered certain countries more susceptible than others. In the case of the African continent, for example, some commentators have put forward the view that certain aspects of former British colonies have rendered them 'less vulnerable to corruption than their Francophone counterparts: these include a tradition of press freedom, durable legal institutions, an emphasis on elite education and British civil service reforms or probity and impartiality' (Robinson 2002: 6). As Robinson (ibid.) notes: 'This would appear to suggest that while contemporary manifestations of corruption in Africa cannot be explained by colonialism per se, colonial regimes left an institutional legacy which has shaped the subsequent form and extent of corrupt practices.'

2.2.3 Degree of international political integration

Theorists have argued that countries that are closed, politically and economically, are likely to experience higher levels of corruption.

Correspondingly, deeper political integration in the international community is thought to diminish levels of corruption. For example, Sandholtz and Gray (2003) report that countries that are politically entwined in the international community – through membership of international organisations and as signatories of international treaties, for example – suffer lower levels of corruption.

According to this view, the advantages of international political integration derive mainly from the creation of common ground rules, which are drawn up to enable and improve the interaction of diverse nations and cultures as they all differ in their traditions, norms and codes of conduct; for example, 'practices that are considered corrupt in one society may be acceptable in another' (Sandholtz and Gray 2003: 7). Therefore, by requiring agreement to a clear set of rules – in the form of an international convention, for example – or by promoting common interests via the creation of international organisations, political integration provides a group of nation states characterised by different practices and customs with common principles by which to abide. This leads theorists to argue that 'countries that are more integrated internationally are likely to be less corrupt' (Sandholtz and Gray 2003: 6).

An example of successful economic and political integration is the European Union (EU). Unfortunately, the EU has not withstood criticism in terms of the above, with some claiming that the complex institutional arrangements and programmes render it *more* vulnerable to corruption. This will be explored in greater detail in Chapter 6.

2.3 TECHNOLOGICAL CHANGE

Glynn *et al.* (1997) state that the globalisation of electronic communication and emergence of an electronically networked international financial system has acted as an enabler of corruption, by making it significantly easier to transfer money across borders and launder funds. Consequently, the globalisation of e-communication can be seen a contributory factor in the increase in corruption internationally. Not only does it make it more difficult to control corruption but also, by transcending national boundaries, the consequences may resonate more widely.

Yet, while technological progress in communication offers new channels for fraudulent and corrupt activity, it may also offer new methods of detection and prevention: 'consider the present day ability of intelligence and other agencies to monitor such electronic traffic – it may offer new opportunities for its exposure and control' (Glynn *et al.* 1997: 14). Furthermore, the globalisation of communication makes life more difficult for perpetrators of corruption because they are constantly under the watchful eye of an unrestrained global media:

> *The global explosion of communication and information not only makes secrecy harder to maintain than ever before, it also forces governments to be more responsive to an influential global audience (investors, journalists, politicians, multilateral officials, and international public opinion in general) that adds to the constraints under which they have to operate (Glynn et al. 1997: 15).*

 For a more detailed consideration of the 'globalisation' of corruption, refer to Glynn *et al.* (1997).

2.4 CRITICAL SUMMARY

One of the difficulties in theorising about the causes of corruption is that it is difficult to engage in the various levels of analysis simultaneously. As Xin and Rudel (2004: 306) note:

> *At different scales one sees different things. At the micro scale, bureaucratic arrangements that give public officials lots of discretion and little accountability seem to increase the incidence of corruption. At the macro scale, poverty, large populations, small public sectors, and earlier historical experiences with autocratic rule appear to increase the incidence of corruption.*

The problem that confronts theorists, therefore, is how to bring together these different sets of observations into a single, comprehensive theory. While this is desirable, theorists identify several areas that require further in-depth research for this to be feasible, including: the contextual correlates of corruption; the effects of state strength and democratic reforms on the perceived incidence of corruption (which is ambiguous at present); and the disparities in the perceived incidence of corruption (Xin and Rudel 2004).

Despite these limitations, we might conclude that corruption can flourish in a variety of political and economic environments, but it thrives when bad government makes it impossible to control, and there is sufficient motivation, opportunity and incentive to engage in corrupt activities. Also, while there may be exceptions to the rule, empirical studies tend to support certain claims that:

> ... there is less corruption where there are fewer trade restrictions; where governments do not engage in favoritist industrial policies ...; and that there is somewhat less corruption where civil servants are paid better, compared with similarly qualified workers in the private sector (Van Rijckegham and Weder 1997, cited by Mauro 1998: 11).

3 Perspectives on the Consequences of International Corruption

A similarly broad range of views has been expressed regarding the consequences of corruption, with analysts theorising how corruption has an impact on economic, political and social development.

3.1 ECONOMIC IMPACT

Corruption drains money from the economy by diverting resources through alternative channels. It is therefore reasonable to suppose that it will have some impact on a state's economy.

At the macroeconomic level, the precise implications of losses to the economy of this kind are hard to determine. This is because, as we have already seen, it is difficult to determine cause and effect in relation to economic performance. The manner in which countries experience the economic costs of fraud and corruption will vary according to the type, scale and frequency of the transactions, but also depending on the ability of that country's economy to bear the brunt of these costs.

In general, however, 'in a large robust dynamic economy, the economic effects of low levels of corruption are minimal' (U4, n.d.a.). In a less robust or stagnant economy, the economic costs are likely to be higher. As the Asian Development Bank (1998: 17) notes, 'some nations can tolerate relatively high levels of bribery and graft and continue to maintain respectable rates of economic growth, whereas others cannot'.

Refer to pages 15–16 of the Asian Development Bank (1998) document, which outlines the effect corruption has had on a number of countries around the world.

Different types of corruption are conceived at different levels of analysis as having different impacts. For example, petty corruption, while imposing disproportionate costs on the poor, may have little effect in wider economic terms. Large-scale or grand corruption, on the other hand, has the potential to adversely affect economies and potentially impoverish entire nations. As Riley (2002: 148) comments:

> Not all types of corruption are equally damaging or objectionable ... A small number of minor instances of petty corruption by public officials does not have a major microeconomic effect, although it can be profoundly alienating for citizens and damages their immediate material circumstances. Other forms of corruption, such as the grand corruption of state elites – in both the mild and malevolent forms of corruption associated with, for example, the Houphouet-Boigny and Mobutu families, in Cote d'Ivoire and Zaire – have had grossly damaging effects in terms of reputation as well as economic growth.

It should be noted, however, that corruption is not universally accepted as having a negative economic impact. Some believe that, in certain circumstances, 'corruption [plays] a useful redistributive role, transferring resources from wealthy individuals and corporations to those of more modest means' (Asian Development Bank 1998: 13). It has also been argued that bribery, for example, can give firms and individuals 'a means of avoiding burdensome regulations and ineffective legal systems' (Gray and Kaufmann 1998: 8). However, this line of argument ignores 'the discretion that many politicians and bureaucrats have (particularly in corrupt societies) over the creation and interpretation of counterproductive regulations' (ibid.).

Overall, economists broadly agree that high levels of corruption have a range of negative consequences, which affect economic performance in the long term. These include the creation of inefficiencies in the operation of markets; the concentration of public spending on activities likely to yield large bribes, which potentially divert funds away from public services; and the reduction of the level of direct foreign investment by adding costs and creating uncertainty

(U4 n.d.a.). These are deemed to have particular salience in the developing world.

3.2 POLITICAL AND SOCIAL IMPACT

High levels of corruption are also viewed by many as a source of social and political instability. Empirical observations seem to indicate that 'on average, countries that are more corrupt tend to be more politically unstable' (Mauro 1998: 13). Furthermore (ibid.), 'Corruption and instability may result from the failure of members of the same government or ruling elite to coordinate their actions. In that sense, corruption and political instability may be two sides of the same coin'.

It is argued that where political cultures are perceived to be characterised by widespread and ingrained corruption, support for democratic processes may be eroded and undermined (Brown and Cloke 2006). This may contribute to:

> ... circumstances where, whether encouraged or sustained by external pressures of internally specific ones, corrupt socio-cultural processes have come to facilitate the existence of a quasi-state (the shadow state) by which a small minority of elites, sustained by extensive clientelistic networks, effectively bypass and subvert official governance structures in a way that excludes and impoverishes the majority of citizens (Brown and Cloke 2006: 282).

It can be argued, therefore, that corrupt activities 'distort the allocation of resources away from those who are legally entitled to them and toward the rich, the powerful, and the politically well connected' (Asian Development Bank 1998: 15).

By contrast, some authors suggest that, in the short term at least, corrupt activities such as political patronage may serve as a stabilising rather than a destabilising force. While there may be some evidence to suggest this, it is not without negative consequence. As Elliott (1997: 2) notes, 'corruption may stabilise a political situation that is repressive and unjust, in which all but a wealthy elite lack the resources to protect themselves from exploitation'. Again, these impacts are thought to be felt particularly keenly in the developing world.

4 Implications for the Developing World

While corruption has consequences for all countries around the globe, there are several factors that make developing countries more vulnerable to its effects, and that make its impact more profound than in the developed world. As Elliott (1997: 1) notes:

> In poor countries, corruption may lower economic growth, impede economic development, and undermine political legitimacy, consequences that in turn exacerbate poverty and political instability. In developed countries, the economic effects may be less severe.

The prevalence of corruption in the developing world has been attributed, in part, to the 'historic dominance of the state in economic and political affairs' (Robinson 2002: 6). In this sense, a tradition of centralised and autocratic rule is believed to have 'created opportunities for rent-seeking and weakened the ability of citizens to hold politicians and state officials accountable for their actions' (ibid.). As Gray and Kaufmann (1998: 9) comment:

> Accountability is typically weak. Political competition and civil liberties are often restricted. Laws and principles of ethics in government are poorly developed, if they exist at all, and the legal institutions charged with enforcing them are ill-prepared for this complex job. The watchdog institutions that provide information on which detection and enforcement is based – such as investigators, accountants, and the press – are also weak.

Furthermore, anti-colonial struggles in many developing countries and the subsequent process of decolonisation created great incentives for corruption as opposing groups struggled to uphold egalitarian rules of entitlement in the face of scarce resources. In the case of Asia, Khan (2002: 19) writes:

> The large gap between demand and supply meant that the actual allocation of property rights often failed the principles of allocation which the law set out. Very great incentives were created for corruption. This was true for the allocation of, land, credit or licenses to emerging industrialists as for the allocation of irrigation water or credit to emerging capitalist farmers.

This contest over public resources and political power frequently led to the creation of large disparities in income and wealth among native populations. These visible inequalities in decolonisation development processes typically led to the formation and mobilisation of opposition groups from those sections of society who felt excluded. Paradoxically, however (ibid.):

> *The opposition of these groups has often resulted in a second set of structural processes generating high levels of corruption in developing countries. The opposition of organised groups has often had to be bought off by payoffs from existing elites or directly from the state to the most troublesome or vociferous opponents in an attempt to 'purchase' support or legitimacy.*

High levels of aid dependence have also been cited as explanatory factors in the prevalence of corruption in developing countries. Robinson (2002: 6), speaking about foreign aid in Africa, states that foreign aid transactions provide 'ample scope for rent-seeking opportunities when alternative sources of income are restricted'. Unfortunately, however, this has the negative effect of discouraging the international donor community from offering vital loans and development aid. As Keuleers (2005: 59) notes:

> *The international donor community has indicated its willingness to increase aid to developing countries to support the war on poverty but given the figures on bribes and money laundering, the impact on these efforts may be limited unless more attention is paid to corruption leakages.*

In the past, academic literature on the subject has attempted to highlight both the positive and negative effects of corruption in the developing world. However, most theorists now concur that high levels of corruption are enormously detrimental to these countries' social, political and economic development in the long-term. For example, one of the perceivably beneficial effects is that in corrupt and inefficient governments the payment of bribes and 'gifts' can offer investors (domestic and foreign) a means of penetrating developing economies, thus facilitating capital formation and economic development (Budima 2006). On the other hand, the prevalence of corruption and expectation of such bribes may actually deter investment in the long-run, by raising transaction costs.

Furthermore, high levels of corruption may allow accumulated capital to leave the country in the pockets of corrupt elites. Unfortunately, in many developing countries, 'the crimes of the powerful have had broad effects: high level corruption has legitimised low level corruption' (Robinson 2002: 147). Country studies have suggested that these two forms of corruption mutually reinforce one another.

Unfortunately, however, as Mauro (1998: 13) states, 'once corruption has become engrained, it's hard to get rid of'. Furthermore, as Johnston (2002: 88) comments, 'even seemingly "petty" corruption, as judged by the sums of money changing hands or the ordinary nature of the situations and participants involved, can be part of a pervasive syndrome of problems that helps keep poor countries poor'.

High levels of corruption can also undermine economic and human capital formation, by allowing elites to allocate national budgets inappropriately. As Gray and Kaufmann (1998: 8) comment, corruption:

> ... impedes long-term foreign and domestic investment, misallocates talent to rent-seeking activities, and distorts sectoral priorities and technology choices (by, for example, creating incentives to contract for large defense projects rather than rural health clinics specialising in preventive care). It pushes firms underground (outside the formal sector), undercuts the state's ability to raise revenues, and leads to ever-higher tax rates being levied on fewer and fewer taxpayers. This, in turn, reduces the state's ability to provide essential public goods, including the rule of law.

Corruption can be seen as unofficial taxes on consumers and producers. The most affected, therefore, are those who are least able to pay: the poor. Furthermore, it is the very poor who bear a disproportionate share of the cost – for example, through the diversion of resources from anti-poverty and other development programmes (Brown and Cloke 2006) and by denying them access to basic services such as healthcare (Chapter 11 will explore the consequences of corruption in relation to healthcare in the developing world).

Corruption can therefore be seen as inextricably linked to persistent poverty in parts of the developing world. In 2005, the United Nations Development Programme's (UNDP) *Human development report* concluded that by 2015, 380m poverty-stricken people worldwide will remain in poverty. One of the reasons given for this dismal projection was 'the significant distributional implications that widespread corruption has on growth, equity and poverty' (Keuleers 2005: 58). As such, it highlights anti-corruption activities as central to the UNDP's efforts to alleviating poverty:

> *Effective democratic governance aimed at achieving sustainable and equitable human development thus requires a comprehensive attack on corruption as a factor of social disintegration and distortion of democratic systems. Because corruption endangers the stability of democratic institutions, discriminates in the delivery of government services, and thus violates the human rights of the people, and the poor in particular, UNDP considers its activities in the area of anti-corruption essential to the strengthening of democratic governance in support of poverty alleviation and human development in its program countries (Keuleers 2005: 58).*

Efforts at political reform, however, have not always yielded positive results. Part of the problem is that some of the political and civil service reforms have occurred without adequate preparation of local bureaucracies. This has been blamed for an increase in corruption in several instances, as the World Bank's vice-president for Asia, Jean-Michel Severino, admitted when stating that, if done badly, 'decentralisation will lead to less governance and more corruption spread around the country, disruption of public service and a fiscal burden' (cited by Hawley, 2000: 13).

As Robinson (2002: 147) comments, 'the admittedly imperfect democratisation of previously authoritarian regimes, including Kenya from 1991 onwards, has not led to a substantial reduction in corruption'. Indeed, some observers have argued that Kenya actually experienced a growth in corruption since its reforms and move to party politics. Similarly, as Riley (2002: 146) noted:

> *In Zambia, as elsewhere, economic liberalisation has created opportunities for corruption. The sale of several government parastatals [government-owned companies or agencies] has not been transparent and has left over 80,000 people jobless.*

The World Bank asserts that attempts to decentralise political systems in transitional democracies are not likely to succeed unless accompanied by adequate resources and training for local governments (cited by Hawley, 2000).

It is argued that these efforts must be conceived as long term and executed with the full support of the local population. Hawley notes (2000: 13) that 'where decentralisation has worked, it has generally been where local governments have been able to raise revenue locally, especially through progressive tax reform'.

CORRUPTION AND POVERTY: SUMMARY OF THEMES

Poverty is a multi-dimensional concept, which not only refers to economic well-being, but also encompasses issues of health, literacy and social inclusion. It is argued that corruption can exacerbate poverty in several ways:

- by reducing domestic and foreign investment by increasing transactions and creating uncertainty and instability in an economy;
- by reducing economic growth;
- by diverting humanitarian and development aid;
- by distorting patterns of public spending and investment;
- by concentrating public spending on activities likely to yield large bribes, which potentially divert funds away from much needed public services such as health, education and other anti-poverty programmes;
- by reducing revenues to government, which in turn further reduces spending on public services;
- by undermining the rule of law, eroding trust in democratic processes, thereby undermining state legitimacy and political stability, and exacerbating social exclusion; and, consequently,
- by preventing the most socially excluded from acquiring access to political power and economic resources, thus exacerbating inequality.

Invariably it is the most marginalised in society – the very poor – who are left most insecure.

Study Questions

- What economic, political and/or social factors do you think facilitate international corruption?

- Do you agree that 'corruption simply mirrors the absence of economic competition' (Lambsdorff 2006b: 6)?

- What are the main arguments for and against economic liberalisation, in terms of its relationship with corruption?

- What are the implications of corruption for the developing world?

- Read Budima (2006). What does Budima conclude about whether economic crime in developing countries can be controlled, and whether it is desirable to control it? Do you agree with this conclusion?

PART II
Challenging Corruption

4

Counter Corruption:
The Role of State Actors

1 Introduction

As the preceding chapters have demonstrated, international corruption has complex social, political and economic implications, which affect all countries around the globe. In a globalised world characterised by increasing flows of goods, capital, people and knowledge across national boundaries, corrupt activity is increasingly taking place both within states and across state frontiers. This has brought about a realisation that international corruption is a problem that can only be addressed effectively by a collaborative approach between international actors. Correspondingly, over the past ten years, visible efforts have been made by the international community to act collectively to counter this growing phenomenon.

This chapter considers the role of state (political) actors in challenging international corruption. It considers the nature and evolution of international regimes and international law, and developments in this field in terms of tackling corruption, and critically assesses these initiatives.

2 The Problem of International Corruption: Global Governance

Tackling corruption has traditionally fallen within the remit of national politics and law-making. Typically, in domestic society, laws and corresponding sanctions are developed and applied by a legislative and executive institution, represented by a head of state; these political institutions are charged with acting on behalf of society (Knutsen 1997). But what happens when policy problems such as corruption spill across national borders? The explosion of corruption *transnationally* has demanded new forms of governance and political decision-making that transcend the confines of the nation-state: global governance.

In practical terms, however, what is meant by the term 'global governance'? In the absence of a world-governing authority, who governs? Halliday (2004: 489) offers a generally accepted definition of the term:

> *'Governance' in its simplest sense refers to the art of governing ... It does not imply that there should be any one institution, but rather, in the present context, refers to a set of interlocking but separate bodies which share a common purpose. Thus it covers the activities of states, but also those of inter-governmental organisations, most notably the UN, and the role of Non-Governmental Organisations (NGOs) and transnational movements: all of these combine, not least through influencing each other, to produce the system of global governance.*

Global governance can be described, therefore, as the international community's efforts to bring order, by collectively attempting to regulate and govern the actions of those operating in the international environment. It covers a range of issues, from security to human rights and the environment.

Recent decades have witnessed a rapid growth in these new forms of political organisation. Commentators believe that this is indicative of the 'rapid expansion of transnational links, and the corresponding desire by most states for some form of international governance to deal with collective policy problems' (Held, McGrew, Goldblatt and Perraton 2005: 50). As Webb (2005: 193) comments, the 'flow, of information, money, drugs, and arms across borders has destroyed the illusion of corruption as a domestic political issue to be left to individual countries'.

For a discussion of the concept of global governance, read Rosenau (2004) and Halliday (2004).

3 Collective Action, International Regimes and International Law

The concept of the *international regime* is central to understanding important changes which are underway in terms of states' collective efforts to regulate the international environment. Hasenclever, Mayer and Rittberger (1997) describe regimes as 'codes of conduct' agreed on by states to govern their relations in specific areas of international politics. Regimes are typically, though not exclusively, constituted by political actors such as governments, governmental departments or other governing authorities. Some are arranged as intergovernmental organisations (most notably the United Nations); others arise from specific conventions, treaties, transnational policy issues or areas of interest (Held *et al.* 2005). The term 'international regime' is best conceived, therefore, as a broad term that encompasses many different types of international organisation, agency, coalition and institution.

In terms of size, membership, functional remit and geographical domain, regimes vary enormously. As Young (cited by Held *et al.* 2005: 51) comments:

> *Functionally, they range from the narrow purview of the polar bear agreement to the broad concerns of the arrangements for Antarctica and outer space. The geographical area covered may be as limited as the highly restricted domain of the regime for fur seals in the North Pacific or as far flung as that of the global regimes for international air transport ... With respect to membership, the range runs from two or three members, as in the regime for high-seas fishing established under the International North Pacific Fisheries Convention, to well over a hundred members, as in the nuclear non-proliferation regime.*

Regimes are therefore not merely ad hoc agreements; often they seek to provide frameworks of legal liability, by collectively developing legal frameworks in response to particular policy issues. One of the consequences of the growth of international regimes, therefore, has been the development of an elaborate body of international law. There are now conventions, treaties and other systems of rule and procedure relating to the land, the sea, the air, outer space, diplomacy, neutrality, warfare, human rights; in essence, almost every aspect upon which a state's existence may encroach upon another's (Evans and Newman 1998).

The United Nations (UN) – an intergovernmental organisation with 192 member states – is perhaps the most striking example of an international law-making regime due to its global reach and broad remit. Chapter 1 of the UN Charter sets out its purpose: to maintain international peace and security; develop friendly relations among nations; cooperate in solving international economic, social, cultural and humanitarian problems and promote respect for human rights and fundamental freedoms; and to be a centre for harmonising the actions of nations in attaining these ends (UN n.d.a.).

The UN's work covers a vast array of collective policy areas relating to economic and social development, and international peace and security. In its time, the UN's International Law Commission has sponsored over 500 multilateral agreements, many of which now form the basis of law governing relations between nations (UN n.d.b.). It has also been instrumental in tackling international corruption by developing a number of legal instruments and collective initiatives.

For a comprehensive overview of the subject of international law, refer to Shaw (2003). For definitions of some of the terms used in international law, refer to UN (1999).

4 Collective Action in Response to International Corruption

4.1 BACKGROUND

The issues of bribery and corruption were brought into view for the first time internationally as a result of political events in the US – events that became known as the 'Watergate scandal'. President Nixon was understood to have authorised an unlawful break-in to Hotel Watergate, the Democratic National Committee's head office. Investigation of this incident created a high level of public awareness regarding the dubious conduct of some of the US's political and business elite, and led to further inquiries into corporate involvement in political campaigns. Several companies were found to have contributed illegally to US political campaigns and also to have channelled resources to foreign governments and political parties. In some instances this led to other nations undertaking their own independent inquiries (Posadas 2000).

Following the resignation of Nixon, the US legislative response was the introduction of the Foreign Corrupt Practices Act 1977 (FCPA), the first national statute to criminalise the bribery of foreign officials. Acutely aware of the international dimensions of the problem at hand, US officials were determined to try to use the FCPA to extend liability to competitor companies in foreign countries. During the mid-1970s, therefore, they also began to propose international rules against corruption. While initiatives in the UN and Organisation for Economic Co-operation and Development (OECD) produced no tangible results until the mid-1990s, US activism certainly started the drive towards placing corruption on the international agenda (Sandholtz and Gray 2003).

Internationally, the first wave of anti-corruption initiatives took place at a regional level. The first multilateral agreement was the Organization of American States Inter-American Convention Against Corruption, in 1996. More recently, the international legal fight against corruption has gained momentum, with the OECD's Convention on Combating Bribery of Foreign Public Officials in International Business Transactions in 2001 and the first global agreement, the United Nations Convention Against Corruption (UNCAC), in 2005.

For a comprehensive account of the evolution of regimes in response to international corruption, refer to Posadas (2000).

4.2 THE UNITED NATIONS (UN)

As described earlier, the UN has a broad international remit. Furthermore, due to its size and membership, it is often viewed as the 'most representative international organisation' (Webb 2005: 192). The UN has made tackling corruption a key priority. Through its activities, the organisation has sought to develop 'a global language about corruption and a coherent implementation strategy' (UNODC n.d.a.).

4.2.1 The United Nations Convention Against Corruption (UNCAC)

UNCAC is known to be 'the first binding global agreement on corruption' (Webb 2005: 191). The draft convention was initially signed in 2003 by 95 different states around the world, and in November 2004 this figure rose to 113. Following the process of ratification, the convention came into force in December 2005.

UNCAC is regarded as the most wide-ranging international legal instrument to date. It has four main components: *prevention, criminalisation, international cooperation* and *asset recovery.*

Prevention – a whole chapter of the convention is devoted to prevention in both public and private sectors. Provisions relate to tackling corruption in the judiciary and public procurement, and the setting up of anti-corruption bodies. It includes model preventive policies – for example, on transparency and accountability in the financing of political parties and election campaigns. It also asks states to actively promote the involvement of NGOs, community organisations and other members of civil society in anti-corruption initiatives.

Criminalisation – the convention requires that state signatories criminalise corrupt acts (if they have not already) under domestic law. It requires that states consider the inclusion of a wide range of corrupt activities, from bribery and the embezzlement of public funds to trading in influence and the concealment and laundering of the proceeds of corruption.

International cooperation – the convention requires that countries work collaboratively in preventing, investigating and prosecuting those committing fraud and corruption. Countries are also required to provide forms of mutual legal assistance to one another, in gathering and transferring evidence for use in court, extraditing offenders, and supporting the tracing, freezing, seizure and confiscation of the proceeds of corruption.

Asset recovery – asset recovery is a particularly pertinent issue for many developing countries where high-level corruption has depleted national wealth and diverted valuable resources from much-needed reconstruction and development. The convention outlines several requirements for how cooperation and assistance should be provided in recovering these national assets (UNODC n.d.a.).

  To read the text of the convention, refer to UNODC (2004a).

4.2.2 The United Nations Global Programme Against Corruption (GPAC)

GPAC was set up by the United Nations Office on Drugs and Crime (UNODC). GPAC acts as a resource to help countries effectively implement the provisions laid out in the convention. It provides practical assistance and helps build technical capacity, in particular in developing anti-corruption policies and institutions, and the establishment of preventive anti-corruption frameworks.

It also assists member countries with vulnerable, developing or transitional economies by promoting measures to counter corruption in the public and private sectors, and financial and political elites (UNODC n.d.b.).

4.2.3 The United Nations International Group for Anti-Corruption Coordination (IGAC)

IGAC was set up by the UN and is a group of organisations, including NGOs, involved in anti-corruption policy, advocacy and enforcement. It seeks to provide 'a platform for exchange of views, information, experiences and best practice on anti-corruption activities for the purpose of enhancing the impact of these activities, including support for the UN Convention against Corruption' (U4 n.d.b.). In providing this platform and strengthening international coordination and collaboration, IGAC seeks to minimise undue duplication of activities and ensure the effective and efficient use of the regional and national systems and resources already in place.

4.2.4 The United Nations Global Compact

The United Nations Global Compact is a voluntary corporate citizenship initiative which works to build the social legitimacy of business and markets. As such, it provides a framework for businesses that are committed to aligning their operations and strategies with ten overriding principles in the areas of human rights, labour, the environment and anti-corruption. Principle 10 dictates that businesses should work against corruption in all its forms, including extortion and bribery (United Nations Global Compact n.d.).

4.3 ORGANISATION FOR ECONOMIC CO-OPERATION AND DEVELOPMENT (OECD)

The OECD's role is to help its member governments compare policy experiences, seek answers to common problems, identify good practice and coordinate domestic and international politics. Its work is diverse and spans several policy areas: finance, governance, economy, environment, employment and education. It is committed to promoting more effective public administration, fighting corruption and money laundering, and improving transparency and ethics in international business (OECD n.d.a.).

Its most notable achievement in the field of counter corruption has been the development of the OECD Convention on Combating Bribery of Foreign

Public Officials in International Business Transactions. It is significant due to the nature of the organisation: the 30 members of the OECD represent 70 per cent of world exports and 90 per cent of foreign direct investment and are home to over 75 per cent of multinational corporations. As Webb (2005: 195) notes:

> *The Convention therefore represents an effort to guide the anticorruption activities of governments that influence the flow of most of the world's investment, trade and goods. Moreover, the OECD probably has even more global reach … through its active relationships with 70 other countries and its engagement with civil society.*

4.3.1 The OECD Convention on Combating Bribery of Foreign Public Officials in International Business Transactions

The OECD Convention on Combating Bribery of Foreign Public Officials in International Business Transactions seeks to control bribery taking place in foreign transactions. Its central objective is to use domestic law to combat the bribery of foreign public officials (Webb 2005). Participating states are required to ensure that the incitement, aiding and abetting or authorising of bribery is criminalised and offences are also applicable to corporations and other legal entities.

As of 12 March 2008, the following 38 countries had ratified the convention: Argentina, Australia, Austria, Belgium, Brazil, Bulgaria, Canada, Chile, Czech Republic, Denmark, Estonia, Finland, France, Germany, Greece, Hungary, Iceland, Ireland, Israel, Italy, Japan, Korea, Luxembourg, Mexico, The Netherlands, New Zealand, Norway, Poland, Portugal, Slovak Republic, Slovenia, South Africa, Spain, Sweden, Switzerland, Turkey, UK and US.

The OECD Working Group monitors and promotes full implementation of this convention. The group comprises government experts from the 38 participating countries. It meets four to five times a year at the OECD headquarters in Paris to conduct a two-phased review. Phase one entails an assessment of the examined country's anti-bribery laws. Particular consideration is given to the degree to which these conform to the OECD convention. Phase two is a practical one-week assessment to see how effectively these laws are implemented in practice. This involves intensive meetings in the examined country with key figures from government, law enforcement authorities, business, trade unions and civil society (OECD n.d.b.).

For more information on the OECD convention, visit: http://www.oecd.org

4.4 EUROPEAN ORGANISATIONS AND INITIATIVES

Several European organisations have also initiated counter corruption measures.

4.4.1 Council of Europe: Group of States Against Corruption

The Council of Europe (COE), founded in 1949, is Europe's oldest political organisation; it consists of 45 countries, including 21 from Central and Eastern Europe (Webb 2005). In 1999, the COE established the Group of States Against Corruption (GRECO). Its objective is to monitor states' compliance with its anti-corruption standards:

> *GRECO's objective is to improve the capacity of its members to fight corruption by monitoring their compliance with Council of Europe anti-corruption standards through a dynamic process of mutual evaluation and peer pressure. It helps to identify deficiencies in national anti-corruption policies, prompting the necessary legislative, institutional and practical reforms. GRECO also provides a platform for the sharing of best practice in the prevention and detection of corruption (GRECO n.d.).*

Its approach is to tackle corruption in a multidisciplinary way. This includes the following:

- setting European norms and standards;

- monitoring compliance with these standards and offering help with capacity building to individual countries and regions; and

- providing technical co-operation programmes

(COE n.d.).

The COE has adopted a number of legal instruments: the Criminal Law Convention on Corruption (ETS 173); the Civil Law Convention on Corruption (ETS 174); the Additional Protocol to the Criminal Law Convention on Corruption (ETS 191); the Twenty Guiding Principles against Corruption (Resolution (97) 24); the Recommendation on Codes of Conduct for Public Officials (Recommendation No. R (2000) 10); and the Recommendation on Common Rules against Corruption in the Funding of Political Parties and Electoral Campaigns (COE n.d.).

4.4.2 Criminal and Civil Law Conventions on Corruption

The Criminal Law Convention on Corruption was signed in January 1999 with a collaborative agreement by all member states 'that an effective fight against corruption requires increased, rapid and well-functioning international co-operation' (COE 1999a).

The Civil Law Convention on Corruption was set up in November 1999, ten months after the Criminal Law Convention was formed. The member states were 'convinced of the importance for civil law to contribute to the fight against corruption, in particular by enabling persons who have suffered damage to receive fair compensation' (COE 1999b). It represents the first attempt to articulate common international rules for civil litigation in corruption cases (Webb 2005). Compliance with the COE conventions is monitored by GRECO.

For more information on these two conventions, visit:

http://www.coe.int/

For more information on the full list of COE legal instruments, refer to Council of Europe (n.d.).

4.4.3 European Union: European Anti-Fraud Office (OLAF)

The mission of the European Anti-Fraud Office (OLAF) is to protect the financial interests of the EU by fighting fraud, corruption and any other irregular activity, including misconduct within the European institutions. It achieves this by conducting internal and external investigations, in line with its treaties:

OLAF carries out all the powers of investigation conferred on the Commission by Community legislation and the agreements in force with third countries, with a view of reinforcing the fight against fraud, corruption and any other illegal activity affecting the financial interests of the European Community (OLAF n.d.).

In addition, it facilitates cooperation between the authorities of its member states so they are better able to coordinate their activities, and supplies its member states with support and technical knowledge to aid their own anti-fraud activities. It also contributes to the development of the European Union anti-fraud strategy and undertakes initiatives to strengthen relevant legislation.

4.4.4 Stability Pact Anti-Corruption Initiative (SPAI)

The Stability Pact Anti-Corruption Initiative (SPAI) was adopted in Sarajevo in 2000 under the direction of the EU to fight corruption in south-eastern Europe. Following political events in the region, corruption was considered to be one of the most serious threats to the recovery and development of south-east-European countries. It aims to adopt and implement international anti-corruption instruments; promote good governance and reliable public administration; strengthen national legislation and the rule of law; promote integrity in business operations; and promote an active civil society (SPAI n.d.).

SPAI member countries are required to take measures in these key reform areas.

4.5 OTHER INTERNATIONAL ORGANISATIONS, COALITIONS AND CONVENTIONS

4.5.1 The Organisation of American States (OAS): Inter-American Convention Against Corruption

The main role of the Organisation of American States (OAS) is to provide a multilateral forum for strengthening democracy, promoting human rights and confronting shared problems such as poverty, terrorism, illegal drugs and corruption. There are 35 member states: Antigua and Barbuda, Argentina, The Bahamas, Barbados, Belize, Bolivia, Brazil, Canada, Chile, Columbia, Costa Rica, Cuba, Dominica, Ecuador, El Salvador, Grenada, Guatemala, Guyana, Haiti, Honduras, Jamaica, Mexico, Nicaragua, Panama, Paraguay, Peru, Saint Kitts and Nevis, Saint Lucia, Saint Vincent and The Grenadines, Suriname,

Trinidad and Tobago, United States of America, Uruguay and Venezuela (while Cuba is a member, the country has been forbidden to participate in the Convention since 1962 as a result of its relations with the US following the Cuban revolution in 1959).

In 1996, the members adopted the Inter-American Convention Against Corruption, which was understood to be the first treaty of its kind. The purposes of the Convention are twofold: 'to promote and strengthen the development by each of the States Parties of the mechanisms needed to prevent, detect, punish and eradicate corruption'; and 'to promote, facilitate and regulate cooperation among the States Parties to ensure the effectiveness of the measures' (OAS n.d.).

The Convention established a set of agreed preventive measures, for example in relation to the criminalisation of certain acts of corruption. It also outlined a number of provisions to strengthen cooperation between signatories, for example in respect of mutual legal assistance, extradition and asset tracing.

4.5.2 The African Union Convention on Preventing and Combating Corruption

The African Union Convention on Preventing and Combating Corruption was signed by the member states of the African Union, which consists of 53 nations in total. It emphasises the need for international cooperation and requires member states to:

- Collaborate with countries of origin of multinationals to criminalise and punish the practice of secret commissions and other forms of corrupt practices during international trade transactions.

- Foster regional, continental and international cooperation to prevent corrupt practices in international trade transactions.

- Encourage all countries to take legislative measures to prevent corrupt public officials from enjoying ill-acquired assets by freezing their foreign accounts and facilitating the repatriation of stolen or illegally acquired monies to the countries of origin.

- Work closely with international, regional and sub-regional financial organisations to eradicate corruption in development aid and cooperation programmes by defining strict regulations for eligibility and good governance of candidates within the general framework of their development policy.

- Cooperate in conformity with relevant international instruments on international cooperation on criminal matters for purposes of investigations and procedures in offences within the jurisdiction of the Convention

(African Union 2003: 21–22).

 For a more comprehensive look at the convention, refer to African Union (2003).

4.5.3 Interpol Group of Experts on Corruption (IGEC)

Dating back to 1923, Interpol is the world's largest international police organisation. Its aim is to facilitate 'cross-border police co-operation, and [it] supports and assists all organizations, authorities and services whose mission is to prevent or combat international crime' (Interpol n.d.a.). As regards corruption specifically, the organisation 'established the Interpol Group of Experts on Corruption (IGEC) in 1998, and is currently in the process of developing the Interpol Anti-Corruption Office (IACO) and International Anti-Corruption Academy (IACA)' (Interpol n.d.b.).

4.6 INTERNATIONAL DEVELOPMENT BANKS

International Development Banks, such as the World Bank and International Monetary Fund, have also become active in the field of counter fraud and corruption. We now consider these in more detail.

4.6.1 The World Bank

The World Bank is owned by its 185 member countries and comprises two development institutions – the International Bank for Reconstruction and Development (IBRD) and the International Development Association (IDA). Its key objective is to provide financial and technical assistance to developing countries. Together, the two institutions provide low-interest loans, interest-free credit and grants to developing countries for education, health, infrastructure, communications and other purposes (World Bank n.d.a.). It finances around 45,000 contracts each year, worth roughly $45–50 billion (Hawley 2000).

Concerns about responsibility for past loans that had been lost prompted the World Bank to consider an anti-corruption strategy. For example, as will be explored in Chapter 10, during General Suharto's three decades of rule, it lent Indonesia a total of $30 billion. The World Bank estimated that at least 20–30 per cent of these development budget funds had been diverted through informal payments to government staff and politicians.

Consequently, in 1997, the World Bank declared its commitment to implementing a 'systematic framework for addressing corruption as a development issue in the assistance it provides to countries and in its operation work more generally' (World Bank, cited by Marquette 2003: 1). This strategy was twofold. The first aspect was related to borrower accountability – for, as World Bank president James Wolfensohn stated while speaking at an anti-corruption conference in 1999, industrialised countries 'do not want to give money for development assistance that ends up in offshore bank accounts' (Hawley 2000: 4). The second element was to focus on internal accountability.

For more information about the World Bank, visit its anti-corruption website: http://www.worldbank.org/html/extdr/thematic.htm

4.6.2 International Monetary Fund (IMF)

The IMF has 185 member countries and was established to promote 'international monetary cooperation, exchange stability, and orderly exchange arrangements; to foster economic growth and high levels of employment' (IMF n.d.). Hawley (2000) highlights the scale of the IMF's activities; between 1998 and 1999, it lent around $90 billion.

Like the World Bank, the IMF came under increasing pressure to take more responsibility for its loans. In Russia, for instance, it was known that President Boris Yeltsin used some $5 billion of multilateral funds, including money from the IMF, for his re-election campaign in 1996. Later, allegations surfaced that

IMF loans were being laundered back into US bank accounts. Following these scandals, the IMF began to take a tougher stance on fraud and corruption issues. In 1997, it stated its intention to take a more proactive approach to eliminate the opportunity for corruption and fraudulent activity. It now requires that borrowing governments draw up anti-corruption action plans and strategies.

> For more information about the IMF, visit http://www.imf.org/external/work.htm

5 Countering International Corruption: A Critical Analysis

5.1 REGIMES AND INTERNATIONAL LAW: THEORETICAL PERSPECTIVES

While it is generally accepted that the emergence of international regimes and their regulatory frameworks can be seen as an expression of the necessity to find new modes of cooperation and regulation for collective policy problems, there is much debate about their effectiveness, particularly from within the academic discipline of international relations (IR).

IR theorists have attempted to explain: which processes and structures foster and sustain international cooperative regimes; how and to what extent international institutions affect state behaviour and collective outcomes in certain issue areas; factors that determine the stability of regimes; and whether explanations exist for the properties of particular institutional arrangements, such as the degree of formalisation and centralisation (Hasenclever *et al.* 1996).

> For an introduction to IR theory, read Brown (2005) and Burchill *et al.* (2005). For a comprehensive glossary of terms used in IR literature, refer to Evans and Newman (1998). For a critical review of the impact or 'consequences' of international regimes, refer to Underdal and Young (2004).

There is also a vast body of literature devoted to the subject of international law and the question of whether it can ever be effective in regulating the actions of the international community. To grasp these different theoretical perspectives, it is important to understand the substantial differences between international law and domestic law. In domestic society, laws are applied and enforced by a legislative and executive institution on behalf of government. In international society, however, there is no world government; there is no world legislature and executive with the power to enforce international law. As such, some argue that compliance with international law is largely voluntary (Webb 2005).

Certainly there is evidence that states and other actors do comply with international regulations, but there are also examples of non-compliance. As a result, commentators have sought to theorise this phenomenon. For example, according to Hathaway (cited by Webb 2005), politically, there are three levels of incentives that affect whether a country will comply with international laws:

- Domestic legal incentives – seeing how other national organisations have enforced the laws in question.

- Transnational legal incentives – seeing how other international bodies and state parties have enforced the laws in question.

- Non-legal incentives – seeing the reactions of other national and international bodies having applied the laws.

 For a theoretical consideration of states' compliance with international law, refer to Raustiala and Slaughter (2002).

Critics such as Keuleers claim that despite new legislation and the establishment of more anti-corruption and integrity regimes and institutions, 'the overall results remain disappointing, intentions still outnumber accomplishments, and tangible successes remain sparse' (Keuleers 2005: 58). Certainly there are some difficulties in relation to the scope of the conventions and how they are monitored, implemented and enforced by the international community.

5.2 COUNTERING INTERNATIONAL CORRUPTION: CHALLENGES AND OPPORTUNITIES

5.2.1 Scope of the conventions

The scope of conventions is negotiated by state parties; ultimately, the outcome depends on the collective political will of member states. Agreement, therefore, has to balance the competing interests, political and legal systems, and often competing conceptual interpretations, of these negotiating parties.

Webb (2005: 228) commented, for example, that negotiation of UNCAC was fraught with controversy, particularly over critical issues such as asset recovery, private sector corruption, political corruption and implementation. As such, she claims, the convention ultimately retreated to the 'safety of noncommittal legal language and deferral of the hard decisions to another day'. This is significant because failure to agree specific requirements can potentially leave conventions open to interpretation, thus undermining their effectiveness.

During the negotiation of UNCAC, while all negotiating parties agreed that the issue of asset recovery should be a high priority, there were significant differences of opinion about how to reconcile the needs of the countries seeking return of the assets with the legal and procedural safeguards of the countries whose assistance is needed. After much debate, mandatory provisions were agreed for establishing measures to allow state parties to recover property through civil actions or via international cooperation in confiscation (Articles 53 and 54 of UNCAC), but not without compromise. For although the seizure and freezing of property was made compulsory for state parties, they are only required to 'consider' preserving property for confiscation (Webb 2005). Some might question, therefore, whether UNCAC was revolutionary or far-reaching enough in this area to be effective.

Similarly, Hawley (2000: 15) outlined the 'loopholes' within the OECD convention. He claims that it failed to:

- prohibit the funding of foreign political parties;

- make parent companies responsible for the corruption their subsidiaries or agents engage in;

- include as bribery non-cash gifts such as shares, trips and other forms of excessive hospitality;

- specify sanctions or means of enforcing the accord; and

- spell out how cases should be brought to the attention of the relevant national authority – by the government of the country whose official has been bribed or by the government of the country whose company has offered the bribe.

5.2.2 Monitoring and implementation

As demonstrated, drafting international conventions can be an enormously complex exercise, since it is necessary to balance the competing interests of state actors. There are also substantial obstacles in monitoring and implementing the conventions once they have come into force. For conventions to be helpful, however, it is important that they are monitored and implemented effectively. As Webb (2005: 218) commented:

> 'Law', in the sense of a set of formal written documents, will be largely irrelevant if the rules are not embedded in an institutional and organisational structure that favours compliance – state parties have to follow through on their decision to sign and ratify the Convention; the UNCAC must be translated into visible, meaningful changes on the ground.

Webb (2005: 228) also commented that it is 'undeniably challenging to design a monitoring mechanism that does not encroach too far on state sovereignty, especially on a subject as controversial as corruption'. While it can be said that the OECD and COE models and monitoring mechanisms have achieved some results, particularly in the area of domestic implementation laws, Elliot (1997: 226) makes the point – in relation to the OECD convention – that there are 'difficulties in observing and documenting illicit payments, which raises concerns about free riders – countries who may commit themselves to sanction such behaviour but then fail to enforce with vigor'.

In terms of implementation, some aspects of UNCAC pose distinct challenges – Mutual Legal Assistance (MLA), for example. MLA is crucial to effectively implementing asset recovery, but it is a complex area. The main obstacle is that MLA implies the coordination of legal systems that might be very different. They could differ, for example, in their conceptions, laws and approaches to police action, the rights granted to the accused, or the independence of the courts. Schmid (2006: 203) asserts, therefore, that 'universal standards in that field have not grown much beyond declaration of good intentions'. Furthermore, in practice, political and legal authorities are often reluctant to embrace MLA:

> *MLA remains characterised by national conceit and international suspicion. Politicians and judges do remain uneasy with the concept that a foreign country's authorities are to be trusted when they ask for cooperation in investigating a criminal matter ... Certain abuses have done little to help promote an open approach to international cooperation (Schmid 2006: 204).*

For more a detailed appraisal of various international anti-corruption conventions and their effectiveness, read part two of TI (2004).

5.2.3 Compliance and enforcement

Theoretically, when a treaty comes into existence, ratifying states are legally bound to comply with it according to the principle of 'pacta sunt servanda' (Webb 2005: 222). As we have seen, however, in the contemporary international system there is no single political authority above the state. In practical terms, therefore, states cannot be forced to comply. As a result, critics such as Austin allege that since the international system is characterised by the absence of a legislature, judiciary and executive, it is not possible to talk of an international legal order. International law, Austin maintains, is not 'law properly so-called', but is at most 'positive morality' (cited by Evans and Newman 1998: 262).

For example, theoretically, those who have ratified UNCAC could be brought before the International Court of Justice (the judicial arm of the United Nations) if they fail to uphold the convention. The court's role is to 'settle, in accordance with international law, legal disputes submitted to it by States and give advisory opinions on legal questions referred to it by authorised United Nations organs and specialised agencies' (International Court of Justice, n.d.). With no central enforcement power, however, the court cannot enforce its judgements; it depends entirely on the country in question to ensure they are followed through.

The issue is further complicated by the fact that many of the requirements conferred upon states are not easily carried out in practice. For example, the recovery of assets derived from grand corruption have been hampered due to several major obstacles:

- the complexity of cases, which often require input from experts in forensic accounting and money laundering;

- the expense of pursuing assets overseas;

- the complexity of reconciling the different civil and criminal laws in different countries; and

- the political will of state parties, particularly if their own legitimacy is called into question

(Webb 2005: 211).

There is often a tension between domestic and international political considerations and compliance.

Between 2004 and 2006, a team of lawyers, accountants, financial investigators and police officers from the UK Serious Fraud Office (SFO), carried out an investigation into allegations of bribery by BAE Systems Plc (BAE) in relation to the Al-Yamamah military aircraft contracts with the Kingdom of Saudi Arabia. Eventually, however, the investigation was halted by the then Prime Minister Tony Blair – a decision that was widely condemned (BBC 2007). Throughout the investigation, BAE had sought to persuade the Attorney General and SFO that pursuing the investigation would be contrary to the public interest because it would adversely affect relations between the UK and Saudi Arabia, thus preventing the UK from securing an enormous export contract. So, while the UK is a signatory of the OECD convention and internationally actively promotes anti-bribery, it appeared to give way to domestic pressures from the Ministry of Defence and the fear of job losses at BAE if its contract was lost.

Despite these difficulties, some commentators remain positive in their appraisal, holding that the convention can be seen as a blueprint for policy reform on a global level. They would argue that international regimes encourage dialogue between nations and therefore provide a vocabulary with which to approach collective policy issues. In that sense, international law, whether enforced adequately or not, can be seen as a benchmark upon which actors know they will be judged and which in turn will affect their behaviour.

 For a critical appraisal of UNCAC, refer to Webb (2005).

Study Questions

- What particular challenge does corruption present for the international community? How is it different from tackling these issues within national borders?

- Critically assess the role of international law in countering corruption.

- What do you think are the main challenges to global governance in relation to tackling corruption?

- Read the Asia-Pacific Economic Cooperation policy brief (2004). What does the brief say about how the convention will be monitored and enforced?

- Do you think international law can be effective in countering corruption?

- Read Webb (2005). According to Webb, what were the main obstacles to negotiating UNCAC? Why were these areas particularly difficult to negotiate and why?

5

Countering Corruption – The Role of Non-State Actors

1 Introduction

This chapter focuses on the role of non-state actors, or Non-Governmental Organisations (NGOs), and their efforts to counter international corruption. It also considers how these organisations interact with the international regimes and regulatory frameworks described in the preceding chapter.

2 What is an NGO?

A Non-Governmental Organisation (NGO) is a legally constituted, non-profit, voluntary group, typically task-oriented in its activities and driven by citizens with a common interest (NGO Global Network n.d.). Like the international regimes that were considered in Chapter 4, NGOs are by no means a homogeneous group but are extremely diverse in terms of their size, function and membership.

NGOs are non-governmental in so far as they are independent of government control, having little or no participation in or representation of any government or political party (Maslyukivska 1999). When NGOs are funded partially or totally by governments, they maintain their non-governmental status by excluding government representatives from membership. NGOs are sometimes also described as civil society, grassroots, private voluntary or self-help organisations or as transnational social movements. In terms of geographical remit, NGOs can be organised on a community, national or transnational level. This chapter is primarily concerned with NGOs that have a transnational reach, whether regional or international.

Most NGOs exist to further the political or social goals of their members or funders, but these goals cover a broad range of political and philosophical positions. Some exist to promote the observance of human rights or the preservation of the natural environment, or to improve the welfare of the disadvantaged. Others exist to further a more corporate agenda. They might also be sub-divided further – for example, according to whether they are religious or secular, and whether publicly or privately oriented.

To demonstrate the diversity of NGOs, some well-known examples are listed below:

- *Red Cross* – a volunteer-led, politically and religiously neutral humanitarian crisis-relief NGO (for more information, visit http://www.redcross.org.uk/).

- *Greenpeace* – an NGO that investigates, exposes and confronts environmental abuse by governments and corporations around the world. To maintain its independence and political neutrality it accepts no donations from governments, corporations or political parties (for more information, visit http://www.greenpeace.org.uk/).

- *Christian Aid* – a faith-based NGO dedicated to fighting the causes of poverty worldwide (for more information, visit http://www.christianaid.org.uk/).

- *International Chamber of Commerce (ICC)* – ICC champions itself as the voice of worldwide business, with thousands of member companies in over 130 countries worldwide. Its members vary considerably in size and represent a broad cross-section of business activity. Its activities range from arbitration and dispute resolution to making the case for open trade and the market economy system, business self-regulation, fighting corruption and combating commercial crime (for more information, visit http://www.iccwbo.org/).

 For a more detailed consideration of different NGO typologies, refer to Maslyukivska (1999).

3 Types of NGO

Several authors have attempted to develop typologies of NGOs in relation to their membership, remit and function. The World Bank's typology is perhaps the most simple and useful, classifying NGOs as either advocacy or operational.

3.1 ADVOCACY

According to the World Bank typology, advocacy NGOs exist to promote a specific cause. These organisations typically engage in campaign work to raise awareness or knowledge of specific issues, or to give them more prominence in international affairs. This might be done through a variety of means, including demonstrations, pilot projects, participation in public forums, formulation of government policy and plans, publicising research results and case studies, press work and other forms of lobbying and political activism (Maslyukivska 1999). As Charnovitz (2006: 348) notes, 'often it has been crusading NGOs that have led the way for states to see the international dimension of what was previously regarded as a domestic matter'.

NGO activism has increased dramatically in recent decades. Frequently, NGOs are now present at international negotiations in order to represent their causes directly and, as such, are increasingly involved in the formation of international conventions. This is certainly true in the field of international corruption. For example, as will be described later in this chapter, Transparency International was involved in the development of the United Nations Convention Against Corruption (UNCAC).

 For a discussion of the NGOs and their role in influencing international law, refer to Charnovitz (2006).

3.2 OPERATIONAL

According to the World Bank typology, an operational NGO's primary purpose is the design and implementation of development-related projects. These are often, though not always, further classified into relief-oriented and development-oriented organisations (NGO n.d.).

Operational NGOs are normally involved in practical interventions. For example, NGOs operating in the field of international corruption might act as a resource for anti-corruption activities, whether by funding project-related activities or by offering information, advice and training for those working in the field. Operational NGOs that represent industries or spheres of business interest might also attempt to regulate the activities of their own members – through codes of conduct, rules and protocol – in a similar way to that in which international law endeavours to regulate the activities of its signatories (states).

In reality, the distinction between advocacy and operational organisations may be blurred, with many NGOs undertaking both operational and advocacy work. However, the typology is useful in terms of delineating the types of activity in which they are involved.

4 NGO Activity in Countering International Corruption

There are many different types of NGO working in the field of international corruption – their number has steadily increased over the last two decades. The following section gives an introduction to some of the most prominent NGOs in the global anti-corruption community. This is by no means an exhaustive list but is intended to give an overview of some of the main types of initiative currently underway.

4.1 TRANSPARENCY INTERNATIONAL (TI)

TI is an international NGO founded in 1993. It is the only international NGO set up solely to combat corruption and is highly prominent in the field due to its high-profile advocacy work. The goals of TI's advocacy are to 'raise awareness about the damaging effects of corruption, advocate policy reform, work towards the implementation of multilateral conventions and subsequently monitor compliance by governments, corporations and banks' (TI n.d.e.).

TI's global network includes more than 90 locally established national chapters and chapters-in-formation. These chapters operate nationally by bringing together other actors from the business world, government, civil society and media to ensure there is 'transparency in elections, in public administration, in procurement and in business' (TI n.d.e.). They also engage in advocacy work to lobby governments to implement anti-corruption reforms.

TI has developed several corruption measurement tools that are widely used internationally – though, as discussed in Chapter 2, not without controversy. These include the Corruption Perceptions Index, Bribe Payers Index and Global Corruption Barometer. TI also publishes the Global Corruption Report and provides online guides for anti-corruption practitioners (TI n.d.f.).

In addition, TI developed a National Integrity System (NIS), which is promoted as part of its holistic approach to countering corruption. NIS, it is claimed, provides 'a framework which anti-corruption organisations can use to analyse both the extent and causes of corruption in a given country as well as the effectiveness of anti-corruption efforts' (TI 2000). The institutional pillars of the NIS are represented in Figure 5.1.

It is suggested that all countries have some kind of NIS in place, but they vary in their effectiveness, depending on the level of corruption found within each of the pillars. The concept of the NIS is proffered as a conceptual

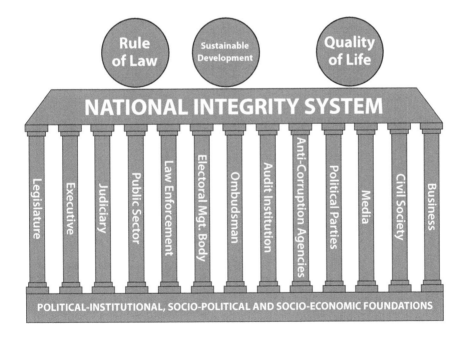

Figure 5.1   Pillars of the National Integrity System

Source: Reprinted from *TI Source Book* 2000 (Berlin: Transparency International). Copyright 24 March 2011 Transparency International: the global coalition against corruption. Used with permission. For more information, visit http://www.transparency.org (TI 2000).

framework which enables reformers take a holistic view of corruption, and encourages them to appreciate the interconnectedness of the pillars and focus efforts on each key area (TI 2000: 31).

For more information about TI and its activities, refer to its website:

http://www.transparency.org/

4.2 GLOBAL TRANSPARENCY INITIATIVE (GTI)

GTI is an international network of civil society organisations which promotes transparency and openness in international financial institutions (IFIs) such as the World Bank, International Monetary Fund (IMF), European Investment Bank and Regional Development Banks. Underpinning its approach is the conviction that people in the international community have the right to information from these public institutions and a right to participate in the development of policies and projects that affect their lives (GTI n.d.a.). Also central to its approach is the belief that transparency can help reduce corruption and, in doing so, contribute positively to economic and social development.

GTI brings together communities of activists and experts from around the world. Together, they campaign on two related issues:

- Full accountability in the use of public power vested in the IFIs.

- The right to access information at state level.

(GTI n.d.a.)

Some of GTI's current projects include:

- The drafting of a 'Transparency Charter', which sets out the standards and norms that, it says, should govern IFI disclosure policy.

- The development of a comprehensive transparency resource, which compares the transparency standards of ten IFIs.

- Case studies and transparency audits illustrating how transparency, or lack of it, has contributed to positive and negative outcomes.

- Comparative legal studies looking at specific exceptions of particular importance to IFI openness.

- Advocacy around ongoing IFI disclosure policy reviews.

(GTI n.d.b.)

GTI also provides small grants to individuals and organisations seeking to contribute to any of these activities.

For more information about GTI and its activities, refer to its website:

http://www.ifitransparency.org/

4.3 TRACE INTERNATIONAL

TRACE is an international non-profit organisation that was set up 'to provide anti-bribery support for companies and commercial intermediaries across all industries and regions' (TRACE n.d.). It aims to provide transparency to companies and organisations around the world. On its website TRACE comments that, due to the implementation of the OECD Convention on Combating Bribery of Foreign Public Officials in International Business Transactions, 30 new laws have been formed which specify that all businesses are liable for corrupt activities when management knows or should have known that an offer of bribery could be made. As a result 'companies are required to conduct sufficient due diligence on prospective intermediaries to ensure that they are committed to ethical business practices regardless of business pressure, local law or custom' (TRACE n.d.).

For more information on TRACE International, visit:

http://www.traceinternational.org

4.4 INTERNATIONAL CHAMBER OF COMMERCE (ICC)

As described earlier in the chapter, the ICC champions itself as the voice of worldwide business, with thousands of member companies in over 130 countries. One of its main areas of work is anti-corruption. Its main objective is to 'encourage self-regulation by business in confronting issues of extortion and bribery, and to provide business input into international initiatives to fight corruption' (ICC n.d.).

The ICC has therefore set up an anti-corruption commission, composed of anti-corruption experts from ICC member companies and business representative organisations. To date, its work has focused on the following:

- the revision and publication of ICC rules of conduct and recommendations to combat extortion and bribery;

- the publication of a *Fighting corruption* handbook;

- raising awareness of the problem of the solicitation of bribes as a key element in fighting corruption; and

- monitoring the latest developments in relation to international conventions against corruption.

(ICC n.d.).

Projects that are underway focus on strengthening links with the World Bank and other intergovernmental organisations engaged in fighting corruption, developing further recommendations on corporate whistleblowing schemes, and the continuing provision of business input in the implementation processes of international conventions (ICC n.d.).

4.5 GLOBAL WITNESS

Global Witness is an NGO that seeks to address the relationship between the exploitation of natural resources, and conflict and corruption. It seeks to expose corruption and exploitation of natural resources and international trade systems, in order to drive campaigns that end impunity, resource-linked conflict, and human rights and environmental abuses. Relevant areas of work are corruption in oil, gas and mining, and the role of financial institutions (Global Witness n.d.).

Global Witness lobbies on these issues and has been involved in the development of international mechanisms and initiatives to address them, including the Extractive Industries Transparency Initiative (EITI). EITI is an international multi-stakeholder effort that seeks to have both sides of a transaction made clear and available to the public so it can see if there are any discrepancies in the figures. In addition to working on policy advocacy, Global Witness actively investigates instances of corruption.

For more information on Global Witness, visit:

http://www.globalwitness.org

4.6 INTERNATIONAL CENTRE FOR ASSET RECOVERY (ICAR)

ICAR is based at the Basel Institute for Governance, an independent non-profit institution that carries out multidisciplinary research and policy advice in public, corporate and global governance. A specific focus of its work has been fighting corruption and money laundering (Basel Institute for Governance n.d.).

ICAR itself specialises in (ibid.):

> *... training and assisting developing countries in the practical work of tracing, confiscating and repatriating the proceeds of corruption, money laundering and related crimes. ICAR assists developing countries in building capacities and setting up necessary procedures and institutions to more effectively make use of international legal assistance in criminal matters for the purpose of recovering stolen assets.*

ICAR intends to act as a permanent resource in international asset recovery cases, by offering advice and assistance and by acting as facilitator. It has also made its primary goal the support of countries in implementing the provisions of UNCAC relating to asset recovery.

For more information about ICAR, visit:

http://www.assetrecovery.org and http://www.baselgovernance.org/icar

4.7 PARTNERSHIP FOR TRANSPARENCY FUND (PTF)

PTF is a non-profit organisation that has three related functions. First, it funds activities and projects initiated by civil society organisations aimed at fighting corruption. Secondly, it helps civil society organisations that are already participating in anti-corruption initiatives. In these instances, PTF is able to fund specialists to assist in specific, finite activities to build their capacity. Thirdly, in some circumstances, PTF supports workshops and seminars aimed at strengthening anti-corruption efforts (PTF 2008).

Some examples of its work include the following:

- monitoring public contracts, public auctions for sale of public assets, or the privatisation of public companies;

- reviewing draft anti-corruption legislation and regulations;

- monitoring activities of official anti-corruption offices;

- participating in inquiries related to corruption; and

- undertaking surveys to track and measure corruption.

For more information about PTF, visit:

http://www.partnershipfortransparency.info

4.8 INTERNATIONAL ASSOCIATION OF FINANCIAL CRIMES INVESTIGATORS (IAFCI)

IAFCI is a non-profit international organisation formed in 1968 by a group of law enforcement officers and special agents of the credit card industry. The association provides 'services and an environment within which information about financial fraud, fraud investigation and fraud prevention methods can be collected, exchanged and taught for the common good of the financial payment industry and our global society' (IAFCI n.d.).

IAFCI works collaboratively with public and private sector organisations, internationally, to counter financial fraud. It hosts annual workshops and training conferences and acts as a resource for information and training.

For more information about IAFCI, visit:

http://www.iafci.org

4.9 GLOBAL INTEGRITY

Global Integrity describes itself as 'an innovation lab for the transparency and accountability community'(Global Integrity n.d.a). Its work is primarily focused on governance, transparency and accountability reforms in public sectors around the world, and its approach based on the premise that these reforms are best achieved when grounded on robust evidence. Its strategy, therefore, is to develop tools, technologies and methodologies which allow reformers to 'make the case' for key reforms, based on their potential to yield positive results (Global Integrity n.d.b.). While its work is tailored to the specific needs of its public, private and civil society 'constituencies', it is based on a common approach:

> *[...] diagnose the specific challenges of corruption and governance at various levels of government; provide those findings to stakeholders who can sue them to implement evidence-based reforms; and build the capacity of others to continue the cycle of research, outreach, knowledge sharing, and monitoring in the future (Global Integritiy n.d.c.).*

The organisation also produces a 'Global Integrity Report', which contains cross-national governance and corruption indicators. Each country assessment comprises two elements: a qualitative report and an 'Integrity Indicator' scorecard, based on quantitative data. The scorecard assesses 'the existence, effectiveness, and citizen access to key governance and anti-corruption mechanisms' (Global Integrity n.d.d.), and considers issues such as transparency in public procurement and media freedom.

For more information about Global Integrity, visit:

http://www.globalintegrity.org/

4.10 GLOBAL ORGANIZATION OF PARLIAMENTARIANS AGAINST CORRUPTION (GOPAC)

Formed in 2002, GOPAC is a network of parliamentarians, organised on a regional basis to fight corruption and promote good governance. It was formed in recognition of the fact that many parliamentarians seek to provide good governance but are limited by parliaments with 'weak support services, limited traditions in playing the core democratic roles of legislation, oversight and representation, and domination by a powerful executive' (GOPAC n.d.).

Its work is underpinned by three main pillars: peer support, political leadership and education. In terms of peer support, GOPAC links together and supports parliamentarians committed to fighting corruption and working towards good governance with their peers. As regards political leadership, it facilitates the transfer of expertise by providing opportunities for parliamentarians to assist their colleagues. Thirdly, in terms of education, GOPAC facilitates various workshops around the world with the aim of building stronger understanding of the duties of parliamentarians (ibid.).

For more information about GOPAC, visit:

http://www.gopacnetwork.org/

4.11 'PUBLISH WHAT YOU PAY'

'Publish What You Pay' is a scheme which was set up to combat corruption in extractive industries in emerging markets. It is backed by both non-governmental and civil society organisations, which aim to help citizens of developing countries to hold governments responsible for the use of revenues from investments. It is underpinned by the notion that payments made by natural resource companies to developing country governments need to be more transparent and officials who are benefiting at the expense of their citizens exposed.

The scheme encourages information disclosure, accountability and asset recovery (Parham 2006) and asks that the following information is disclosed: net taxes, fees, royalties and other payments.

5 The Role of NGOs: A Critical Analysis

5.1 EXPOSING CORRUPTION, ENCOURAGING TRANSPARENCY

In terms of exposing corrupt practice, NGO activity has been significant. For example, Global Witness wages international campaigns to expose companies which perpetuate corruption – whether directly or indirectly – in their search for profits, and 'the brutality and injustice that results from the fight to access and control natural resource wealth' (Global Witness 2010b: 1). They begin from the premise that companies are often able to act with impunity in their search for income maximisation, and this acts as a major driver of the overall problem. By exposing corrupt practice and highlighting the negative spin-offs of such activity, their intention is to exert pressure on those actors involved and ultimately force them to change their business practice.

For example, in 2009 Global Witness published a report about the militarisation of mining in the eastern Democratic Republic of Congo (DRC), *Faced with a gun, what can you do?* (Global Witness 2009). The report documents findings of field research carried out in the region, detailing the groups involved in plundering minerals, how they have used them to extort illegal 'taxes' from the civilian population, and how violence and intimidation has been used against civilians working for them, to ensure they comply. In addition to naming the armed groups involved and those involved in smuggling/transiting the minerals, the report also names foreign companies which sell the minerals on to a range of processing and manufacturing companies, thereby facilitating the corrupt trade (Global Witness 2009: 7).

Among the named companies was Thaisarco, a subsidiary of British-based trading company Amalgamated Metals Corporation (AMC). Shortly after it was named, the company publicly announced that it would suspend sourcing from the DRC, citing 'the threat of misleading and bad publicity' (Global Witness 2010a: 7). The tin industry body (International Tin Research Institute, or ITRI) also announced that it would bolster its effort to 'agree guidelines for supply chain traceability for companies sourcing from the DRC' (Global Witness 2010a: 7).

Global Witness has claimed this cessation of the company's involvement with the DRC, and ITRI's increased emphasis on tackling this problem, as a victory in its efforts against natural resource-related corruption. Though it is difficult to determine whether these outcomes can be seen as a direct consequence of the pressures exerted by Global Witness's campaigning activity, it is reasonable to assume that the organisation was influential. To echo the sentiments expressed by Thaisarco representatives, bad publicity is bad for business.

For more information about the recent work of Global Witness, see Global Witness (2010a).

For more information about the investigation in eastern DRC, see Global Witness (2009).

NGOs have also been at the forefront of initiatives to encourage transparency in international business dealings. For example, various NGOs have been engaged in initiatives that promote information disclosure, accountability and asset recovery in extractive industries in emerging markets (Rose-Ackerman 2004: 334–335) – 'Publish What You Pay', for example. The difficulty for programmes like this is that all the multinational contractors and concessionaries in an industry need to agree on the voluntary procedure and to enforce mandatory standards, such as participating countries making disclosure a condition for doing business. Also, disclosure by firms and governments could become a condition for receiving investment guarantees and subsidies from the international aid and lending organisations such as the World Bank (Rose-Ackerman 2004: 334–335).

Certainly, efforts to monitor host country use of funds generated from oil and mineral extracting industries have increased globally and are supported by international organisations such as the World Bank (Rose-Ackerman 2004: 335). Independent watchdog revenue oversight committees have also been established to scrutinise how the natural resources money is spent (for example, in Chad). However, these organisations do not have universal leverage. Some claim, for example, that only very poor, aid-dependent countries such as Chad – which are dependent on loans from international financial institutions such as the World Bank and IMF – can be pressured into complying with these monitoring initiatives, while leaders of less aid-dependent countries with weak democratic institutions may not be willing to cooperate (Rose-Ackerman 2004: 335).

5.2 INFLUENCING INTERNATIONAL LAW, SETTING ANTI-CORRUPTION NORMS AND STANDARDS

NGO advocates have had an enormous effect on the development of international law. By campaigning and acting as consultation partners, they are able to feed into the processes of development, implementation and monitoring. In a recent study, Alvarez (cited by Charnovitz 2006: 359–60) observed that 'although the impact of NGOs on legal development ebbs and flows, no one questions today the fact that international law – both its content and its impact – has been forever changed by the empowerment of NGOs'.

This is certainly true in the field of international corruption. For example, TI has participated in almost all of the anti-corruption programmes developed by international regimes. Its advocacy work is often cited as a key factor in the emergence of a powerful international norm of anti-corruption, which has subsequently underpinned the increasing legalisation of the international anti-corruption regime. In the case of the OECD convention, for example, Gutterman (2005: 19–20) states that 'TI advocated in favour of a multilateral agreement to curb bribery in international business and is largely responsible for swaying recalcitrants among business and government – in Europe in particular – in favour of an OECD instrument to criminalise foreign bribes'.

In terms of monitoring, too, TI chapters in Latin America have made significant contributions to the follow-up of the Inter-American Convention. Evaluations of countries' anti-corruption policies have been conducted by TI chapters in Argentina, Colombia, Nicaragua, Uruguay, Panama, Ecuador and Chile. These documents, which were submitted to the Inter-American Convention Committee, have been used by the group and published on its official webpage (Gutterman 2005).

For a more detailed discussion about the role of Transparency International in the development of anti-corruption treaties, refer to Gutterman (2005).

Interestingly, despite its involvement in the development of a legislative approach to countering corruption, legalistic and punitive approaches are not part of TI's preferred strategy. To be effective, TI claims, anti-corruption agencies require a broader institutional framework for maintaining and promoting good government. It therefore favours an approach which builds coalitions between government agencies, NGOs and private sector organisations, rather than targeting individuals suspected of corruption (Hindess 2009: 22).

It is in this context that TI developed the NIS, referred to earlier in this chapter. The system is outlined in detail in TI's National Integrity Source Book, which also proposes practical reforms, with examples of best practice, that can be applied to each pillar of society in the fight against corruption. Writing about this publication, Dahl (2009: 162) observes that 'the Source Book ... provides ideas on what sort of activities a national chapter might engage in. It can thus be used as a support in the daily work at the national chapters: project leaders can find theoretical grounding for their projects by reading the book'.

Part of the reason TI favours such an approach over legalistic and punitive measures is that it views the latter as 'politically problematic' and carried out 'at the expense of addressing more difficult and challenging areas', notably, broader institutional and societal reform (TI 2000: 34). Hindess describes the NIS, therefore, as a framework designed 'to enable anti-corruption activities to take root without directly confronting powerful individuals and political forces' (2009: 23). He suggests that while there may be certain advantages to avoiding political confrontation, because TI seeks to avoid singling out 'dangerous' targets, the NIS approach allows the corrupt practices of well-connected, high profile individuals to remain unchallenged (2009: 24).

A second criticism of the NIS approach is that it is based on flawed assumptions. TI proposes that corruption – particularly that which occurs in the public sector – invariably undermines political legitimacy and economic growth (Hindess 2009: 28). However, as was highlighted in Chapter 3, analysts who write on the consequences of corruption are divided; the idea that corruption necessarily impacts negatively on the economic growth or political legitimacy of a country is by no means a given. Therefore, as Hindess states, 'it is potentially misleading to suggest that public sector corruption will always have the dire consequences that the Source Book identifies' (Hindess 2009: 28).

Leaving aside the matter of whether NIS can be unequivocally championed as an appropriate model for reform, critics have questioned the capacity of TI to implement the model, and the extent to which the creation of the model can claim to have had any impact in terms of reducing corruption. Hindess (2009: 29) writes:

> TI combines different levels and styles of organisation. Internationally, it is an organisation of 'suits' discreetly lobbying international public servants in the World Bank, OECD, and the UN, and suggesting how to tackle corruption. At another level it is an organisation of small national chapters relying on the work of a few local activists and engaging, like many NGOs, in projects funded by national and international agencies. At neither level, however, is TI really in the game of implementing the NIS design.

Like other NGOs described in this chapter, without the capacity to impose its views on the states in which it operates, TI has limited leverage. It might be said, therefore, that while the NIS can be conceived as an 'ideal' to work towards, there is no reason to suppose that its existence will necessarily have an impact on the problem at hand.

Despite these challenges, TI remains well regarded by many on the anti-corruption scene. Luis de Sousa (2009: 204), for example, writes:

> *TI stands today as the world's best-known anti-corruption actor. It has been able to both institutionalise the anti-corruption norm and spread its doctrine at global level via the action of its constituencies. Its role in the global anti-corruption scene is neither marginal nor expendable.*

5.3 MOUNTING LEGAL CHALLENGES

In November 2009, a collection of NGOs launched a legal case to a public prosecutor. In this landmark case, Sherpa, Greenpeace France, Global Witness, Amis de la Terre and a prominent Liberian activist collectively lodged a complaint in France against the timber company Dalhogg Larsen Horneman (DLH), which is one of the world's leading wholesalers of timber and wood products. The collective alleged that the company had 'bought and traded illegally-obtained timber during the civil war in Liberia from companies known to have been providing support to Charles Taylor's brutal regime' (Global Witness 2010b: 18). It is alleged that DLH imported and distributed wood originating from Liberian timber companies which were involved in corrupt and illegal activity:

> *... the companies DLH purchased from were named in numerous UN reports as committing gross human rights violations, breaching UN arms sanctions, and engaging in environmental destruction and corruption. It is alleged that DLH's suppliers did not even have the legal right to fell the timber it was selling (Global Witness 2010a: 2).*

The complainants allege that DLH continued to use corrupt Liberian suppliers in the face of strong evidence which linked them to the above corrupt activities, only ceasing its Liberian wood imports following a United Nations Security Council embargo on wood which came to force in July 2003 (Global Witness 2010a: 2).

It is not yet possible to evaluate the relative merits of this challenge – how it will be played out remains to be seen. If successful, however, it could pave the way for further collective action in the field of anti-corruption.

For more information about the background to this case, refer to Global Witness (2010a).

Study Questions

- Summarise some of the activities of NGOs in relation to countering corruption.

- What are the main differences between the activities of operational and advocacy NGOs?

- Critically assess the role of NGOs in countering corruption.

- Do you think the NGOs behind the 'Publish What You Pay' initiative are right in pushing for a mandatory disclosure system managed by an international organisation?

PART III

Sector Analyses and Case Studies

6

Corruption and World Politics

1 Introduction

Corruption in world politics has erupted into visibility over the last two decades. As the wave of scandals exposing corrupt heads of state and high-level public officials worldwide demonstrates, corruption is becoming harder to hide. 'Hostility towards corruption is growing worldwide. The post-Cold War era has brought an opening up of governmental processes, freer and more aggressive news coverage and increased independence of prosecutors and judges' (Brademas 1999).

'Until the mid 1970s, with very few exceptions, analyses of political corruption focussed on the specifically national and sub-national aspects of the phenomenon' (LeVine 1999: 685). However, with the increase of intergovernmental organisations and the spread of globalisation, corruption in the political sphere needs increasingly to be examined from a transnational perspective. Closely linked with other cross-border sectors such as international business, global finance and transnational organised crime, political corruption has transcended its national context and fully entered the realm of world politics.

This chapter provides an overview of the different forms of political corruption before looking at each level where it can occur. At the governmental level, world politics are sometimes shaped by corrupt heads of state or governments and this can affect the wider political landscape in a region or how the international community interacts with it. On the intergovernmental level, the European Union, the United Nations and other international political bodies become new arenas in the fight against corruption and are themselves often very vulnerable to becoming entangled in fraud and corruption scandals.

2 What is Political Corruption?

Transparency International defines political corruption as 'the abuse of entrusted power by political leaders for private gain, with the objective of increasing power or wealth' (Hodess 2004: 11). It encompasses a wide range of illegal activities committed by politicians before, during or after they have been in office (ibid.). Corruption by politicians and other public officials can be regarded as a particularly immoral crime, as it involves the abuse of the public authority these individuals have been entrusted with.

Corruption in the political sphere can take many forms and ranges from accepting bribes from lobbyists and companies to secret party financing and electoral fraud, bribing judges, vote-buying and the looting of state assets. Political finance is an area particularly vulnerable to corruption: it includes, for example, 'vote-buying, use of illicit funds, sale of appointments and abuse of state resources' (TI 2004: 1).

Vote-buying is often connected to the misappropriation of public funds or the use of illegal campaign contributions to pay voters. Vote-buying 'refers to the moment an inducement is offered by a candidate or a candidate's agent with clear intention of harvesting the recipients vote. Voters may also be asked to commit to vote in favour for or against a particular candidate; they may also commit to abstain from voting ... The object of the transaction is not always cash' (Pfeiffer 2004: 77).

Another form of political corruption is the sale of public offices, for example lucrative or influential positions, and paying bribes to the judiciary, police, army, supporters or journalists to buy their goodwill or compliance.

In terms of illicit funds, politicians are vulnerable to bribes from lobbyists and companies in exchange for political concessions, such as change of policy, the introduction, amendment or halt of legislation, or simply to steer lucrative contracts in the bribe-payer's direction. The transactions involved do not have to be cash bribes, but can also take the form of holidays, gifts or kickbacks. At the same time, dubious political donations can go undeclared towards election campaigns and 'the lack of transparency about money flows; the potential of the private sector to purchase influence, distorting both the marketplace and the fair representation of the public interest' (Hodess 2004: 12). Breeding grounds for political corruption are in particular the arms, energy (oil and gas) and public contracting sectors (TI 2004: 3).

Transparency International reported in its 2004 Global Corruption Report that 'one in three countries still has no overall system in place to regulate political party finance' (TI 2004: 1). In the United States it is compulsory for candidates in high office and political parties to disclose financial information. The Washington-based Centre for Responsive Politics, an independent non-profit organisation, analyses this information to trace the influence of money on public policy and elections in the United States. By publishing all political donations, fundraising and spending activities as filed with the Federal Election Commission, the centre aims to advocate transparent government and empower citizens with knowledge.

For more information on the Centre for Responsive Politics, visit its website at:

www.opensecrets.org

The media plays an important role in uncovering corruption and holding politicians to account, but being at the same time a tool for political power, it has itself become vulnerable to political corruption. Access to airtime and favourable coverage is highly important for politicians, therefore there is a logical nexus in this area for collusion, corruption and bribes. Corrupt politicians will sometimes try to control the media and prosecute, intimidate or censor journalists who report critically or withdraw licences for media organisations that oppose their politics.

There is also the problem of conflict of interest, when politicians hold corporate stakes in media organisations while being in office. In Italy, for example, Silvio Berlusconi did not only hold the office of prime minister but was at the same time also owner of the largest private broadcaster and regulator of three public networks (TI 2004: 1).

It is still very difficult to hold politicians and powerful heads of state to account, either while there are still in office or, even more so, when they have left the country for exile abroad. In order to curb political corruption and enable successful prosecution, national and international laws need to be reformed. With corrupt state leaders often depositing millions or billions of their countries' siphoned-off wealth in secret offshore accounts (so-called 'grand corruption') and enjoying exile abroad, the available counter measures need to match the international character of this form of political corruption. In particular, international laws and cooperation concerning the areas of bank secrecy, money laundering, extradition and immunity need tightening.

Transparency International (2004: 1–5) believes the following conditions need to be in place to effectively deter and fight political corruption:

- Independent judiciary

- Change of national immunity laws that prevent (ex-)state leaders from being prosecuted

- Improvement of repatriation laws for looted national wealth

- Reform of extradition laws

- Regular public disclosure of income, assets and expenditure by politicians and political parties, in particular before and after elections

- Conflict of interest regulation (politicians should not hold senior positions in private or public companies).

In addition to the above criteria, in order to keep politicians in check and hold them accountable it is also vital for states to develop a strong civil society and independent media which enables access to information. However, both of these features are usually lacking in states with strong political oppression.

3 Corruption in Government: Corrupt Political Leaders

As awareness of corruption in general has increased since the 1990s and several high-profile cases of corruption by political leaders have been pushed into the media spotlight, political leaders have come to realise that they can lose their position in office over allegations of corruption.

There are numerous prominent examples of political leaders entangled in corruption. Indonesian president Suharto was toppled by allegations of corruption in the 1990s after protests against his use of government power to enrich his family (Reuben 2008). Charges of corruption also helped in the late 1990s to defeat Benazir Bhutto of Pakistan and Narasimha Rao, then prime minister of India, who was accused of bribing lawmakers to win a confidence vote in parliament. After Rao's term as head of state expired, he was formally charged in 1996 (*The New York Times* 1997).

In South Korea, two former presidents were jailed following disclosures that they had received large bribes from Korean companies (Scanlon 1997). In Italy, the bribery charges brought by Milanese magistrates in 'Operation Clean Hand' led to the overthrow of the entire political elite that had ruled Italy for more than 40 years. In Japan, over a period of 38 years (1955–1993), nine out of the 15 prime ministers were involved in corruption scandals (Budima 2006).

In recent years, the world has witnessed a long list of current or former heads of state being investigated for corruption and some of them were even charged and convicted. The following examples give an overview of some of the most prominent cases over the last decade.

In Israel, former Prime Minister Ehud Olmert was plagued by corruption scandals during his three years in office from 2006 to 2009. Six months after leaving office, he was charged with fraud, breach of trust and concealing fraudulent earnings (McCarthy 2009a). Olmert was accused of accepting secret donations from an American businessman from 1997 to 2005 and defrauding Israeli charities, among them the World Jewish Congress, Yad Vashem and the Simon Wiesenthal Centre, by falsifying expenses and over-claiming on travel. In 2010, Olmert was accused of involvement in another corruption case, the so-called 'Holyland affair', which dates back to before 2006, when he was still a minister and major of Jerusalem. (McCarthy 2009a) Current Israeli foreign minister, Avigdor Lieberman, was also investigated by police over corruption charges relating to money-laundering charges and using front companies in Cyprus in 2009 (McCarthy 2009b). He has denied all charges and the inquiry is still ongoing (McCarthy 2009b). In April 2011, Israel's attorney general announced that Lieberman will be indicted on charges of fraud and money laundering, pending a final hearing (*The Guardian* 2011).

In Germany, former chancellor Helmut Kohl's long political career ended in a series of corruption allegations when he was investigated in 2000 for accepting illegal cash contributions of $1m for his party, the Christian Democratic Union, from a German-Canadian arms dealer, Karlheinz Schreiber, which were allegedly linked to an arms deal with Saudi Arabia. (BBC News 2000). Kohl was never prosecuted for corruption, but made a settlement with German courts in 2001, in which he admitted to have broken party financing laws and agreed to pay a fine of $142,000 (BBC News 2001). The investigators had also examined corruption allegations linked to the sale of Eastern German oil refinery Leuna to the French oil company Elf Aquitaine after German reunification, which allegedly had involved bribes to Kohl's political party (BBC News 2000).

> Read about the 'Elf Aquitaine scandal' which broke in 1994 and
> the alleged involvement of France's and Germany's political elite:
> Roeber, 2004 and Shaxson, 2004.

In France, current president Nicolas Sarkozy has come under pressure in the so-called 'Bettancourt affair' in 2010, in which he has been accused of accepting illegal donations for his 2007 presidential campaign from France's richest woman and L'Oreal heiress, Liliane Bettancourt (Davies 2010a). The investigation is still ongoing, but Sarkozy has strongly denied Bettencourt's claims that she had given cash envelopes of up to $190,000 to the treasurer of his political party (ibid.).

In Italy, recently resigned prime minister Silvio Berlusconi has long been accused of involvement in several cases of corruption and attempts by Italian courts to prosecute him on money laundering, bribery of police and judges, tax evasion, mafia collusion, false accounting and other corruption charges have so far not been successful (Freedom House 2009). Most charges eventually resulted in acquittal or had to be dropped, which was also due to new immunity laws passed by the Italian parliament in 2008, which grants the prime minister and other elected officials immunity from prosecution while in office (ibid.). As mentioned earlier, in a clear conflict of interests, Berlusconi also controls an Italian media empire (for example, the country's largest private broadcaster, Mediaset) in addition to his political office (Pujas 2009). Currently, he is facing trial over allegations of sex with an under-age prostitute and abuse of authority trying to cover the scandal up (Hooper 2011).

In Thailand, former prime minister Thaksin Shinawatra was sentenced in his absence to two years in prison over a corrupt land deal worth £12.9m in 2008. Thaksin, who was ousted by a military coup in 2006 and currently lives in exile in England, was the first Thai president convicted of corruption. He has however dismissed the ruling as politically motivated (MacKinnon 2008).

In Pakistan, the late Benazir Bhutto served twice as prime minister and in both cases had to resign from office over allegations of corruption. Bhutto and her husband, Asif Ali Zardari, then minister of investment, allegedly received regularly large kickbacks from foreign companies contracted by the Pakistani government and held $100m in offshore accounts and foreign property (Burns 1998). While in exile, in 2003 Bhutto and her husband were convicted of money laundering and given a suspended three-year sentence in Switzerland, which also returned $12m of her assets, the aggregate they had received in bribes, to Pakistan. Pakistan is estimated to have lost more than $2bn in tariff revenues as a result of the corruption (Carver 2004). Bhutto denied the charges and maintained that the claims were politically motivated. She and her husband were granted amnesty in Pakistan and returned to the country in 2007, where Bhutto was assassinated in the same year while taking part in another presidential election campaign. After her death, husband Asif Ali Zardari returned to the political scene and won Pakistan's presidential election in 2008.

For more information on the Bhutto corruption case, read Burns (1998).

At the start of 2011, the world witnessed political unrest and mass protests in North Africa and the Middle East, which led to the overthrow of two long-standing authoritarian regimes in both Tunisia and Egypt. A major contributing factor to the popular uprisings, which have become known as the 'Arab Spring', was deep frustration and anger at the endemic corruption and nepotism of the ruling elites, along with socio-economic factors such as poverty, unemployment and inflation and the desire for political reform (Spencer 2011).

Inspired by the uprisings and resulting political change in their neighbouring countries, the protests spread to other states in the region with similar long-standing authoritarian regimes, such as Yemen, Bahrain, Syria, Libya, Algeria and Jordan. The pro-democracy protests were nervously watched by the region's leaders and in response to the developments in Tunisia and Egypt, rulers in countries such as Jordan, Yemen and Syria hastily announced concessions and reforms in order to appease the public and gain control. However, in the cases of Syria and Yemen the civil uprisings had already gained momentum and in Libya even resulted in civil war which led a few months later to the overthrow of the Gaddafi regime.

The recent examples of Tunisia, Egypt and Libya show that anger at state corruption can fuel revolutions and be a catalyst for political change. The outcomes of the 'Arab Spring' have also given new importance to asset recovery movements which seek to fight impunity linked to grand corruption and recover stolen assets from past heads of state (Vlasic 2011).

CORRUPTION AND POLITICAL UNREST – THE CASES OF TUNISIA AND EGYPT

The widespread corruption and nepotism in Tunisia under President Zine el-Abidine Ben Ali, who ruled for 22 years, created major economic problems for the country. As business confidence declined and fewer foreign investments were attracted to Tunisia, unemployment rose.

It is alleged that Ben Ali's extended family and that of his wife, the Trabelsi clan, acted in a quasi-mafia manner and controlled between 30 and 40 per cent of the Tunisian economy, profiting from almost every sector (Lewis 2011). The regime even risked harming the banking sector because 'the family threw lots of bank loans (presumably on favourable terms) to cronies who never paid them back' (Cole 2011). While the rich elite were flaunting their wealth, the poor and unemployed took to the streets, enraged by the social divisions (Cole 2011). After losing the support of the military and being forced to resign in January 2011, Ben Ali and his family fled to Saudi Arabia.

The BBC reported that Swiss officials estimated that Tunisian government officials had deposited $620m in Swiss banks (BBC News 2011a). The Ben Ali-Trabelsi family wealth is however estimated at $10bn to $12bn and suspected to be spread across several countries, such as France, Switzerland, Argentina and the United Arab Emirates (Lewis 2011). A Tunisian judge has already started investigations into the alleged self-enrichment of the former leader to trace his foreign assets. Ben Ali's wife allegedly fled the country with $50m worth of gold bars from the Tunisian central bank (Willsher 2011).

President Hosni Mubarak, who ruled Egypt for 30 years, was ousted only a few weeks after Ben Ali, when protests swept through the country demanding his resignation and free elections and reforms. Since 1967, Egypt had been under emergency law, which was designed to oppress any political opposition and resulted in weak rule of law and flourishing corruption.

It is estimated that Mubarak's family fortune could be as much as $40bn–$70bn, with much of his wealth invested in real estate or offshore in Swiss and British banks (Inman 2011). 'Experts say the wealth of the Mubarak family was built largely from military contracts during [Mubarak's] days as an air force officer. He eventually diversified his investments through his family when he became president in 1981' (Kim 2011).

Business projects by foreign companies in the Middle East usually need a local sponsor, which gives government the opportunity to request kickbacks. Profits from those deals and corrupt investments, for example, turned Mubarak's sons into billionaires (Inman 2011). In February 2011, Switzerland froze any assets of Mubarak and his family in Swiss bank accounts to prevent any risk of embezzlement (*Sydney Morning Herald* 2011). Swiss authorities had weeks before also frozen the assets of Tunisian former president Ben Ali and his entourage (BBC News 2011a). In August 2011, Mubarak was charged with corruption and the unlawful killing of protestors in Cairo and became the first leader ousted in the 'Arab Spring' to stand trial in court, along with his sons and other senior regime figures (Owen and Shenker 2011).

Mubarak and Ben Ali have joined the likes of other corrupt heads of state accused of embezzlement. Transparency International has created a corruption league table (see below) which lists some of the most notorious self-enriching state leaders over the last 20 years who have looted state assets. They are ranked by the amount each allegedly stole from public funds, in US dollars.

List 6.1   The world's ten most corrupt leaders over the last 20 years

1.   Former Indonesian president Suharto (1967–1998): $15–35bn
2.   Former Philippines president Ferdinand
     Marcos (1972–1986): $5–10bn
3.   Former Zairian president Mobutu Sese Seko (1965–1997): $5bn
4.   Former Nigerian president Sani Abacha (1993–1998): $2–5bn
5.   Former Yugoslav president Slobodan Milosevic (1989–2000): $1bn
6.   Former Haitian president J-C Duvalier (1971–1986): $300–800m
7.   Former Peruvian president Alberto Fujimori (1990–2000): $600m
8.   Former Ukrainian prime minister Pavlo
     Lazarenko (1996–1997): $114–200m
9.   Former Nicaraguan president Arnoldo Aleman (1997–2002): $100m
10. Former Philippines president Joseph Estrada (1998–2001): $78–80m

All sums are estimates of alleged embezzlement.

(*Source*: Adapted from 'Where did the money go?', *Global Corruption Report: Political Corruption* (TI 2004). Copyright 24 March 2011 Transparency International: the global coalition against corruption. Used with permission. For more information, visit: http://www.transparency.org)

Some of the money has since been recovered and returned to the looted states' treasuries.

For example, in 2003 the Swiss government repaid $618m belonging to Sani Abacha's accounts to the Nigerian people. In the same year, former Nicaraguan president Aleman was fined $10m and sentenced to 20 years in prison (later converted to house arrest on health grounds) for money laundering, fraud, embezzlement and electoral crimes. However, former Peruvian president Fujimori is exiled in Japan, where he holds citizenship, and has so far been able to escape extradition to Peru.

Former or current public officials with links to corrupt authoritarian regimes are often termed as 'Politically Exposed Persons' (PEPs) by financial institutions as they pose an increased money-laundering risk in their efforts to loot their states' assets. Chapter 9 looks in more detail at PEPs and the international efforts to stop money laundering.

4 Corruption in Intergovernmental Organisations

Corruption is not just taking place at the national level of politics – the international and intergovernmental level is also affected. International organisations and intergovernmental structures often create unintended new opportunities for fraud and corruption.

Both the EU (often also referred to as a supranational organisation) and the UN are institutions which have over time created unintended incentives for corruption and have distinctive structural weaknesses. In the case of the ever-evolving European Union (EU), institutional and programmatic changes are constantly creating new opportunities for corruption (Warner 2002).

4.1 CORRUPTION IN THE EUROPEAN UNION

Shleifer and Vishny (1998) and Ades and Di Tella (1997) suggest that some EU member state governments deliberately tolerate fraud in those sectors where they can expect some economic or electoral benefits to key constituents. Some even go as far as stating that the EU has created a 'transnational, internal market for fraud' (Warner 2002: 14).

Putnam (1993) suggests that member states bring national patterns of corruption into international organisations and that cultural sources of fraud and corruption are significant. The view among some cultural anthropologists is that fraud and corruption in international organisations are 'national exports' (Warner 2002: 13). They argue that most fraud and corruption in EU programmes occurs in member states with a culturally embedded tradition of fraud and corruption.

4.1.1 EU policies, programmes and funds

One of the most common explanations for the occurrence of fraud within the EU focuses on institutional arrangements and programmes that may contribute to fraud and explain why it is so difficult to tackle. Most of the EU's funds are collected by its member states (for example, the Common External Tariff and Value Added Tax) and, therefore, most of the detection, investigation and prosecution of fraud and corruption is dealt with by the policing and judicial systems of the member states. 'Thus should a member government find it politically useful to tolerate fraud in a particular economic sector (e.g. agriculture), the fact that it has jurisdiction over EU funds within its territory lowers the risk of discovery' (Warner 2002: 11). This allows member states to 'free-ride' and defraud the EU because the harm caused is spread out across all members, while the gains are country-specific (Frey 1991). Warner (2007: 167) points out that 'EU funds are sometimes regarded by member-state governments and citizens alike as free money'.

An example of widespread fraud affecting the EU is the exploitation of the complicated system of corrections and subsidies available through the Common Agricultural Policy (CAP). The CAP was intended to protect the EU's internal agricultural market from cheaper foreign imports, and it subsidises the export of surpluses to poorer countries. 'Widespread frauds involve exaggerating the amount of land or produce cultivated, exceeding quotas or failing to meet prescribed conditions. At a more sophisticated level, hundreds of thousands of pounds can be earned by misclassifying the type or quality of product for which subsidy is being claimed' (Nelken 2003: 221).

Procurement is also a highly vulnerable area within the EU. Warner (2007: 161) points out that 'within the EU member states, corruption most often occurs through kick-back schemes on public work contracts issued by member-state authorities. These contracts account for 10–20 per cent of the combined GDP of the EU states'.

Another weak spot for corruption is the exploitation of EU structural funds – especially in light of the recent EU enlargement eastwards. These funds make up a third of the entire EU budget and are designed to modernise the infrastructure of new member states as well as create new employment opportunities.

In contrast with the previously mentioned areas of fraud against outflows, however, the majority of frauds in the EU are committed against inflows – the revenues collected by customs and indirect tax payments (Nelken 2003).

The potential for fraud is high because the implementation and monitoring of EU programmes and policies is strongly influenced by those groups in member states that are meant to be regulated. Warner (2007: 166–167) highlights an example:

> Take agriculture, for instance. Until the early 1990s its multitude of subsidy programs consumed almost 80 percent of the EU's annual budget. Administration of the subsidy programs was in the hands of the states; the programs, in turn, were tightly linked with agricultural interests. In France, for example, the national farmers' unions have official voice on the many national, regional, and local farm administrative bodies that write the rules and manage the programs.

Opportunities for fraud and corruption often result from 'an inadequate international legal system; enforcement largely left to the very governments that may be directly involved in corruption; and low risk of discovery and penalty, partly because the states seldom if ever intervene in each other's affairs' (ibid.: 173).

Another obstacle in countering fraud in the EU is the lack of a common definition:

> There is considerable variation among the [member] states as to how the EU's interests may be represented in a legal standing, from the EU's perspective it is best if the fraud occurred in Belgium, France, Luxembourg, or Spain. There is also considerable variation in applicable penalties, with member states obligated only to ensure that penalties have a deterrent effect – an unenforceable obligation (Warner 2007: 167).

The EU is vulnerable not only to fraud and corruption committed against it from the outside, but also to that committed from within – two of the EU's major institutions, the European Commission and the European Parliament, have both been shaken by fraud and corruption scandals in the past.

4.1.2 The European Commission

In 1999, the entire European Commission (EC) led by ninth president Jacques Santer, had to resign because the commissioners had lost the confidence of the public and European Parliament over charges of fraud, nepotism and mismanagement.

The scandal was uncovered when an EC auditor, Paul van Buitenen, passed dossiers with evidence he had discovered of fraud and mismanagement to the European Parliament. The European Parliament commissioned independent experts to investigate the scandal and forced the Santer Commission to accept and act on any recommendations made.

Although damning overall, the report showed that all 20 commissioners had been unaware of the malpractice within their respective directorates and criticised them for losing control within the services they were running. It also singled out individual commissioners with accusations of nepotism (see example of Edith Cresson below), as they had employed close friends in fictitious posts. The report set in motion the resignations of all 20 commissioners, which was seen at the time as a 'political act of taking responsibility' (BBC 2003).

The Committee of Independent Experts (1999) noted in its final report that while the Commission was transformed in the 1990s from a proposer of policy to a policy implementer, its administrative and financial culture did not develop at the same speed. In addition, senior staff remained more concerned with the political aspects of the Commission's work than with management.

THE CASE OF EDITH CRESSON

In 2003, Edith Cresson, former French prime minister and European Commissioner for Education and Research from 1995 to 1999, was the most senior EU official charged with corruption relating to her time in office and the resignation of the Santer Commission. She was accused of embezzlement of EU funds for personal gain, falsification of contracts and nepotism over hiring a close dentist friend as highly paid EU advisor on HIV/AIDS, even though he had no specialist knowledge on the topic (Osborn 2003). A year later, the embezzlement charges were dropped by a Belgian court, but Cresson was taken to the European Court of Justice over the nepotism allegations. In 2006, the court ruled that she had violated her official duties by appointing the personal advisor, however no penalty was ordered against her and Cresson was able to keep her EU commissioner pension (BBC News 2006).

The Santer Commission scandal is an example of the problems associated with the unique institutional structure of the EU, with the Commission not being fully responsible to a legislative body, contrary to common standards in parliamentary democracies. The membership of the Commission is not derived from the European Parliament and, even though the Commission has to justify its expenditure and contracts to the Parliament and Court of Auditors, it is not held fully responsible for its actions. The Parliament can only oust the entire Commission, which is a very unlikely move, and member states can only recall their respective commissioners (Warner 2002).

However, addressing the EU's structural weaknesses and increasing the powers of each body might not be the sole cure for curbing fraud and corruption within the EU institutions. One theory is that the European Parliament only attracts less fraud and corruption than the Commission because it is less powerful and influential, with no relevant expenditure in comparison to the Commission. 'If institutional position and opportunities are what fuel fraud, strengthening the Parliament could result in yet another locus for activities the EU would like, in principle, to discourage' (ibid.: 28).

Looking at the outcome from the Santer scandal, Warner (2002: 28) concludes:

> Unfortunately, the Santer Commission's failings have taken the focus away from the areas where most costly fraudulent activities take place: the programs administered by the member states, including the preferential tariff agreements.

The Code of conduct for commissioners was introduced in 2004 and can be found on the European Commission's website:

http://ec.europa.eu/

The European Parliament has used the issue of fraud to justify its attempts to gain more control over the Commission but, subsequently, the increased spotlight on fraud and corruption revelations has backfired and highlighted some of its own members' misuse of expensive accounts. While the Court of Auditors criticises the Commission's failing to keep the levels of fraud under control and stresses that 'auditing should not be confused with policing', the Commission puts blame on the Council of Ministers for 'last minute political compromises which make it impossible to fraud-proof the resulting legislation' (Nelken 2003: 223).

4.1.3 The European Parliament

In 2008, Paul van Buitenen, the whistleblower in the EC scandal, by now a Member of the European Parliament (MEP) and fittingly seated on the Budgetary Control Committee, entered the spotlight again by publishing a confidential internal audit report that highlighted the abuse of staff allowances by MEPs.

The report revealed that money was paid for non-existent staff or assistants already working for another MEP, including lay-off payments made to staff of MEPs who were not re-elected, transfers of staff salaries to political parties and non-payment of social security costs (BBC 2008a).

The report also referred to abuse of travel expenses. Every MEP is eligible for about £130,000 a year to pay for staff. It appears that abuse of these allowances was widespread in the European Parliament before 2006 due to lax rules, but that these deficiencies have since been addressed due to public pressure and the system has now improved (BBC 2008b).

There are several agencies responsible for preventing, detecting and investigating fraud within the EU, such as the European Anti-Fraud Office (OLAF), Group of States Against Corruption (GRECO) and the European Court of Auditors referred to in Chapter 4.

Visit the following websites for more information on their work:

OLAF – http://ec.europa.eu/anti_fraud/index_en.html

GRECO – www.coe.int/greco

4.2 CORRUPTION IN THE UNITED NATIONS

International political bodies face various forms of corruption due to their institutional structure. They are mainly vulnerable because of their size, institutional make-up, the complexity of their policies and programmes and the conflicting interests of member states.

International organisations are one of the main arenas where nations struggle for international political influence and their committees and elections are often politicised. The problem of vote-buying has also been particularly evident in the management of international environmental resources over the last 20 years (see the International Whaling Committee case study at the end of this chapter).

The elections for top posts at intergovernmental organisations are often marred with allegations of cronyism, nepotism, bribery and so-called 'cheque book diplomacy', promising aid or threatening to cut it off. Two prominent examples are the World Health Organisation (WHO) and the United Nations Educational, Scientific and Cultural Organisation (UNESCO).

In 1993, WHO faced a vote-buying scandal during the elections for the director-general post with member state Japan accused of using aid promises to developing countries to secure votes for a second term of its candidate Nakajima (Deen 2000).

A few years later, in 1999 – again during director-general elections, this time at UNESCO – both the Japanese and Saudi governments were accused of the same controversial methods, namely offering aid to countries that would in return support their candidate. *The New York Times* (Riding 1999) wrote at the time that 'the Unesco headquarters ... has been buzzing with rumours that the Japanese and Saudi Governments had promised generous aid packages to several third world countries in exchange for their votes. Japanese and Saudi diplomats strongly denied engaging in such 'chequebook diplomacy' (Riding 1999).

Over the last decade UNESCO has faced several controversies over alleged nepotism and cronyism. In the same year as the elections, an independent audit, commissioned and carried out by Canadian government, found that cronyism was endemic, with 40 per cent of UNESCO appointments and promotions failing to meet the organisation's own criteria for fair election (Henley 1999).

The organisation has implemented many reforms since then but ten years later, in 2009, allegations of bribery during the election of the first female director-general, Bulgarian Irina Bokova, re-emerged. Several member states reportedly complained of bribery bids and one person was ejected from the UNESCO headquarters, allegedly for trying to bribe delegates (Montesquiou 2009).

4.2.1 The UN 'Oil-For-Food' programme in Iraq

The so-called 'Oil-For-Food' (OFF) scandal has been the most highly prominent and embarrassing corruption scandal for the United Nations to date. With the overthrow of Saddam Hussein's regime in Iraq in 2003, allegations of corruption in the $60bn UN-administered programme emerged.

The OFF programme was set up in 1996 in the years after Iraq's invasion of Kuwait and the resulting Gulf War of 1990–1991 which imposed sanctions on Iraq. The scheme was supposed to allow Iraq to sell oil in exchange for humanitarian supplies that the country lacked due to the imposed sanctions. The programme allowed Iraq to sell its oil without breaking the sanctions and was supported by a UN Security Council resolution.

After the US-led coalition invasion of Iraq in 2003 and the handover of the OFF programme to the new Coalition Provisional Authority, allegations of widespread corruption within the scheme were made public. In 2004 an Iraqi newspaper published a list of 270 people, including UN officials, politicians and companies, from over 40 countries who had allegedly profited from the OFF trade. Saddam Hussein was believed to have made $13.6bn in illicit gains by selling oil to neighbour states keen to breach the sanctions and another $4.4bn through kickbacks on the humanitarian goods (BBC 2005).

Several investigations in the US and Iraq were launched, of which the most high profile was a $30m independent inquiry set up by the UN with 100 investigators and headed by former US Federal Reserve Chairman, Paul Volcker. A year later, in 2005, the panel published its findings and concluded that there was inadequate administration and widespread corruption in the OFF programme (BBC 2005).

Several UN officials were accused of taking bribes or turning a blind eye. The former head of the OFF programme and Under-Secretary General of the UN, Benon Sevan, was accused of having ignored a severe conflict of interests, by 'using his contacts with the Iraqi leadership to steer millions of dollars in contracts to an Egyptian businessman' (Lynch 2007).

The brother-in-law of former UN Secretary General Boutros Boutros Ghali, Fred Nadler, allegedly channelled nearly $160,000 in commissions from these oil sale proceeds to him. Sevan strongly denied taking cash bribes between 1998 and 2002, but was suspended after the allegations. He later resigned before the Volcker panel's findings were published in 2005 and claimed he was a political scapegoat for the US's own mismanagement in Iraq (BBC 2005; Lynch 2007).

In 2007, after a two-and-a-half-year criminal investigation, both were charged in their absence; Sevan was indicted of bribery, wire fraud and conspiracy to commit wire fraud and could face up to 50 years in prison. However, as Sevan has been living in his native Cyprus since the UN scandal broke, it is still unclear if he will ever be extradited because Cyprus has no extradition treaty covering financial crimes with the United States (Lynch 2007).

In another case, a Russian former UN procurement officer, Alexander Yakolev, admitted accepting bribes of $1m from oil contractors (BBC 2005). Even Kofi Annan, the then UN Secretary General, had to face intense scrutiny over his son's employment at Swiss company Cotecna, which had a contract under the OFF programme. Questions raised over Kojo Annan's integrity caused a great deal of embarrassment for the Secretary General (ibid.). While there was no evidence of any wrongdoing by Kofi Annan, the Volcker report blamed him for not exerting enough control over the OFF programme and highlighted general mismanagement as well as unethical and corrupt behaviour of UN officials (ibid). 'However, it found no evidence that the secretary general had made personal gain or influenced the Cotecna contract' (ibid.).

The OFF programme involved 4,500 companies from 60 countries. The Volcker report estimates that more than 2,000 of these companies were involved, some of them unknowingly, in kickbacks or surcharges and made illicit payments to the Iraqi regime (BBC 2005). Firms receiving contracts for humanitarian goods paid kickbacks to the Iraqi regime and companies buying oil at reduced prices would pay a surcharge. By inflating the prices of humanitarian import contracts by 5–10 per cent, the Iraqi regime received the difference in cash from the contractors (Gordon 2004).

One of the crucial administrative errors was that it was Iraq and not the UN that chose its oil buyers, which 'empowered Iraq with economic and political leverage to advance its broader interest in overturning the sanctions regime. Iraq selected oil recipients in order to influence foreign policy and international public opinion in its favour' (Volcker, Goldstone and Pieth 2005: 2). Between 2000 and 2002 Saddam Hussein imposed a surcharge of $0.10–$0.50 for every barrel of oil allocated by the regime. This money was then deposited in bank accounts around the Middle East (Winnett 2004). 'Dozens of private individuals were given oil at knockdown prices. They were able to nominate recognised traders to buy the cheap oil from the Iraqi state oil firm and sell it for a personal profit' (Winnett 2004).

It was also suspected that politicians in the UK, France and Russia were being bribed to lobby against the sanctions on Iraq's behalf (BBC 2005). While possible military action was discussed at the UN, Iraq sold oil to influential figures in these countries in the hope of influencing their governments and, ultimately, the decisions in the Security Council.

> *Iraq preferred to sell its oil to companies and individuals from countries that were perceived as 'friendly' to Iraq, and, in particular, if they were permanent members of the Security Council in a position potentially to ease the restriction of sanctions. Russian companies received almost one-third of oil sales under the Programme ... French companies were the second largest purchaser of oil under the Programme (Volcker, Goldstone and Pieth 2005: 2).*

Both France and Russia, along with China, were opposing any UN-backed invasion of Iraq and, as permanent members of the UN Security Council, had veto powers. Some commentators believe that the OFF scandal needs to be seen in the context of the power struggle between the US and the UN over the invasion of Iraq and the aim of US neo-conservatives with a dislike of the UN to cast the organisation as incompetent, as well as their desire for Kofi Annan to resign (Gordon 2004). They also point out that it was a failure of the superpowers in the politicised Security Council that the policing of UN sanctions against Iraq were not effective (ibid.).

Did the UN have no checks in place to oversee such a large programme? The organisation did indeed have a monitoring system for the OFF programme and UN staff did flag up 70 cases of price irregularities to the UN Sanctions Committee; however, the Security Council did not take effective action to review and block those contracts (ibid.). The OFF programme also required Iraq to list all items to be purchased as humanitarian goods for approval and conducted spot checks on deliveries to prevent military equipment from being smuggled (UN n.d.c.). In response to the Volcker report, the UN promised to learn lessons and increase the levels of transparency and accountability in its administered programmes.

The OFF scandal is unlikely to be the last large corruption case that will come to light in connection with Iraq. The BBC reported in 2005 that 'billions of dollars are unaccounted for in the Iraq reconstruction fund set up to replace the OFF programme – which was under the stewardship of the US-led coalition in Iraq'.

List 6.2   UN Oil-For-Food scandal: Facts and figures at a glance

- $64.2bn of oil was sold by Iraq to 248 companies.
- 3,614 companies sold $34.5bn of humanitarian goods to Iraq.
- Oil surcharges were found in contracts of 139 companies.
- Humanitarian kickbacks were paid in contracts of 2,253 companies.
- Saddam Hussein made an estimated $13.6bn in illicit gains by selling oil in breach of the sanctions and another $4.4bn through kickbacks on humanitarian goods.

(*Source*: Volcker Goldstone and Pieth 2005; BBC News 2005)

For more information, read the full Volcker report (Volcker, Goldstone and Pieth 2005).

5 Case Study: 'Vote-buying' in International Organisations – The International Whaling Commission

The International Whaling Commission (IWC) is presented as a case study as it illustrates vote-buying, bribery and corruption used by member states to succeed in the political bargaining process.

Established for the sustainable management and conservation of whales, the IWC is responsible for compiling data on whale stocks and coordinating national policies on whaling. In 1948 the International Convention for the

Regulation of Whaling, an international environmental agreement, came into force and the IWC was established with 15 member states. Membership of the IWC is open to any country that abides by the Convention, and states that want to join the IWC do not necessarily need to be involved in whaling.

This lack of clearly defined membership criteria has led to both whaling opponents and proponents starting to recruit more members to join the organisation and a fierce struggle to influence their voting. The number of members has been growing rapidly over the last ten years; as of January 2011 there were 88 member states.

In 1986 the IWC adopted a moratorium banning commercial whaling that is still in force today. Limited whaling for scientific research purposes is, however, permitted. This provision remains controversial as the opponents of whaling claim it is being used as a disguise for commercial whaling. Currently, the three main whaling nations, Japan, Iceland and Norway, have continued whaling despite the international moratorium. Since the ban has been in force, they have hunted some 35,000 whales, which is around 3,000 whales annually (*The Sunday Times* 2010a).

In 2001, allegations of bribery surfaced; Japan was accused by anti-whalers of bribing poor nations to support its pro-whaling stance and using its aid budget to buy votes. Several countries with no apparent interest in whaling issues but which were recipients of Japanese aid or fishery grants, such as Mongolia and Mali, were allegedly recruited by Japan over the last decade to gain a majority in the IWC and overturn the ban on commercial whale hunting. 'Many of the Commission's 20 newest members, such as the Marshall Islands and St Kitts and Nevis, have no history of whaling and several, including Mongolia and Mali, have no coastlines' (McNeill 2006). There have been claims that Japan was using its aid budget to persuade 24 small or landlocked IWC member states, including St Lucia, Grenada, Dominica, Antigua and Barbuda, Nauru and Mongolia, to vote against a whaling ban (Kerbaj 2010).

In response, however, the pro-whaling side, led by the USA, Europe, New Zealand and Australia, quickly adapted similar methods to swing votes in their favour. In 2006, Lord Ashcroft, then treasurer of the Conservative Party in the UK, donated money to pay for Belize's annual membership fees to the IWC and Belize returned the favour by voting to uphold the ban (Hassell 2007).

A year later, a British diplomatic campaign persuaded six Caribbean IWC member states to withdraw their support for whaling and to vote against Japan and its allies. These island states had previously received $16m in fisheries aid from Japan and consistently voted with Japan and Norway to overturn the moratorium (Hassell 2007). 'What once seemed a moral imperative has become a grubby game of vote-bargaining, which defenders of the whale must play' (MacIntyre 2007).

Allegations of bribery and corruption at the IWC were in the headlines again just weeks before the IWC's 2010 annual meeting in Morocco. UK's *Sunday Times* newspaper sent two undercover journalists posing as anti-whaling lobbyists for a Swiss billionaire conservationist. The reporters offered ministers and fisheries officials from Japan's key alliance states in Africa, Asia, the Pacific and Caribbean £25m in aid over ten years if they voted against the proposed lift of the commercial whaling ban (*The Sunday Times* 2010b). The newspaper reported that when offered aid packages to change their vote, St Kitts and Nevis, Marshall Islands, Kiribati, Grenada, Republic of Guinea and Ivory Coast all entered negotiations.

A Guinean fishery department official is reported to have admitted that his country had been persuaded by Japan to join the IWC ten years previously and that Japan not only paid them millions in fisheries aid but also paid for Guinea's annual IWC membership fees and attendance at the meetings, including all-expenses-paid travel costs. Delegates were allegedly paid $300 a day spending money (the average annual wage in Guinea is $1,000) (ibid.).

The Tanzanian IWC commissioner revealed that key people in his fisheries department had been educated in Japan and spoke fluent Japanese, having had their tuition fees and living costs paid for by Japan, which had also paid Tanzania £80m in development aid over the past two years (*The Sunday Times* 2010b). 'Such backroom stitch-ups at the IWC have been rumoured, but they have never before been captured on a video camera' (ibid.). Japan has always denied buying IWC members' votes or covering any IWC expenses for other countries (ibid.). Since the new allegations broke in 2010, pressure on the IWC has been growing to investigate the claims.

It was hoped to find a compromise between the two opposing sides at the 2010 annual meeting and bring an end to the escalating battle for votes, by replacing the ban with a legalised quota that would be monitored by the IWC. This would put in place enforceable limits (1,800 whales a year) on whaling which, it was hoped, would result in fewer whales being killed (Tedmanson 2010). It would have allowed the first legal commercial hunts in 25 years, albeit with limited quotas, in exchange for an end to killing whales for so-called scientific research.

As no consensus was reached, it was agreed to pause work on this topic until the 2011 annual meeting, where it is likely that the same tactics will be repeated by both sides. There are still no effective deterrents, such as penalties or expulsion from the organisation, to nations implicit in vote-buying available by the international community.

Study Questions

- How does corruption affect democracy and rule of law in world politics?

- What are the challenges of holding corrupt political leaders to account and recovering stolen state assets?

- What are the implications of corruption in the EU or the UN?

- How can the practice of 'vote-buying' be challenged?

7

Corruption and International Business

1 Introduction

In the search for profit, and under pressure from international competition, many companies involved in business abroad are willing to engage in illicit behaviour and pay bribes to secure deals. The list of alleged corporate bribery and corruption scandals in the international business world is long, including, to name just a few, Parmalat, BAE, Exxon Mobil, Halliburton, Boeing, Texaco, Siemens and DaimlerChrysler.

Bribery, which 'is often considered to be synonymous with corruption' (Shichor and Geis 2007: 409) has become increasingly subtle. The truth is that 'for multinationals, bribery enables companies to gain contracts [particularly in the public sector and extractive and defence industries] or concessions which they would otherwise not have won, or to do so on more favourable terms' (Hawley 2000: 3).

Bribes are often disguised as commissions, 'success' fees, 'facilitation' fees, expenses, inflated prices, presents or donations. Langseth (2006: 10) defines bribery as 'the bestowing of a benefit in order to unduly influence an action or decision'. With the expansion of competitive international markets and the rise of new emerging markets, companies have often resorted to bribery and corruption to win lucrative contracts (Hotchkiss, cited by Moran 1999: 142).

2 The Costs of Corporate Bribery to International Trade

'The international business community is beginning to recognise the costs of corruption to the global investment environment' (Rose-Ackerman 2004: 334–

335). Corruption distorts international trade and investment flows, since the best contender no longer wins, and cash and influence prevail. 'Bribery not only raises moral concerns; it also runs counter to the long-term interests of business, because it increases costs and risks, undermines efficiency, lowers country credit rankings, and deters investors' (Asian Development Bank and OECD 2004: 26). Many successful international companies with a high reputation to lose are deterred from an otherwise attractive investment because of host countries' reputation for corruption. If reputable companies avoid investing because of corruption concerns, host countries lose out: the investors that they attract are likely to have lower standards, both of integrity and of professional competence.

In 2006, risk consultancy Control Risks and law firm Simmons & Simmons jointly commissioned a survey on international business attitudes to corruption, which involved telephone interviews with 350 international companies. Respondents were asked to estimate the maximum percentage increase that corruption can have on the costs of an international project:

> A quarter of respondents said that it was between zero and 5% – already a high figure on a multi-billion dollar project. However, 9.7% said that corruption could amount to up to half of the total project costs, and 7.1% said it could be even higher. The companies estimating maximum corruption at more than a quarter of the total project cost were most likely to come from the construction (29%), defence (25%) and finance (18%) sectors (Control Risks and Simmons & Simmons 2006: 9).

These figures illustrate how corruption can distort business and inflate costs and risks. Bribery of foreign government officials in international business transactions is a serious threat to the development and preservation of democratic institutions. Not only does it undermine economic development, it also distorts international competition by seriously misdirecting resources. Corruption has very negative effects for public authorities because it makes services more costly for the public, and therefore undermines development. 'The amount of money lost to corruption which could, and should, be directed towards public services [improving basic living standards] and to the development of democratic institutions is significant' (Hawley 2000: 3). Instead, expensive projects with lucrative commission potential are undertaken.

The single greatest source of corruption is that of large public sector contracts and concessions to private companies (TI 2009). Any bribe adds to the price of a public contract awarded (such as to run a power station) and, ultimately, these costs will have to be recovered by transferring them directly to the customer (for example, through higher electricity or water charges). 'Bribery puts up the prices of projects. When these projects are paid for with money borrowed internationally, bribery adds to a country's external debt. Ordinary people end up paying this back through cuts in spending on health, education and public services' (Hawley 2000: 6).

Hawley also points out that where money buys influence, the poor are left out of the decision-making and remain at the political margins. 'Corruption makes the rich richer and the poor poorer' (Hawley 2000: 3). Overall, corruption is seen as an enemy of development because it is known to be 'the single greatest obstacle to economic and social development' (Eigen 2003).

Morino and Iyer (2003: 1) believe that globalisation 'has led to the internationalisation and increase of illegal activities, transcending international boundaries' and that when multinationals seek to do business in countries with low governance standards and high levels of corruption they ultimately face moral challenges (ibid.).

WESTINGHOUSE ELECTRIC AND THE BATAAN NUCLEAR CONTROVERSY

In the early 1970s, the US electrics firm Westinghouse won a contract to build Bataan, the first nuclear power plant in the Philippines, at a cost of $2.3 billion. This was actually three times the price of similar plants built by the company in other countries, and the high fee was allegedly mainly due to $80 million in kickbacks for the Philippines President Ferdinand Marcos (Hawley 2000). Westinghouse vehemently denied that money went to Marcos and justified the high price of its plant with escalation provisions and the building of housing for employees at the remote site (Dumaine 1986).

Westinghouse entered the competition for the Philippines project late, after another US company, General Electric (GE), had a head start in the bidding. Eager to move the business away from its competitor, Westinghouse contacted a Filipino well-connected with President Marcos – Herminio Disini, the Chairman of Herdis Management & Investment, a Philippines conglomerate. In 1974, Disini enabled Westinghouse's salesmen to make their pitch directly to Marcos and his cabinet. 'By this time, GE had spent nearly nine months wooing the Filipinos, but had not sought an audience with the President' (ibid.).

'Instead of getting a twin-reactor plant for $650 million, the Philippines were paying $722 million for a single-reactor plant with half the power output. Another $387 million for interest and escalation costs raised the total contract price to $1.1 billion' (ibid.). Even though it was never proven that Disini also took bribes from Westinghouse, he nevertheless profited from his arranged nuclear deal when Westinghouse awarded major subcontracts on the plant to him.

Over time, the Filipino taxpayers have spent $1.2 billion for the plant's debts, even though it never produced any electricity at all after its completion in 1985, for the simple reason that it was built at the foot of a volcano, near several earthquake fault lines. Until 2018, the Philippines government will have to pay $170,000 a day in interest on the loans taken out to finance the nuclear plant (Hawley 2000). This heavy burden for the low income nation illustrates all the money lost through corrupt business deals that should have gone into education, healthcare or infrastructure.

In 1986, the US Justice Department reopened a bribery investigation (which it had dropped in 1978 after a grand jury voted not to indict Westinghouse over Bataan), this time with eager cooperation from the then new Philippines government, which had ousted the dictator Marcos. Westinghouse faced conviction for violating the Foreign Corrupt Practices Act 1977. However, a Federal District Court found no evidence of bribery and the Philippines government filed an appeal in 1993 (Bloomberg 1995). The Philippines government later even banned Westinghouse equipment when settlement talks broke down. Finally, in 1995, a settlement was reached between the two parties, which ended the litigation over the power plant; the Philippines dropped their lawsuit and the ban was lifted. Westinghouse agreed to pay $45 million for the settlement, considerably less than the $200 million payment Manila proposed (ibid.).

For more information and analysis on the Bataan scandal, read the article 'Nuclear nightmares in the Philippines' (Beaver 1994).

3 Bribery by Multinationals in Emerging Markets

With the end of the Cold War, the scramble for new markets, which were expanding but still unstable, created a competitive environment for international business. Today, many firms engage in bribery in order to secure lucrative deals and contracts. 'Every year, Western businesses pay huge amounts of money in bribes to win friends, influence and contracts. These bribes are conservatively estimated to run to US$80 billion a year' (Hawley 2000: 2).

Bribes are mostly requested by service providers, police or the judiciary, but also by public bodies such as customs and tax revenue authorities and registry or permit offices. Arvis and Berenbeim (2003: 7) believe that companies are pressured to emulate corrupt competitors: 'in a situation of competition in a corrupt environment, the firm will fear that if it does not pay bribes, it may lose business to competitors willing to pay, and so everyone pays bribes'.

Multinational corporations (so-called multinationals) routinely pay commissions to gain contracts from governments in emerging markets and are often assisted by their own political leaders (Hawley 2000). For example, in 1999, the former UK Minister of State for Defence Procurement, Jonathan Aitken, was jailed for negotiating contracts for an arms deal between three UK companies (GEC, Marconi and VSEL) and Saudi Arabia. The three arms firms had paid bribes into a Swiss bank account for Saudi agents, to help facilitate the deal (Pallister *et al.* 1999).

Apart from securing business deals, bribes can also enable foreign companies to circumvent regulations, permissions and local laws. 'Bribery can be a useful way of getting around local opposition to a project and of bypassing the usual democratic process involved with awarding contracts' (Hawley 2000: 6). Often, this results in serious damage for the environment (for example, the pollution of drinking water), ruins livelihoods and displaces local communities when they lose their land. It often involves paying off local leaders and politicians, allowing the flouting of environmental laws and regulations in order to conduct, for example, illegal mining or logging (for instance, in Cambodia, Nicaragua, Papua New Guinea, Mexico, Brazil or the Philippines) (Hawley 2000). Developing countries are particularly vulnerable to corporate bribery and corruption due to their weak governance systems, large informal sector, reliance on natural resources and extractive industries and major privatisation programmes. (TI 2009: 10).

EXAMPLE: MINDEX

In the late 1990s, the Norwegian mining company Mindex was accused of bribing local officials in Mindoro, a Philippines island, with the aim of dampening local protest against its nickel and cobalt mining plans on the island (Hawley 2000). Local organisations of indigenous peoples and other citizen groups opposed the proposed project due to environmental concerns: it would have required the stripping of at least 1,000 hectares of the rare remaining forest cover in central Mindoro, the ancestral land of the Alangan and Tadyawan and their farms. 'It is also a watershed for downstream farmers. The forest is home to rare and endemic species including the Tamaraw-Mindoro buffalo' (Mines and Communities 2001).

In 1999, Mindex gave gold watches to members of the local authorities, built a new house for the local priest, and paid for district leaders to go on luxurious holidays, which the company claims were all 'signs of friendship' (Hawley 2000). However, its opponents believed such gifts were obvious bribes trying to manipulate the project's Environmental Impact Assessment. As it was revealed two years later, Mindex had been granted a mining licence, despite not having completed the environmental clearance process, nor gaining the necessary social acceptability. It was announced in 2001 that the company's licence was to be revoked, which proved to be a massive victory for opponents of the project (Mines and Communities 2001).

However, not only Western companies engage in bribery and corruption abroad. The main emerging market multinationals from Brazil, China and India also play an increasing role in international business. 'Firms from India, China and Brazil are regarded by their peers as among the most corrupt when doing business abroad' (TI 2009: 29). For example, China's huge investment in Africa has come under a lot of public scrutiny recently as its companies are seen to have fewer reservations when dealing with corrupt and oppressive regimes. 'Western oil and mining companies, having started to improve their behaviour in Africa under pressure from NGOs, now face competition from Chinese, Indian and Russian rivals that seem willing to cut deals with even the most unsavoury African politicians' (*The Economist* 2008).

A survey supporting that trend is Transparency International's 2008 Bribe Payers Index which found that companies in emerging economies are most likely to pay bribes. Of the 26 countries surveyed, Russian firms came out on top, followed by Chinese, Mexican and Indian companies, as being the most prone to engage in bribery when doing business abroad (TI 2008: 5). A ranking of industry sectors showed that the likelihood of bribes being paid to a public official is particularly high in the following five areas: public works contracts and construction; real estate and property development; oil and gas; heavy manufacturing; and mining (ibid.: 11).

Read the full Bribe Payers Index 2008 report with breakdown by industry sector and type of bribe on Transparency International's website:

www.transparency.org/news_room/in_focus/2008/bpi_2008

The extractive industries sector is particularly vulnerable to corruption and bribery. Developing countries have seen a recent boom in commodities, and demand for natural resources is steadily growing. 'In 2006 exports of oil and minerals from Africa were roughly $249bn, nearly eight times the value of exported farm products ($32bn) and nearly six times the value of international aid ($43bn)' (Hayman 2009: 54).

The revenues raised by governments from the sale of natural resources could be used to ease poverty, but countries depending on oil and mining are often prone to instability and lack accountability, rule of law and good governance standards, which means that local populations unfortunately do not seem to benefit much from the boom. 'To give just one example: from 1970 to 2000 the Nigerian government received over $300 billion from oil sales while the percentage of citizens living in extreme poverty (on less than $1 per day) increased from 36 to 70 percent' (Hayman 2009: 54).

So far the international response to the corruption problems facing this sector has been rather muted because geopolitical competition is strong. However, the OECD Anti-Bribery Convention and international initiatives such as the Extractive Industries Transparency Initiative (EITI) and Publish What You Pay are trying to make a difference. EITI seeks to make information on how much money governments are paid by oil and mining companies available to citizens, so they can hold their governments accountable and ask what these public funds were used for. Publish What You Pay provides the opposite information by informing the public how much resource extraction companies paid foreign governments. These initiatives combined make it harder for corruption to take place and money from natural resources to be diverted into private pockets.

Learn more about both initiatives by visiting:

www.eiti.org

www.publishwhatyoupay.org

These international efforts to improve governance standards and business ethics, as well as regulatory oversight in emerging market economies, were initially made by NGOs in developed countries; however, the approach has now also been adopted by many grassroots organisations in the affected emerging market countries (*The Economist* 2008).

> *It seems that these local and international initiatives, combined with stricter bribery laws, have started to have an impact on multinationals in the extractive industries sector: Gradually firms in the oil industry and the mining industry are developing better standards of corporate responsibility in Africa. No more should diamond companies do deals with rebel armies. No more should oil firms pollute the local environment. Pay bribes in Africa and you risk being arrested back home in America or Britain (Roberts 2010).*

4 Criminalisation of Bribery in Business Transactions

The international expansion of multinationals operating across national borders has created a need for regulation, since there is no longer a formal authority of the nation state (Held *et al.* 2005). 'While bribery has been tolerated by law and even encouraged by tax regulations for many years, the view on bribery in international business transactions has dramatically changed over the past two decades' (Fulgeras 2003: 64).

This section looks at different legislative changes that have taken place internationally to combat bribery in foreign business transactions.

4.1 THE US FOREIGN CORRUPT PRACTICES ACT

When it was revealed in the 1970s that US aircraft manufacturer Lockheed paid bribes to secure contracts in foreign countries, the public in the US was shocked. Subsequent investigations by the US Securities and Exchange Commission found that over 400 US companies admitted making questionable or illegal payments in excess of $300 million to foreign government officials, politicians and political parties (Fulgeras 2003). In order to restore public confidence in the integrity of the US business system, the Foreign Corrupt Practices Act (FCPA) was passed in 1977, which introduced sanctions against US businesses that intentionally bribed foreign public officials in international business transactions. Since 1998, the sanctions have also applied to foreign firms and individuals who take any act in furtherance of such a corrupt payment while in the United States.

International awareness of the harmful effects of corruption on the world economy gradually rose in the 1980s and 1990s and, with the increased promotion of good governance, legal frameworks similar to the US FCPA were implemented internationally (Fulgeras 2003). Most of these international frameworks, such as the OECD Convention on Bribery and the UN Convention Against Corruption (UNCAC), came about through pressure from the United States, which felt that US firms were losing business deals due to bribery and corruption by their mostly European competitors. 'US companies consistently complained that FCPA put them at a disadvantage vis-à-vis companies from other countries. In Germany and Belgium, for example, bribes were effectively tax deductible' (Moran 1999: 142).

4.2 OECD EFFORTS TO END TAX DEDUCTIONS FOR BRIBES

As Hawley (2000: 3) points out, 'until … [the mid-1990s], bribery was seen as a normal business practice. Many countries including France, Germany and the UK treated bribes as legitimate business expenses which could be claimed for tax deduction purposes'. While domestic bribery has long been prohibited in all EU member states, most states did not criminalise bribery of foreign officials. The 1990s brought about a growing understanding among European and OECD governments of the negative impacts of bribery (Wehrlé 2005). In 1996, the OECD took the first step towards eliminating tax deductions for bribe payments by adopting a recommendation urging member states to stop the practice and to pass legislation that criminalised such conduct. The OECD states eventually amended their tax legislation and the resulting non-deductibility has sent a strong signal to companies ever since that bribery is no longer an acceptable business practice.

4.3 THE OECD CONVENTION ON COMBATING BRIBERY

In 1997, 20 years after the FCPA came into force, OECD countries adopted the OECD Convention on Combating Bribery of Foreign Public Officials in International Business Transactions, which has been a milestone in the efforts to combat corruption in international markets. It was the first legally binding international anti-bribery instrument and requires its signatories to penalise the payment of bribes to foreign public officials:

> ... the decision of political leaders to ban foreign bribery has led to a radical change in the mentality of large corporate groups when deciding to invest abroad, making them aware of new risks and giving rise to the development of internal corporate control mechanisms aimed at banning the giving of bribes to foreign public officials by their staff (Wehrlé 2005: 4).

For more detailed information on the OECD anti-bribery convention, see:

www.oecd.org/corruption

4.4 THE UK BRIBERY ACT

The Bribery Act has been designed to reform existing UK bribery laws and bring the UK into line with its obligations under the OECD Convention, which requires all signatories to introduce legislation that penalises paying bribes to a foreign public official. Since signing the Convention in 1997, the UK government has been strongly criticised for continuously delaying the enactment of the treaty for over a decade (OECD 2008).

The Bribery Act was drafted by a joint committee of both Houses of Parliament and published in March 2009. The new anti-corruption law aims to provide a more effective legal framework and demonstrate the UK's commitment to stricter bribery regulation. It is designed to fight corruption in both the public and private sector, and includes provisions for both offering and requesting bribes. The Act applies to all UK-based companies and individuals doing business anywhere in the world, as well as foreign companies doing business in the UK. Offenders will face penalties of ten years' imprisonment and unlimited fines, blacklisting from EU contracts and in some cases even charges under money-laundering laws (which carry harsher penalties than bribery).

As required by the OECD Convention, it also introduces the new offence of bribing foreign public officials and private citizens. In comparison with the FCPA in the United States, the UK Bribery Act is wider in its definition of bribery and includes penalties for failure to prevent a bribe being paid on the company's behalf by intermediaries, such as agents, consultants or lobbyists (Sokenu 2011).

Concerns among the UK business community increased in the months before the planned enforcement of the Act. They feared that it was too restrictive and would result in British companies losing out to less regulated global competitors. In particular, the Act's defence provisions were criticised: businesses complained that, unlike the FCPA, the Bribery Act will not allow any exceptions from prosecution for facilitation payments and corporate hospitality. Instead, the key defence under the Bribery Act is that the company has implemented adequate compliance procedures to prevent bribery (ibid.).

After extensive consultation, the Act was passed in the final days of the last parliament on an all-party consensus before the 2010 UK general election. The Bribery Bill received royal assent in April 2010 and was due to come into force a year later, in April 2011. However, coming under intense pressure from media and businesses in late 2010, the new Conservative government announced in January 2011 that it would delay the bill and conduct a review (Leigh 2011).

The OECD expressed its concern about the delay of the Act in a press statement in February 2011 in which it reminded the UK to honour its commitment to fighting bribery and to meet its international obligations under the terms of the OECD Convention. In the statement (2011), Mark Pieth, Chair of the OECD Working Group on Bribery, stressed that: 'Establishing a level playing field for international business is as important now as ever and will help strengthen the global economic recovery. As a G20 country, the UK bears a special global responsibility and should lead by example.'

To read more information on the Bribery Act visit:

www.justice.gov.uk/publications/bribery-bill.htm

4.5 EFFECTIVENESS OF ANTI-BRIBERY LAWS

Internationally, laws and regulations can be set in place, but whether they have impact depends entirely on the ability of nations 'to change the discourse inside member countries and in the international business communities in ways that also change behaviour' (Rose-Ackerman 2004: 333–334).

Results from the 2006 survey *International Business Attitudes and Corruption* by Control Risks and Simmons & Simmons revealed that despite an increasing awareness and rising number of laws against foreign bribery, the number of prosecutions is still low and honest companies risk losing out to the illicit activities of their competitors (Control Risks and Simmons & Simmons 2006).

Companies in the construction, oil, gas and mining sectors are the most likely to have lost business to corrupt competitors – mainly due to the high value of projects and the involvement with government officials in the deals.

Respondents felt they were powerless in cases where competitors paid bribes and won the contract, which is reflected in some of the responses in the survey: they 'would avoid working again with the same customer and simply look elsewhere in the future' or 'make no public complaint, hoping to be more successful next time' (Control Risks and Simmons & Simmons 2006: 6).

Unfortunately, only a small minority seem willing to take action by making enquiries, lodging an appeal or contacting the tendering authority or law-enforcement authorities. These results show that the existing bribery laws need to be promoted and implemented more effectively in order to make any impact and change the attitudes within the international business world.

For a full summary of the 2006 '*International Business Attitudes to Corruption Survey*' by Control Risks and Simmons & Simmons, visit:

www.crg.com/pdf/corruption_survey_2006_V3.pdf

When it comes to awareness of the OECD anti-bribery convention amongst the international business community, findings by Transparency International (2008) in its 2008 Bribe Payers Index survey raised concerns:

> *It is both surprising and alarming that three-quarters of senior business people surveyed revealed that they were not at all familiar*

with the OECD Anti-bribery Convention, the foremost international legal instrument for tackling the supply side of international bribery. Governments need to work to build awareness of the Convention within the business community and ensure that it is backed up with solid enforcement.

In particular, respondents from Western Europe and the United States, and high income countries in general, indicated they were the least familiar with the convention (TI 2008: 9).

The success of the UK Bribery Act will depend on its enforcement and on whether the UK government bows to domestic corporate pressure and weaken its provision. It is hoped that the Act will have as strong an impact as its US sister law, the FCPA, in terms of deterrence and compliance but also increase the number of successful prosecutions in corporate bribery cases.

Overall, there are signs that international companies are becoming aware of the fact that being subject to an investigation or even a simple allegation of bribery can have considerable financial and reputational repercussions. Companies fearful of the vigilance of their competitors and wanting to avoid being reported to prosecution authorities, have begun to adopt various anti-bribery strategies:

Those strategies include written company codes of conduct circulated among staff, rigorous selection of the agents and intermediaries who are to be involved in the commercial process, implementation of financial monitoring and internal control procedures (Wehrlé 2005: 4).

The former general counsel of US company General Electric, Ben Heineman, argues in *The Economist* (2008):

As developed-country multinationals enter emerging economies, it is crucial they do not lower their standards on corruption. ... behaving consistently ethically is in their self-interest. Successful global companies need uniform global cultures, in which everyone adheres robustly to the same rules, even in places where local companies do not. If people in one part of the company start adopting a lower ethical standard, it can have a corrosive effect on the entire corporate culture.

After the Foreign Corrupt Practices Act was more strongly enforced in the United States during the 1990s, increasing numbers of multinationals, particularly in the US, started to introduce stricter guidelines for corporate governance. This might have cost them some business in notoriously corrupt regimes but at the same time helped them to avoid being dragged into large reputation-damaging bribery scandals in the same way as some of their rivals, such as Germany's Siemens (*The Economist* 2008).

EXAMPLE: SIEMENS BRIBERY SCANDAL

One of the biggest bribery scandals in German corporate history was revealed in 2007 with the news that Siemens, a large German telecommunications and engineering group, had paid millions of Euros in bribes to cabinet ministers and other officials in Nigeria, Libya and Russia in order to win lucrative telecommunication contracts.

Two Siemens managers were given suspended sentences for bribery and breach of trust in 2007 and Siemens was ordered to pay a fine of EUR 201m. As a reaction to the court ruling, Nigeria has suspended all dealings with Siemens. However, only a year later, German courts lifted the verdicts against the employees as bribery of foreign public officials only became an offence in 2002 and the payments were made in 2000 (Matussek 2008).

To avoid further reputational damage, the company decided to hire a US law firm to investigate the widespread corruption within the company in over 65 countries where it was operating (Jameson 2007).

In a second court case in 2009, to settle charges for routinely using bribes and slush funds since the mid 1990s for public work contracts, Siemens paid $1.34bn in fines to US and European authorities. While the company admitted it had violated the FCPA, it avoided a guilty conviction for bribery and the consequential blacklisting from future public procurement contracts in the USA (Lichtblau and Dougherty 2008).

---

5 Business Ethics and Corporate Governance

The emergence of international treaties to combat global corruption has seen an increased concern with reputation among the international business community and made corruption a more widely discussed issue at the top management level. 'The international business community ... recognise the costs of corruption to the global investment environment' (Rose-Ackerman 2004: 334–335) and, as a result, is aiming to provide greater transparency and corporate responsibility. Corporate compliance offers many benefits to firms, such as lower costs and increased brand value and it also helps to market the company to a growing number of sensitive customers (TI 2009: 5).

Major corporate scandals involving companies such as Enron and WorldCom have ensured that 'the corporate governance in a globalised economy has become one of the most important topics for the business environment' (Yuksel 2008: 101). There is now far greater importance placed on legislation in both Europe and the US, ensuring 'ethical standards rather than just free market principles' (ibid.). Corporate governance can ultimately provide greater accountability and transparency in today's corporate environment and help to prevent fraud and corruption. Corporate responsibility is about how companies manage the business process to produce an overall positive impact on society and this includes ensuring that companies and employees do not engage in corrupt activities. Iyer and Samociuk (2006: 34) outline the growing role of corporate responsibility: 'the underlying requirement for an ethical tone at the top is also a principle for good corporate governance, as is the goal of preventing irresponsible behaviour by companies, their officers and employees'.

To this end, many firms – especially larger companies with more than 250 employees – have introduced anti-corruption training. In the US, for example, it is common practice for senior managers to sign formal compliance statements declaring that they have abided by anti-corruption laws and reported any incidents – unfortunately, this practice does not yet extend to many other countries.

The US is still leading the way on corporate governance; however, in the emerging market regions, Asia is starting to emerge as a driving force. For example, Chinese companies are also increasingly aware that corporate integrity is important for their international reputation. Many major Chinese firms have signed up to the UN Global Compact (Bräutigam 2009: 69), the largest voluntary corporate responsibility initiative in the world, comprising over 8,700 companies from more than 130 countries. The policy initiative includes an important principle against corruption and urges its members to commit to the fight against it.

Another example of a similar corporate responsibility initiative is the Partnering Against Corruption Initiative (PACI) of the World Economic Forum. In 2005, 47 companies signed a zero-tolerance pact against bribes (*CFO Magazine* 2005). Large multinational companies from three sectors (energy; engineering and construction; and mining and metals) signed in support of the Partnering Against Corruption Principles for Countering Bribery (PACI Principles). The signatories include Bechtel Group, Rio Tinto, Vattenfall, Petronas and De Beers.

The PACI Principles are derived from Transparency International's Business Principles for Countering Bribery and call for two fundamental actions (World Economic Forum 2005):

- a zero-tolerance policy towards bribery; and

- the development of a practical and effective implementation programme.

The companies agreed either to implement anti-bribery and anti-corruption practices based on the PACI Principles or to use them to benchmark and improve their existing programmes. The World Economic Forum hopes that the adoption of PACI Principles will raise business standards across the world and contribute to the goals of good governance and economic development (ibid.).

A growing number of multinationals from emerging markets such as China, India and Brazil have also increased their business in established markets of developed countries and will therefore be exposed to stricter corporate governance standards. Some commentators believe that this will slowly force these companies to adopt their host countries' integrity and anti-corruption standards. Even more so, they hope that it will feed back over time to improve their business practices in their own home countries (*The Economist* 2008)

5.1 CORPORATE CODES OF CONDUCT

Many multinational companies communicate written codes of conduct to staff which apply not only to the company's employees but also to its agents, intermediaries, consultants and contractors (Fulgeras 2003).

The International Chamber of Commerce (ICC) actively promotes self-regulation and anti-corruption by international business. Its *Rules of conduct to combat extortion and bribery in international business* addresses the use of agents and sub-contractors, which are a common channel for illicit payments. The ICC and its national chambers have prepared model codes of conduct for their member companies, which should encourage enterprises to develop and implement their own codes of conduct consistent with the ICC rules (Asian Development Bank and OECD 2004: 28).

Other examples of efforts to foster ethical business include initiatives by countries such as Hong Kong, China, Indonesia, Japan, Korea and Singapore. Singapore, for instance, established special anti-corruption commissions to develop guidelines and best practices for corporate codes of conduct and to offer training to international corporations. Even if compliance is not mandatory in all countries, in some, such as Singapore, companies have to give reasons in their annual reports for deviating from these guidelines. Other countries use 'integrity pacts' – voluntary commitments developed by Transparency International to prevent corrupt practices in public procurement (Asian Development Bank and OECD 2004: 27).

List 7.1   Example: British Petroleum (BP) Code of Conduct

Anti-bribery and anti-corruption laws:

- Apply to BP employees worldwide.
- Forbid making, offering or promising to make a payment or transfer anything of value, including the provision of any service, gift or entertainment, to government personnel and other officials for the purpose of improperly obtaining or retaining business, or for any other improper purpose or business advantage;.
- Forbid making improper payments through third parties – BP personnel must therefore be diligent in selecting and monitoring contractors, agents and partners.
- Require that companies keep accurate books and records so that payments are honestly described and company funds are not used for unlawful purposes.

Basic rules you must follow – *never*:

- Offer or make an unauthorised payment, or authorise an improper payment (cash or otherwise) to a local or foreign official, or any related person or entity.
- Attempt to induce a local or foreign official to do something illegal.

- 'Shrug off' or fail to report any indication of improper payments.
- Offer or receive money (or anything of value), gifts, kickbacks or commission, in relation to obtaining business or awarding contracts.
- Establish an unrecorded 'slush' fund for any purpose.
- Do anything to induce or facilitate someone else to break these rules.
- Permit an agent or representative of BP to take questionable actions ('looking the other way').

BP rules on facilitation payments:

- BP policy does not permit so-called 'facilitation' or 'grease' payments to be made to government officials, even if such payments are nominal in amount.

Commercial bribery:

- Bribery of government officials is a serious matter, but bribery of those working in the private sector is also often illegal and always against BP's own standards of business conduct. In the end, bribery is bribery regardless of the recipient.

(*Source*: BP 2005: 48–49)

 For more information about business codes read Kapstein (2009: 83–88).

5.2 CONTROLLING AGENTS AND COMMERCIAL INTERMEDIARIES

The management of agents and other commercial intermediaries is particularly ripe for bribery and corruption. Despite increasing due diligence procedures to assess the integrity of agents, many international corporations still prefer to rely on trust and close relationships that have been built over years. Nevertheless, multinationals whose agents have paid bribes can be prosecuted under the FCPA in the United States – even if the employer denied any knowledge of the payments. Therefore, some multinationals try to control their agents' conduct via contracts in which they explicitly forbid the payments of bribes to secure a business on their behalf. This is difficult in sectors where the identity of 'middle men' is confidential, such as the arms and defence industries.

5.3 WHISTLEBLOWING AND REPORTING HOTLINES

Awareness-raising and staff education and training campaigns also aim to encourage the reporting of suspicions: so-called whistleblowing. Top-level management has come to recognise how important it is to support and protect whistleblowers. Many corporations have realised that in the case of fraud and corruption, insiders to the company, such as its employees, are a particularly valuable source of information (Wheeler 2003). Due to their unique insight into their company's complex business procedures, they are more likely to be able to detect illegal activities and companies generally prefer to deal with disclosures internally rather than in the eye of the media.

The most common way that integrity issues are brought to light is through whistleblowing by a disaffected employee or former employee, or even by a relative or friend of an employee (ibid.). Such disclosures have long been regarded as malicious and an act of betrayal, prompting no further action. However, as Wheeler (2003: 128) points out, at least initially, until it is established whether the information is accurate:

> ... the fact that a whistleblower's motive may be improper or inappropriate often has little bearing in practice on whether the information provided ... is of value. What is crucial is the content of the disclosure. It is important to separate the message from the messenger.

Anonymity and confidentiality are crucial preconditions for whistleblowing and management needs to deter reprisal practices by staff or management against the whistleblower by criminalising such actions.

As part of providing effective whistleblowing provisions, multinationals have introduced confidential reporting hotlines for employees to report fraud and corruption. Any shortcoming in a company's preventive mechanisms may be interpreted as a tacit incentive to commit acts of bribery and warrant the implication of their criminal liability. Therefore, many multinationals established such hotlines as part of corporate ethics programmes to reduce liability and fines if convicted of corrupt and unethical business practices. A warning system that supports whistleblowers, such as a fraud hotline, encourages employees to act when others do wrong. It can inspire confidence in employees that reporting misconduct is in their best interest and will benefit them, other employees and the company. It helps to create a culture that values ethical behaviour, is committed to preventing and detecting fraud, and will respond decisively and appropriately to misconduct. Other methods to implement corporate ethics programmes include the appointment of chief ethics officers or ombudsmen to address complaints and allegations of wrongdoing.

BRIBELINE: BUSINESS REGISTRY FOR INTERNATIONAL BRIBERY AND EXTORTION

Trace International's Business Registry for International Bribery and Extortion (BRIBEline) provides a secure and anonymous place to report bribe requests worldwide and help to combat bribery. BRIBEline is a multilingual online tool that focuses on demand-side bribery only, and does not request or collect information about those who pay, or offer to pay, bribes. No names are required and the information collected is not used to take legal or investigative action. Instead, aggregate information is published by the NGO to highlight trouble spots and allow companies to better manage risk.

Between 2008 and 2010 BRIBEline published six country studies on bribery demands in emerging economies, such as Brazil, Mexico, India and China. The reports show that the majority of reported bribery demands in most of these countries were for avoiding damage to personal or commercial interests rather than gaining an advantage. To read the full reports, visit the website: www.traceinternational.org

---

 For more information on Trace International's BRIBEline project, visit the website: www.bribeline.org

6 Case Study: BAE Systems and the Al Yamamah Scandal

The UK defence company BAE Systems (formerly known as British Aerospace), Europe's largest arms firm, has long been the subject of allegations of bribery in relation to its business in Saudi Arabia. The company was accused of maintaining a secret £60 million Saudi slush fund, which resulted in an investigation by the Serious Fraud Office (SFO). The SFO focused its probe on the so-called Al Yamamah arms deals which date back to 1986 and cover the sale of Tornado and Hawk jets and an airbase construction programme, estimated at £50bn and allegedly the result of bribes to members of the Saudi royal family.

BAE Systems, the world's third largest defence contractor, has sold fighter jets to Saudi Arabia since the 1960s, but the Al Yamamah deals that began in the 1980s and continued for decades were of a much larger scale. They included not only the supply of fighter jets, but also the sending of staff and maintenance facilities, which locked BAE Systems into a long-term agreement with thousands of UK citizens living and working in Saudi Arabia to support the deal (BBC 2007a). It has been claimed that the deal was crucial for BAE at the time as it allowed the company to stay afloat for more than two decades.

When it was revealed by *The Guardian* newspaper in May 2004 that BAE Systems had allegedly won the deals with the aid of a secret slush fund, the SFO announced that it was considering opening an investigation. *The Guardian* claimed that payments of £60m were made during the course of the Al Yamamah deals with BAE Systems. It was alleged that a Saudi prince who negotiated the £40bn arms deal between Britain and Saudi Arabia had received secret payments for over a decade (BBC 2007b). A few months later, BAE Systems confirmed it was being investigated by the SFO under Part 12 of the Anti-terrorism, Crime and Security Act 2001, but denied any misconduct.

In the following two years, the SFO collected documents that illustrate how BAE Systems had transferred £1bn to Washington bank accounts controlled by Prince Bandar of Saudi Arabia, son of the Saudi defence minister, and another £1bn to Swiss bank accounts linked to agents acting for Saudi royals (Leigh 2007). The purpose of one of these accounts was to pay the expenses of the Prince's private Airbus. It has been alleged that these payments were made with the full knowledge of the Ministry of Defence (BBC 2007b). According to a BBC *Panorama* investigation, the payments were written into the arms deal contract in secret annexes, described as 'support services'. They were then authorised on a quarterly basis by the MoD (ibid.).

The SFO discovered these secret annexes during its investigation, but it remains unclear if the payments were actually illegal. This depends partly on whether they continued after 2001, when the UK made bribery of foreign officials an offence. If there was indeed any evidence of bribery or corruption in arms deals since 2001 – when the UK signed the Organisation for Economic Cooperation and Development (OECD) Anti-Bribery Convention and the British Parliament passed the Anti-terrorism, Crime and Security Act, which bans the bribery of officials abroad – this would be a criminal offence. Payments made before these laws were passed did not result in prosecutions.

In November 2006 it was announced that the long-running SFO investigation was likely to continue for another two years in order to probe Swiss bank accounts. At the same time, BAE Systems was about to finalise a further estimated £10bn sale of 72 Eurofighter jets to Saudi Arabia, negotiated between the MoD and the Saudi government.

On 14 December 2006, the Attorney General, Lord Goldsmith, announced in a statement in the House of Lords that the SFO was discontinuing its investigation into BAE Systems and that the team had been ordered to turn in its files. The wider public interest 'to safeguard national and international security' outweighed any potential benefits of further investigation (*Hansard*, Lord Goldsmith, 2006). 'It has been necessary to balance the need to maintain the rule of law against the wider public interest. No weight has been given to commercial interests or the national economic interests' (ibid.). These words were carefully chosen, as Britain had signed up to the OECD Convention on Combating Bribery of Foreign Public Officials in International Business Transactions, which states in Article 5 that 'national economic interest' cannot stand in the way of stopping corruption.

However, the reversal had suspiciously followed reports that the Saudi royals were angered by the British corruption probe and considered pulling out of the new Eurofighter deal with BAE Systems. Instead, the Saudis entered talks with BAE defence competitors in France (BBC 2007c).

The termination of the investigation became hugely controversial, not only domestically with opposition MPs, the public and the media, but also abroad. The director of the anti-fraud section at the OECD addressed the decision in a formal complaint letter to the Foreign Office on behalf of the United States, Japan, France, Sweden, Switzerland and Greece in December 2006, harshly criticising the end of the investigation. In 2007, the OECD conducted an inquiry into whether Britain violated the OECD anti-bribery convention it signed in 2001 and published a 79-page report one year later, criticising the UK government and stating it was 'disappointed and seriously concerned' (Peel 2008).

Meanwhile, the Head of the SFO, Robert Wardle, acknowledged that the decision to terminate the investigation may have 'damaged the reputation of the UK as a place which is determined to stamp out corruption' (Pfeifer and Power 2007). Media commentators and anti-corruption campaigners accused the British government of only opposing corrupt practices when the UK's own interests are not at stake (BBC 2007a). Furthermore, the revelations surrounding the Al Yamamah defence contract seem likely to damage BAE Systems' sales in other countries. A deal to sell 18 typhoon jets to Austria had already become the subject of intense controversy in Vienna (BBC 2007a).

The then Prime Minister, Tony Blair, justified the termination of the probe by stressing diplomatic reasons: 'Our relationship with Saudi Arabia is vitally important for our country in terms of counter-terrorism, in terms of the broader Middle East, in terms of helping in respect of Israel and Palestine. That strategic interest comes first' (Brady 2006). The MoD had claimed that public discussion of the Prince Bandar payments could cause the Saudi royals to cut off intelligence links and would have generally slowed down cooperation unless the investigations were halted (Leigh 2007).

Despite the SFO insisting that it was not motivated by commercial factors, Tony Blair and other politicians were openly concerned about the impact in case of a commercial boycott by the Saudi royals on the British economy, BAE Systems and other British exports such as Rolls Royce (Peston 2006). The Prime Minister explained that a continuation of the SFO investigation would have led to 'the complete wreckage of a vital strategic relationship and the loss of thousands of British jobs' (BBC 2007b).

Ultimately, it became clear that the investigation was ended in order to maintain good relations with Saudi Arabia and the 50,000 jobs at stake in the manufacture of the Eurofighter jets.

A significant example to illustrate the secrecy displayed in this case is the probe of the National Audit Office (NAO) – another UK authority that investigated the Al Yamamah contracts. Its findings – drawn up in a report in 1992 – have never been published. In July 2006, the Head of the NAO, Sir John Bourn, refused to release a copy to the SFO investigating the arms deal. The NAO report has been repressed because the Ministry of Defence feared it would anger Saudi Arabia and stated that 'the report remains sensitive. Disclosure would harm both international relations and the UK's commercial interests' (Leigh 2007).

In 2007, the US Department of Justice opened a probe into BAE Systems' compliance with anti-corruption laws within the US – including its business with Saudi Arabia. Washington formally demanded mutual legal assistance, meaning that Britain should hand over all evidence of secret BAE Systems payments to the Saudi royal family to secure arms deals (ibid.).

Despite the earlier charges being dropped by the SFO in 2006, the SFO stepped up its investigations in 2009 into other BAE contracts and arms deals in Tanzania, South Africa, the Czech Republic, Chile and Romania. That BAE Systems finally had to agree to a settlement is due to the persistence of the then newly appointed SFO Director Richard Alderman, who offered the company a plea bargain whereby BAE would admit guilt and pay a large fine. (Leigh and Evans 2010a). 'Although BAE was prepared to accept a limited fine, the company stood firm against admitting guilt [to corruption] for fear of its impact on future contracts' (Hotten 2010). In the US, Alderman's counterpart at the Department of Justice, Mark Mendelsohn, was also still keen to enforce the US Foreign Corrupt Practices Act to bring charges against BAE.

In 2010 negotiations finally reached a breakthrough and BAE Systems agreed to a plea bargain, settling cases in both the UK and the US by agreeing to pay penalties. However, pleading guilty to only a single accounting offence in relation to a £28m radar contract with Tanzania in 2002, the company avoided having to admit to corruption. This was particularly important for BAE as a conviction for corruption would have affected its chances of winning future contracts and risked the company being blacklisted. Originally, prosecutors in the UK had tried to charge BAE over several allegations of corruption in various countries (Leigh and Evans 2010b).

The settlement seemed to be a relief for all sides: 'Prosecuting BAE through the courts would not just have been damaging for Britain's biggest manufacturing company, but also intensely embarrassing for the government and Ministry of Defence' (Hotten 2010).

For the UK it was also important to bring an end to international accusations of violations of the OECD convention and enable the SFO to keep face.

The judge in the case concluded that BAE Systems had made secret payments to a Tanzanian middleman, Sailesh Vithlani, to facilitate the radar deal for the company. However, no individual person was charged, despite the actions being apparently approved by BAE's then chairman, Sir Richard Evans (Evans and Leigh 2010). Vithlani was paid a third of the contract's value ($12.4m over five years) via two offshore companies to secure the overpriced radar deal – an astoundingly large amount for a mere lobbyist, as BAE tried to claim (ibid.). The judge in the case questioned 'if it really is the case that legitimate lobbyists could be paid 30% of the value of a $40m contract simply as recompense for their time and trouble' (ibid.).

BAE was eventually fined £500,000 for the accounting offence of hiding the payments to Vithlani from auditors and ordered to pay some of the SFO's legal costs. The fine was kept comparatively low compared with the contract value, as BAE had agreed in the plea bargain to pay £30m in corporate reparations and fines and subtract any fine from that sum (ibid.). This means that a £29.5m 'gesture of goodwill' will now be paid to Tanzania to compensate for the overpriced deal.

In the US however, BAE Systems did have to pay a much larger fine and to settle all corruption investigations it was ordered to pay a much larger fine of $400m to the US government.

BAE also seems to have been treated less harsh when compared with the German company Siemens, which was fined $1.34bn in 2008. As in the case of Siemens, BAE was able to escape being blacklisted from future EU or US contracts as it was not convicted of corruption but merely false accounting. 'BAE, the SFO, and the UK government will no doubt hope that one of the most controversial episodes in corporate British history has now been resolved' (Hotten 2010).

List 7.2   Timeline of BAE Systems controversy

1985:   First phase: BAE Systems signs Al Yamamah arms deal, worth £50bn.

1993:   Second phase: Saudi Arabia purchased 48 Tornados off BAE.

2004:   Allegations by *The Guardian* newspaper that the Al Yamamah deal was won with the aid of a £60m secret slush fund; Serious Fraud Office (SFO) begins its investigation.

2005:   Third phase: Saudi Arabia orders 72 Eurofighter jets from BAE Systems.

2006:   Talks over order of Eurofighter jets have stalled and Saudi Arabia is in talks with BAE's competitors. SFO drops its investigation in light of national security interests.

2007:   Saudi Arabia and BAE Systems resume Eurofighter deal.

The OECD voices serious concerns over the British investigation.

The US State Department opens a formal investigation into BAE Systems.

2009: SFO starts investigations to prosecute BAE for corruption linked to contracts won from Tanzania, the Czech Republic, Romania and South Africa.

2010: BAE Systems pleads guilty to charges of false accounting in simultaneous settlements in the UK and the US. The firm is fined £286m, however, it avoids admitting corruption and bribery.

(*Source*: BBC News 2010a)

Study Questions

- In what ways does corruption take place in the international business environment, in particular in emerging markets?

- What are the implications of bribery by multinational corporations for developing countries in particular? Are there incentives for multinationals to improve on corporate governance?

- Evaluate the international community's attempts to counter corruption in the international business sector and the effectiveness of the main international anti-bribery legislation.

8

Corruption and Global Finance

1 Introduction

The world of global finance and, within it, the international banking and financial market sector are very vulnerable to fraud and corruption.

Fenner (2009: 139) describes the different forms of corruption that can take place in financial institutions:

> Either the financial institution itself or an employee directly commits an act of corruption by bribing or by accepting bribes (employee risk); or the financial institution is misused by one of its clients to disguise the corrupt origin of funds or to commit tax fraud (client risk).

Fraud and corruption can be a serious problem, damaging the financial integrity and prove to be time-consuming and costly for public funds to investigate.

> If a case is complicated and involves the international movement of funds, then the investigation costs can be very complex. It is not unusual to spend $1 million or more on investigating a $10 million fraud. When cross border money transfers and offshore tax havens are involved, this can cost more than the amount lost (Samociuk et al. 2006: 3).

Fraud and corruption in the financial sector can often have huge international implications across the financial markets as well as an impact on economic and political stability. It is not unheard of for banks to collapse due to corruption-related fraud (the British Barings Bank is a prominent example) and cause turmoil on the global financial markets.

2 Rogue Trading

Financial institutions and banks have become increasingly dependent upon profits from trading activities (such as trading currencies, bonds or futures) as opposed to the traditional business of lending. Barely a year goes by without a major bank or financial entity losing millions, and sometimes billions, due to a fraudulent trader acting outside of their authority.

Rogue trading is when an employee makes unauthorised trades on behalf of their bank, often resulting in the loss of enormous amounts of money for that organisation. This activity is often hard to identify, because the perpetrator is a legitimate employee and their actions will sometimes go unnoticed as he or she usually covers up the losses (sometimes in secret accounts) or hopes to recover them through more risky trades. The motivation behind these acts is often to boost their own earnings by increasing their bonuses, which are linked to their trading profits.

The following list of rogue traders provides an overview of the central figures in the world's largest bank frauds. The traders were charged with covering up huge trading losses so that they could boost their own earnings in bonuses and were sentenced to between two and eight years in prison for their illegal activities.

List 8.1   Overview of some the most famous rogue traders

- **Jérôme Kerviel** – lost French Société Générale approximately $7.2bn in 2008.
- **Yasuo Hamanaka** – lost Japanese Sumitomo Corporation $2.6bn in 1996.
- **Nick Leeson** – lost British Barings Bank approximately $1.4bn in 1995.
- **Toshihide Iguchi** – lost Japanese Daiwa Bank Group approximately $1.1bn in 1995.
- **John Rusnak** – lost Allied Irish Bank approximately $691m in 2002.
- **Peter Young** – lost Deutsche Morgan Grenfell approximately $600m in 1996.

(Wearden 2008; BBC 2008d)

The losses listed in List 8.1 occurred in some of the world's most sophisticated financial institutions, which are publicly traded and subject to the full weight of global regulatory oversight. Despite this and most of the banks' own risks management systems, compliance checks and internal audits, they were unable to prevent or detect the unauthorised trades before they created huge financial losses and reputational damage. One of the most recent cases, not contained in the list above, is 31-year-old trader Kweku Adoboli, who is alleged to have lost Swiss bank UBS an estimated $2bn and was charged in London with fraud by abuse of power and two counts of false accounting in September 2011. If Adoboli will be convicted, this latest disclosure of unauthorised trades is thought to become the third largest rogue trading scandal since Kerviel and Hamanaka (Murphy and Gill 2011).

2.1 EXAMPLE: JÉRÔME KERVIEL AND SOCIÉTÉ GÉNÉRALE

In 2008 the banking sector was shaken by the biggest rogue trading scandal it had seen at that point surrounding Jérôme Kerviel. The junior trader had lost French bank Société Générale (SocGen) EUR4.9bn, which equates to almost two years of pretax profit at the bank's investment-banking unit (Viscusi and Chassany 2008).

Kerviel's method was to remove all personal trading limits and balance each real trade with a fictitious one. Having worked for six years in the back office, his knowledge of the bank's controls allowed him to avoid detection by colleagues and supervisors (ibid.). He was only found out when a compliance officer noticed that a trade had exceeded bank limits and alerted the bank's senior management.

When Société Générale called the counterparty, they were told the trade didn't exist (ibid.). Kerviel immediately confessed to his unauthorised trading activities. By then, he had already lost the bank a record sum, and even though he did not siphon any money off for himself, his main motive was to impress the other traders and increase his bonus (BBC 2008c). His actions had risked over 100,000 jobs at SocGen and the solvency of the bank, which dates back to 1864. In his defence, Kerviel claimed that his superiors had known about his risky trading and claimed he had been made a scapegoat for a corrupt banking system (Allen 2010).

In 2010, Kerviel was convicted of breach of trust, computer abuse and forgery, and sentenced to five years in prison, of which two years were suspended. He was also ordered to pay back the EUR4.9bn in damages that his risky betting strategies had cost the bank. 'It is understood that the bank views the granting of damages as a symbolic payment, and may not intend to force its erstwhile employee into a lifetime of unpayable debts' (Davies 2010b). Kerviel's lawyer slated the ruling as unreasonable and pointed out that responsibility did not lie only with Kerviel but also with the bank for not having installed effective control mechanisms and allowed the excesses (ibid.). Two years earlier, SocGen was fined in this regard EUR4m by financial regulators for failing to conduct proper checks which would have uncovered Kerviel's illegal trading (ibid.).

Jérôme Kerviel's illegal trading is not a one-off scandal to hit the banking sector. One of the first rogue traders who came into the public spotlight was Nick Leeson, who lost Barings Bank £860m in 1995, leading to the collapse of one of the oldest London merchant banks, dating back to 1762. SocGen was fortunate in this respect not to face a similar demise, despite even larger losses.

2.2 HOW TO COMBAT ROGUE TRADING?

After 1995, alarmed investment banks increasingly started investing in risk management systems to prevent rogue trading, in the aftermath of the high-profile Nick Leeson case and the resulting Barings Bank bankruptcy. More sophisticated technology has made banks' internal controls tougher and at the same time quality standards and knowledge of auditing also vastly improved in the banking sector (Hunt 2008).

However, high-profile cases of rogue trading still make the headlines, and in the case of Jérôme Kerviel, the trading losses amassed were even higher than those of Nick Leeson. How is this possible? Kerviel – who, according to Bloomberg, made a salary and bonus combined of less than EUR 100,000 a year (which is small by investment banking standards) – had joined the trading floor from the firm's back office in 2006, and used that knowledge to manipulate SocGen's accounting systems to conceal his trades (Viscusi and Chassany 2008). This suggests corporate governance failures and a lack of control procedures within banks. However, 'complacency and a market culture that rewards excessive risk-taking', combined with a systemic lack of ethical values in this sector, could also be at fault (Hunt 2008).

It is questionable whether occurrences of rogue trading are really just isolated incidents, and not far more widespread (Chrisafis, Treanor and Allen 2008). It is suspected that many small- and large-scale illegal trading activities go unreported every year and this activity seems to be fuelled by the bonus culture within investment banks. Often the bad trades go on over a long period of time, as in the cases of both Iguchi and Hamanaka (see overview of rogue traders, above), who accumulated their losses over a period of over ten years, without anyone noticing (Leith 2002).

Most of the above rogue traders had control over the front and back offices; another common feature is that they worked in small understaffed branches remote from the bank's head office (ibid.). Front and back offices should always be separated to avoid collusion and covering up bad trades.

Another factor is often that senior bank executives are sometimes not fully aware of what is happening on the trading floor. 'They are like dads asking their sons to explain the new generation of computer games' (ibid.).

With the increased complexity of today's financial markets, rogue trading is often facilitated by a lack of internal controls or accountability concerning traders who are rarely routinely checked. Banks need to invest heavily in risk management and encourage internal whistleblowing. Another possible solution to reduce the risk of rogue trading is the introduction of trading and credit limits, which seems unlikely, as banks usually encourage risk-taking and would not want to reduce their profit margins.

3 The Role of Accountancy and Auditing Firms

Usually, cases of fraud and corruption in the financial services industry are revealed by external auditors (market leaders in this field include consultancy firms such as PricewaterhouseCoopers, KPMG, Deloitte and Ernst & Young). Their role is to examine their clients' financial statements, check compliance with laws and provide shareholders with independent information – if necessary, raising the alarm if they discover fraud. But what if the accountants and auditors are themselves part of the scam and bribed by their clients?

The most prominent case came to light in 2002, following the collapse of failed energy giant Enron. US accountancy firm Arthur Andersen was found guilty of obstructing justice by shredding documents relating to Enron and illegally destroying thousands of computer records belonging to its scandal-hit client over a period of several weeks. Arthur Andersen, which audited Enron's accounts, was also accused of questionable accounting that kept hundreds of millions of dollars in debt off its books (BBC News 2002a). Following the conviction, several Enron investors and shareholders brought multi-million lawsuits demanding compensation, and the firm was subsequently banned from auditing publicly traded companies, prompting its bankruptcy. In 2003, US banks Citigroup and J.P. Morgan Chase were also fined $236m in compensation to betrayed Enron investors for their role in helping Enron cover up its actual debt (SEC 2003).

THE ENRON AND WORLDCOM SCANDALS

In 2001 US energy giant Enron, once the seventh largest company in the United States, went bankrupt with debts of $31.8bn (£18bn). Around 21,000 employees lost their jobs in a scandal that shook corporate America, and shareholders lost billions of dollars in stocks and retirement savings. Former Chief Executive of Enron, Jeffrey Skilling, was sentenced in 2006 to 24 years in prison for fraud, conspiracy and insider trading (he is currently awaiting resentencing). 'Accounting schemes he approved masked huge debt and cash flow problems at the company that led to its ultimate demise' (Barrionuevo 2006).

Only one year after Enron's downfall, US telecommunications company WorldCom collapsed as a result of fraud in 2002 and nearly 17,000 employees lost their jobs. In 2005 former WorldCom Chief Executive, Bernard Ebbers, was sentenced to 25 years' imprisonment for his role in the largest accounting fraud in the United States – an $11 billion scheme to bury expenses and inflate revenue (Johnson 2005).

 For more detailed information on Enron's downfall and the conviction of Arthur Andersen, read 'Enron: Who's Accountable?' (Kadlec 2002).

The Arthur Andersen case highlighted inappropriate accounting practices and tarnished the reputation of the accounting profession, which failed to detect widespread fraud (Johnson 2007). The example illustrates how accountants, but also auditors, analysts and rating agencies, are particularly vulnerable to corruption. 'They are paid by the very clients on whose information disclosure they are meant to pass an independent judgement' (TI 2009: 132). Transparency International argues that this risk could reduced by making the disclosure of conflict of interests mandatory, rotating auditors, segregating the auditing function from other consulting services, and introducing proportionate liability for auditors and accountants (ibid.: 133).

Many industry commentators believe there is a conflict of interest when auditing firms try to make money from consulting, rather than solely from providing auditing services:

> *They have (at least in the short run) an incentive to go easy on their clients or even, as consultants, to help their clients think of ways to improve the appearance of profits – 'within' the rules. Analysts at investment banks that earn large fees from stock offerings may, as we have seen, have an incentive to tout the stocks, even when they have their doubts. And if they have a commercial bank division, they may have an incentive to maintain credit lines beyond the level which is prudent, simply because were they to cut them, they risk losing high potential future revenues from mergers and acquisitions and stock and bond issues (Stiglitz 2002).*

It is difficult for investors to sue audit firms, because the companies which hire them have primary responsibility for their own financial reports. Over the years, courts in the US have forced investors to prove that auditors took part in fraudulent conduct in order to prevail in court. However, for the vast majority of accounting-firm partners, officials who did not engage in misconduct generally are protected from having their personal assets seized (Johnson 2007).

FRAUD AND THE US SUBPRIME MORTGAGE CRISIS

Lehman brothers

The collapse of investment bank Lehman Brothers in 2008, the largest bankruptcy filing in US history, left thousands of staff jobless and 100,000 creditors in debts. The bank had suffered unprecedented losses due to the subprime mortgage crisis in the United States and the events sparked the beginning of the world-wide financial crisis (Mamudi 2008).

In a 2010 report by the US court-appointed bankruptcy examiner, the bank's ex-directors and its UK accounting advisors were accused of accounting and securities fraud in relation to the Sarbanes-Oxley Act. Lehman Brothers had allegedly exploited a legal loophole which allowed the bank to use cosmetic accounting gimmicks to hide its financial losses and make their accounts appear more robust than they actually were. The bank temporarily removed $50bn in risky loans from its balance sheets to other institutions, with a guarantee to buy them back a few days later under so-called repurchase agreements, which the bank classified as sales, not accounting tricks (Pagano 2010). However, the bank has been accused of deceiving investors and regulators by this action of its real financial situation in 2007 and 2008 with this action.

Charges were filed against the bank's auditors, Ernst & Young, who advised the bank on the transactions on the ground of having assisted in accounting fraud by approving the accounts (Scannell 2010).

Goldman Sachs

In 2010, investment bank Goldman Sachs was ordered to pay $550m to settle a fraud suit with the US Securities and Exchange Commission (SEC) – the largest fine the SEC has ever handed to a company (Goldfarb 2010). The bank was accused of betting against clients and misleading them to invest in subprime mortgage securities in 2007 which were likely to lose value, while marketing it to buyers as lucrative investment opportunity. Investors lost subsequently $1bn a year later, when 99 per cent of the mortgages in the so-called Abacus portfolio were downgraded in the credit crunch. The SEC criticised Goldman Sachs for failing to disclose this information to its clients and of 'fiddling investors out of $1bn by wilfully mis-marketing toxic sub-prime mortgage-related securities' (Clark 2010). The bank was blamed by the SEC for wrongly permitting a client, hedge fund Paulson & Co, which was betting against the mortgage market, to strongly influence which mortgage securities to include in the investment portfolio. (Clark 2010) It also emerged that the bank had been paid $15m by Paulson & Co for marketing the dubious portfolio. Goldman Sachs was among the very few banks to void major losses on mortgages during the credit crunch in 2008.

Does the threat of liability prompt auditors to do better work? Should there be liability caps for auditing firms in lawsuits where investors sue them? Read the article 'Accounting for the Future' (Johnson 2007).

4 The Sarbanes-Oxley Act in the United States

The Sarbanes-Oxley Act of 2002 is also referred to as the Public Company Accounting Reform and Investor Protection Act. Within the financial sector, prior to 2002, there was no specific regulation set up to deal with fraud and corruption. It was only due to the financial scandals that led to the collapse of Enron, WorldCom and Arthur Andersen in the United States between 2001 and 2002 that the Sarbanes-Oxley Act was introduced. The purpose of the Act is to introduce corporate governance standards to ensure that companies are managed in the best interests of stakeholders (Hibis 2003).

Aldrighi (2009: 89) describes the benefits of the law as follows:

The law provides for a wide array of corporate governance reforms, including stronger liability for management in case of corporate fraud, extended reporting and disclosure requirements, additional checks and balances through more independent audit committees, and clearer responsibilities and liabilities for accountants and auditors to improve the accuracy of financial information.

However, this Act only applies to companies in the United States with US parent companies and non-US parent companies that have a listing on the US stock market. A similar law has not been introduced in Europe, mainly because some of its main provisions would be incompatible with some of the national laws in individual EU member states or risk double regulation of EU audit firms. In most EU countries, it is already the shareholders, not management, who appoint auditors (Gumbel 2002).

5 European Financial Market Regulation

In order to maintain the integrity of the financial system, the supervision of financial institutions is highly important. Internationally, according to the UK Financial Services Authority (FSA) 'because of the increasingly global nature of markets, regulators have been increasing the levels of regulatory communication and co-operation and enhancing the role of international standard setting regulatory organisations' (FSA n.d.a.).

Many jurisdictions have set up their own national regulators to oversee the financial services industry in their respective country. Two large national regulatory authorities are:

- The Financial Industry Regulatory Authority (FINRA), formed in 2007 and based in Washington DC, 'is the largest non-governmental regulator for all securities firms doing business in the United States' and regulates 4,570 brokerage firms (FINRA n.d.).

For more information on FINRA visit: www.finra.org

- The Financial Services Authority (FSA) in the United Kingdom is another self-regulatory body, financed by the firms it regulates and accountable to UK Treasury ministers. The FSA was created in 2000 and is independent from the government while regulating around 29,000 firms in the UK. Its objectives are to increase market confidence, financial stability and consumer protection, and to reduce financial crime (FSA n.d.b.).

For more information on the FSA visit: www.fsa.gov.uk

There are many others, such as the US Securities and Exchange Commission (SEC) and Federal Reserve System in the United States, the Financial Supervisory Authority in Germany, the Financial Services Agency in Japan, the Swiss Financial Markets Supervision and the China Banking Regulatory Commission.

Financial regulation at the European level is moving towards the creation of a new integrated financial European market. However, the relationship between European financial regulations and national regulators has been reported to be quite complex. Frison-Roche (2005) argues that 'there is a distortion between the substantive rules, elaborated at the European Union level, and the institutional rules because regulators are still national'.

This specific issue (which is also the case for the energy or tele-communications sectors) of whether there should be a pan-European financial regulator to coordinate regulation, has been heavily debated in Brussels for years. In the wake of the global financial crisis, more urgency fuelled the debate and the European Union eventually decided to establish a single financial regulator that would supervise national ones. Three new European regulatory boards for banking, securities and the insurance sector (the European Banking Authority based in London, European Securities and Markets Authority based in Paris and the European Insurance and Occupational Pensions Authority based in Frankfurt) were created in January 2011 to oversee financial markets and European governments hope that with this centralised measure they will be able to 'avoid a recurrence of the risky behaviour that led to the credit crunch' (Stewart 2009).

The three financial watchdogs will be independent institutions. EU governments can contest decisions by the new regulators, but such veto power can only be evoked in a crisis. In normal circumstances, the European regulator can overrule the national regulators and authorities (Traynor 2009).

6 Case Study: Bernard Madoff's Ponzi Scheme

The famous Wall Street trader Bernard Madoff (born 1938) came from a middle-class New York background and started his career aged 22 with $5,000 saved from summer jobs (BBC News 2009a). He set up Bernard L. Madoff Investment Securities in 1960, matching buyers and sellers of stocks. His company grew very successfully within a decade and soon had an impressive client list. By the early 1990s, Madoff had branched into investment banking with his reputation gaining even more when he became chairman of the Nasdaq stock exchange.

However, behind the façade of impressive financial success, the reality was that Madoff defrauded his investment clients with an elaborate $64.8bn 'Ponzi' scheme, the biggest fraud Wall Street had ever seen, which bankrupted investors around the world. A 'Ponzi' scheme operates by using money from new investors to pay off the old investors instead of to generate new returns. Madoff's victims were individual investors, charities, big banks and pension and hedge funds, which were attracted by the continuously high win margins in all market conditions. Madoff promised investors a positive return of over 10 per cent annually and certain clients even 46 per cent (Chibber 2009). Big hedge funds and banks were keen to invest with him because the consistent annual returns meant steady fees for them. These were not the highest return seen on Wall Street but the attraction lay in their consistency, which portrayed Madoff as a safe bet for investors.

PONZI SCHEME EXPLAINED:

A 'Ponzi' scheme is an investment scheme in which no real profits are generated. It is named after Charles Ponzi, who first used this scheme in the 1920s in the United States.

Investors are paid from other investors' money and large returns act as bait to attract new investors. The scheme is different from pyramid selling as all investors invest with the same person. When no more new recruits can be found, the scheme collapses, with the newest investors losing everything (Wilson 2008).

In late 2008, the con finally unravelled as a large number of clients, feeling worried by the global financial crisis, wanted to withdraw their investments and left Madoff with $7bn in redemptions. As all his clients wanted to cash in on their investments at once, Madoff's scheme imploded as he could not fulfil their requests (BBC News 2009a).

Problems had already started a few years before the credit crunch, when the pricing of securities changed at Wall Street and new competition entered the market. However, it seems that if the credit crunch had not happened, Madoff's scam would have continued undetected for quite some time. In the end, the Madoff scandal came to symbolise the excesses of Wall Street and was the first truly global financial fraud case.

Madoff was arrested in December 2008 after telling his sons that his business was a scam. He was freed on $10m bail and placed under house arrest, with his assets frozen and his mail searched. Madoff was subsequently charged with fraud, money laundering and other offences. In the 2009 court trial Madoff pleaded guilty to all 11 charges and was sentenced to 150 years in prison (BBC News 2009b). It turned out that his fraud had run since the early 1990s and that, over the 40 years in business, Madoff never traded a single share for his investment clients (Nasaw 2009). One of his employees, Frank DiPascali Jr, also pleaded guilty to falsifying office records and customer accounts to cover up the non-existent trades. He now faces up to 125 years in prison.

Another person charged was Madoff's accountant, David Friehling, who had been his auditor since 1991. He pleaded guilty to nine criminal charges, among them securities fraud and investment adviser fraud. 'In essence, [Friehling] admitted that he had never adequately audited the Madoff operation and, as an investor in the scheme, had never been a truly independent auditor. Nevertheless, he produced the supposedly professional and independent audits that sustained the Madoff fraud year in and year out' (Henriques 2009). Friehling denied, however, having been involved in the Ponzi scheme and stated he had 'simply trusted Mr. Madoff, taking whatever figures he was given and plugging them into his supposedly independent audits' (ibid.). Both Friehling and DiPascali Jr were released on bail and are still awaiting sentencing. Facing a 144-year prison sentence, Friehling, like DiPascali, agreed to assist the prosecutors in return for leniency.

In June 2011, Madoff's former payroll manager, Eric Lipkin, also admitted to his part in the Ponzi scheme and pleaded guilty to falsifying documents and bank fraud. By summer 2011, he was the 9th person to be charged in connection with the Madoff scandal and could face up to 70 years in prison (Kollewe 2011).

Other financial white-collar fraudsters in the United States have received less severe sentences: Former WorldCom CEO Bernard Ebbers was sentenced in 2005 for 25 years for accounting fraud and former Enron CEO Jeffrey Skilling was sentenced in 2006 to 24 years in prison. In addition to his prison sentence, Madoff was ordered to pay back $171bn in assets and his wife $80m in assets. His wife was accused of having withdrawn $45.5m and another $10m from his brokerage firm shortly before her husband's arrest (BBC News 2009c).

Apparently, Madoff showed remorse in court, reportedly saying, 'I left a legacy of shame … I cannot make an excuse for my behaviour' (Teather 2009). He insisted that he had run the fraud scheme alone, despite having his close family, such as his sons, working for him (Rushe 2010a).

How was he able to fool so many investors and financial regulators? There were warning signs: back in 2000, financial analyst Harry Markopolos tried to alert the US Securities and Exchange Commission (SEC) to Madoff's suspicious trading and high returns, but his repeated warnings were ignored over the years. Even after handing the SEC a document outlining Madoff's Ponzi scheme, the Commission concluded that there was not enough evidence and that Madoff had only violated regulations by not being a registered advisor (Chibber 2009). Overall, Madoff was investigated eight times by the SEC over the last 16 years but nothing was ever found.

Madoff's offices in New York were split across three floors and the fraud was run from one of them, the 17th floor, to which Madoff's employees seldom had access. It was here that the fake account statements for clients were printed on old computer technology, as updating would have meant a risk of exposing the con. 'Madoff was trusted by his victims because of his sterling reputation on Wall Street. Alongside his fraud, he ran a legitimate share-trading business that provided the perfect cover' (BBC News 2009a).

Madoff's personal charm, his social connections and his establishment credentials aided him in concealing his fraud from investors, financial regulators and the SEC, who all seem to have trusted him (BBC News 2009a). Many of his victims were recruited at an exclusive Palm Beach country club, where he was a member (Chibber 2009). The exclusivity meant that many clients trusted Madoff with their money due to personal recommendation. Madoff threw out investors who asked too many questions (Teather 2009). 'Madoff appears to have cultivated the air of a brilliant financial mind, which won over the people into whose ears he whispered at golf clubs. Access to his funds was considered exclusive. Madoff chose his clients, not the other way round' (Chibber 2009).

So far, nearly 9,000 victims have filed claims for losses. Many of them lost their life savings. Madoff had strong connections with New York's Jewish community; having acted as the former treasurer of the American Jewish Congress, many Jewish investors felt particularly betrayed by Madoff, whom they regarded as one of their own (ibid.). Having been a philanthropist donating to hospitals and charities, Madoff provided 'the security of investing with a man they knew and trusted' (Creswell and Thomas 2009).

Among the victims were several Holocaust survivors, including prominent victim Ellie Wiesel, Nobel Peace laureate, who lost his life savings and $152m of his charity's money. Hollywood film director Steven Spielberg invested nearly 70 per cent of his charity's Wunderkinder Foundation funds with Madoff (Chibber 2009). Madoff deceived many working class people as well, such as teachers, mechanics and farmers who were saving for their retirement. 'Many invested in so-called "feeder funds", which often did little to advertise their connection to Madoff, and they had little or no idea that their money had been lost until they received letters from their financial advisors' (Teather 2009). Even employees at the London and New York offices were allowed to invest with Madoff and lost their savings (Creswell and Thomas 2009).

Several of Madoff's victims committed suicide. In December 2008 a French hedge fund manager killed himself after his firm, Access International Advisers, lost £1.4bn of his clients' money in the fraud. Half a year later, in

June 2009, another victim, William Fox, committed suicide, unable to cope with the shame of losing his family savings. In Madoff's court case, more than 100 victims described in statements the impact the fraud had had on their lives and the devastation it caused (Teather 2009).

After sentencing Madoff, the spotlight of the investigators moved to his two sons, who had both worked for the business, and Madoff's wife. There were doubts that Madoff could have kept his elaborate scheme secret over decades or run it without help (ibid.). Madoff was accused of trying to hide his assets to keep them from being frozen and to prevent compensation for betrayed investors by giving away jewellery worth $1m to friends and relatives. Investigators also found signed cheques worth $173m in Madoff's desk when he was arrested and it was suspected that he and his wife had transferred funds to their sons. His wife's $69m assets were also frozen and she had to surrender her passport to prevent her escaping the country with the money. 'Rumours persist that Madoff has billions of dollars deposited with overseas banks, but if this is true they are likely to prove almost impossible to track down' (Griffiths 2009).

Irving Picard was named as court-appointed trustee, responsible for recovering assets on behalf of Madoff investors and deciding how to distribute them. After initially looking into Madoff's own assets, Picard soon realised he needed to focus more on Madoff's business partners who profited from their links or investments with him in order to recover some of the large amounts lost (ibid.). However, some victims already started suing Picard over the speed of the recovery and size of his bill (Rushe 2010b).

By summer 2009, 15,400 victims had filed claims for compensation and by the end of 2010 Picard had recovered nearly $10bn of funds (ibid.). The two biggest settlements were from the widow of one of Madoff's closest friends, the billionaire and philanthropist Jeffry Picower, who had made $7.2bn over 20 years investing with Madoff (receiving in one year a 950 per cent return on the money he invested) (ibid.). His widow returned the profits as a gesture of goodwill by way of declaration that her husband had been in no way complicit. The family of another old friend of Madoff, Carl Shapiro, agreed to pay $625m in a settlement (ibid.).

In December 2010, a US high court complaint against Madoff's sons and an Austrian banker, Sonja Kohn, who had promoted Madoff's feeder funds in

Europe, was filed in an attempt to recover $80m (Rushe 2010a). Irving Picard explained his actions:

> MSIL [London subsidiary Madoff Securities International] was part of Madoff's global shell game. Funds stolen in the Ponzi scheme travelled around the world, but ultimately ended up in the pockets of Madoff, his family and confederates like Sonja Kohn. The London operation was a critical piece of the façade of legitimacy that Madoff constructed to conceal BLMIS [Bernard L Madoff Investment Securities, the main US firm]'s lack of actual trading activity (Goodley 2010).

Law-suits were also filed against top banks Citigroup, HSBC and JP Morgan, which are accused of enabling the fraud.

In December 2010, two years after the fraud was revealed, Madoff's son Mark committed suicide. Both sons had always claimed to be victims of the scam and had cut ties with their parents (Rushe 2010a). Despite this, they had come under increased scrutiny from liquidators who were seeking to recover the lost funds from those seen as having enabled Madoff. The brothers had high-profile positions in their father's firm and were blamed for not noticing the fraud and raising the alarm earlier.

In October 2011, nearly three years after the fraud was discovered, the first compensation payments, a total of $312m, were finally paid to 1,230 Madoff victims, while the remainder of the recovered money is currently still being held up by ongoing legal appeals (Rushe 2011).

Study Questions

- In what ways does corruption affect the banking and finance sector?

- Critically assess the measures that have been taken to counter corruption in international finance.

- What are the lessons to be learned from the Madoff 'Ponzi' scheme?

9

Corruption and Transnational Organised Crime

1 Introduction

Corruption has strong linkages with transnational organised crime networks involved in money laundering, terrorist financing and the trafficking of humans, drugs and arms. The criminal business of money laundering is complex and highlights the challenges for financial organisations and the international community to be well informed when dealing with 'politically exposed persons' or offshore financial centres. The growing concerns about elaborate ways of terrorist financing and money laundering are often linked with the international fight against corruption and all three areas should be examined together in order to develop effective counter measures.

2 What is Transnational Organised Crime?

Transnational organised crime describes criminal activities that reach across national borders and involve transnational criminal organisations, often supported and enabled by corrupt public officials. The United Nations Office on Drug and Crime (UNODC) uses the following definition, which includes a range of organised crimes:

> *Transnational organized crime is considered as one of the major threats to human security, impeding the social, economic, political and cultural development of societies worldwide. It is a multi-faceted phenomenon and has manifested itself in different activities, among others, drug trafficking; trafficking in human beings; trafficking in firearms; smuggling of migrants; money laundering; etc. (UNODC n.d.c.).*

The 2003 United Nations Convention against Transnational Organized Crime (UNTOC) is one of the main international instruments to counter organized crime. The Convention promotes frameworks for mutual legal assistance and extradition and encourages cooperation in law enforcement. It also includes additional protocols which cover specific areas, such as human and arms trafficking.

The UNTOC Convention can be read in full at UNODC's website:

www.unodc.org

Corruption is an important aspect of transnational organised crime; along with violence and extortion, criminals use corruption as means to facilitate their criminal activities and launder the proceeds of crime and corruption into the legal economy (Chêne 2008: 2). Collusion between criminals and corrupt public officials allows criminals to infiltrate state structures and the economy. Organised crime networks rely heavily on corruption 'to ensure the circulation of illicit goods, facilitate money laundering and minimise the risks of successful prosecution' (ibid.).

The strong linkages between organised crime and public sector corruption become evident in bribes to various public officials in the areas of border control, law enforcement, government and the judiciary, areas where criminals block investigations, avoid raids and work undisturbed. In short, through corruption criminals gain control over the political arena and business world (ibid.).

In 2003, a study by Edgardo Buscaglia and Jan van Dijk on 'Controlling Organized Crime and Corruption in the Public Sector' examined the links between the growth of organised crime and that of corruption in the public sector. The study looks at the influential factors behind the growth of both by analysing qualitative and quantitative information from several countries. Buscaglia and van Dijk (2003) found that the two types of crime reinforce each other.

 For more information on the study read: Buscaglia and van Dijk (2003).

The next sections explore briefly three different types of organised crime and their close links to corruption: the illicit drug trade, human trafficking and the illegal trade of arms.

2.1 CORRUPTION AND ILLEGAL DRUGS TRADE

Similar to transnational organised crime in general, the international trade in illegal drugs such as heroin, cocaine and amphetamine-type stimulants flourishes in corrupt national political systems. Drug cartels reinvest their criminal proceeds in bribes to police, politicians, judges and other public officials to buy their compliance or silence (Harris 2003: 176–178).

Narcotic drugs are usually grown in impoverished regions with little rule of law and high corruption. For example, Afghanistan was in 2010 still the world's largest producer of opium poppies and a major source of heroin (The White House 2010). The administration involved in processing and distributing the drugs opens up many opportunities for bribes and corruption. Analysis of international drug routes has shown that the illegal substances are being trafficked from producing countries via weak and corrupt transit states in, for example, Central Asia or South America, to be distributed in Europe, Russia and North America (Aranaga 2009). It was estimated that by 2008, the European market, valued at around $34bn, was almost as valuable as the North American market at $37bn (UNODC 2010).

The UNODC World Report 2010 analyses different transnational drug markets and is available at:

www.unodc.org

In Mexico, for example, where the war between the government and various drug cartels has cost the lives of 35,000 Mexicans between 2006 and 2010 (15,000 assassinations were counted in 2010 alone), local drug barons corrupt local and state authorities and rule whole towns and regions (Ackerman 2011). In some Mexican provinces many police, military and government officials have been found to be on the drug cartels' payrolls (Harris 2003: 178). Corrupt local governments often depend on drug money to finance their election campaigns and bribe supporters. Those corrupt officials often seek the protection of armed drug gangs to stay in power and in return offer them protection from prosecution.

Drug-related corruption is not confined to Mexico but also affects its neighbour, the US, where 46 law enforcement officials were convicted of drug trade-related corruption in the late 1990s (Harris 2003: 178). There has been a longstanding concern in the US about collusion and drug money corrupting politicians and law enforcement officials at home. In 1998, for example, widespread drug-related police corruption was reported in the US states of Illinois, Ohio and Pennsylvania, 'while in the same year in Zapata County, Texas, most political leaders, including the Sheriff, Judge and Clerk, pleaded guilty to drug corruption charges' (ibid.: 180).

There are also strong links between the illegal drugs trade and money laundering as the illicit proceeds from the sale need to be transferred into the legitimate economy. Harris (2003:180) points out the linkage: 'the political power of the drug barons and the complex interrelations among drugs, terrorism, money laundering and political corruption can scarcely be overstated'.

An interesting example of the various links between the illicit drugs trade and corruption is provided by the case of notorious drug lord Pablo Escobar, who terrorised Colombia from the 1970s to the early 1990s. The example illustrates how political instability, corruption and the international drugs trade can feed off each other. Read Escobar's brother's account (Escobar 2010).

2.2 CORRUPTION AND HUMAN TRAFFICKING

Human trafficking is a very profitable crime and the US government estimates that traffickers make around $32 billion annually (US Bureau of Public Affairs 2010). The Terrorism, Transnational Crime and Corruption Centre (TraCCC) at George Mason University in the US estimates that most victims are trafficked annually from Asia (375,000), the former Soviet Union (100,000), Eastern Europe (75,000), Latin America and the Caribbean (100,000) and Africa (50,000) (TraCCC n.d.).

UNODC (n.d.d.) defines human trafficking as a crime against humanity. The UN Protocol to Prevent, Suppress and Punish Trafficking in Persons defines it as an act that involves:

... the recruitment, transportation, transfer, harbouring or receipt of persons, by means of the threat or use of force or other forms of coercion, of abduction, of fraud, of deception, of the abuse of power or of a position of vulnerability or of the giving or receiving of payments or benefits to achieve the consent of a person having control over another person, for the purpose of exploitation (UNODC 2004b: 42).

Exploitation in connection with human trafficking can mean prostitution or other forms of sexual exploitation, forced labour, slavery or even the removal of organs.

The UN Protocol to Prevent, Suppress and Punish Trafficking in Persons, also known as the Palermo Protocol, is available at UNODC's website:

www.unodc.org

A working group at the 14th International Anti-Corruption Conference (IACC) 2010 in Bangkok examined the linkages between corruption and human trafficking. In the IACC report that summarises the meeting, corruption is identified as 'the lubricant that allows the wheel of human trafficking to adequately operate, imbedding itself at all levels, from the planning to the aftermath of the actual trade. Human trafficking wouldn't be as epidemic if it wasn't for the leverage corruption offers' (Tremblay 2010: 1).

Half of the victims are women and children, who are often too afraid to report to the police and there are cases of collusion when corrupt public officials, such as police officers, immigration officers, members of the judiciary or politicians are being bribed to 'turn a blind eye'. Men also comprise a significant number of trafficking victims and are mainly used for forced labour in mines or to fight in war zones (US Department of State 2010).

Corruption and human trafficking are interconnected and elements of corruption can be found in each phase of human trafficking, from recruitment to transportation and exploitation (Tremblay 2010: 2). The working group established that corruption has four main purposes in human trafficking: '... to allow the crime to be invisible, to facilitate the impunity once a case of human trafficking is detected, to facilitate the different circuits in the country, and to assure the re-victimization of the trafficked victims' (ibid.: 2).

In 2010, the US government published the tenth annual 'Trafficking in Persons Report'. Read the comprehensive report US Department of State (2010), which examines human trafficking in 177 countries.

2.3 CORRUPTION AND ILLICIT ARMS TRADE

Due to the lack of transparency in the legal arms trade it is even more difficult to establish the exact scale and size of the illegal market for arms but it has been estimated that, in 2007, the value of illicit arms sales worldwide amounted to approximately $5bn (Stohl and Grillot 2007: 187).

Illicit trafficking of arms is responsible for some of the worst human rights violations, civil bloodshed and prolonging of violent conflicts, as these deliveries are mostly destined to countries under international arms embargoes (for example, Sudan, Somalia, Republic of Congo, Ivory Coast). Previously, countries under international arms embargoes have included South Africa, which was under a UN arms embargo during Apartheid, and China after the Tiananmen Square massacre in 1989, which led to an embargo by the US and the EU. UN mandatory arms embargoes, despite being legally binding, have not proven to be very effective, as many member states have not made their violation a criminal offence (Sprague 2006: 2).

The demand for weapons is fuelled by oppressive regimes, militias, civil conflicts and terrorist activities and a wide range of arms are smuggled, ranging from small firearms and AK47s to sophisticated military equipment (for example, radar or satellite technology), heavy weaponry (such as parts for tanks, jets and missiles) and even nuclear material (Stohl and Grillot 2007: 99). The secret weapons transfers can be arranged by individuals, companies or even governments.

Corruption plays a big role in illegal arms trading, from bribes paid by arms brokers to border control agents, transport officials and law enforcement and also routinely involves corrupt government officials who 'turn a blind eye'. 'Corrupt or negligent government officials may sell weapons for personal gain. ... Corrupt officials may also accept bribes to overlook weapons documentation and allow illegal shipments to proceed without scrutinising' (Stohl and Grillot 2007: 100).

In 2009, several leading French politicians and business figures, including the former Interior Minister Charles Pasqua and the son of the late President Francois Mitterrand, were convicted of selling arms worth £450m to Angola, while under UN embargo during its civil war from 1975 to 2002 (Sage 2009). The case shows how illegal arms deals involve the corruption, embezzlement and illegal lobbying of political elites. The sales were facilitated by business tycoons and arms dealers paying in bribes and kickbacks to the French establishment (ibid.).

> *[The ex-president's son, Jean-Christophe] Mitterrand, for example, received $2.6 million (£1.6 million) in kickbacks because he was a former chief of his father's secretive Africa cell, which oversaw relations between France and its former colonies. ... But the subplot to a trial that Angola and France both sought to derail ... involved accusations that two French presidents, François Mitterrand and Jacques Chirac, had turned a blind eye to the trade (Sage,* The Times *2009).*

In terms of companies involved in supplying arms illegally, research by DellaVigna and La Ferrara in 2008 has found that companies based in high-corruption countries are more likely to engage in illegal weapon sales, and profit from the increase in hostilities. In contrast, companies in low-corruption countries are more to likely to restrict themselves to the legal arms trade (DellaVigna and La Ferrara 2008: 2).

The illegal transfer in arms often goes hand in hand with human and drug trafficking, employing similar corrupt methods and means, with transnational crime organisations often being involved in several of those criminal activities simultaneously (Stohl and Grillot 2007: 94). It is believed that this weapons trade is run by transnational organised trafficking networks, which are guided by only a relatively few individuals (Sprague 2006: 3). Private arms dealers often broker the sale and then organise the trafficking by forging documents, diverting shipments, bribing officials and setting up shell companies to hide the origins of the delivery (Stohl and Grillot 2007: 108–109).

> *Typically, the individuals behind these deals will set up a labyrinth of front companies, make frequent use of fraudulent or misleading official paperwork, utilise a myriad of shipping companies' freight forwards and handling agents, and hide payments via offshore banking and financial services. They may also route the actual deliveries via third countries (not subject to embargo restrictions) (Sprague 2006: 3).*

TALES OF CORRUPTION AND CRIME – TWO NOTORIOUS INTERNATIONAL ARMS DEALERS

Leonid Minin: An Ukrainian arms broker, who delivered arms to various war zones, for example Sierra Leone and Liberia during violent conflicts in 1990s. Minin was arrested in 2000 in Italy and charged with arms trafficking and illegal possession of diamonds. But despite being found with incriminating evidence against him, was eventually released, because of a legal loophole. (Sprague, 2006: 3; Traynor 2001)

For more background information on Leonid Minin, read Traynor (2001).

Viktor Bout: Bout, a former Red Army officer, acquired surplus aircrafts and weapons after the Soviet Union's collapse and sold them on to conflict hotspots around the world. The Russian arms broker created a private fleet of transport planes to deliver the weapons quickly to Africa, Asia and Latin America, without the need for middle men (Borger 2008). He supplied for example, Liberia, Sierra Leone, Angola and Congo despite arms sanctions. He also flew weapons to the Taliban, and years later, even carried out flights for the Pentagon to Iraq and Afghanistan (Fallon 2010). When the UN froze his assets and ordered a travel ban, he still enjoyed high-level protection in Russia. Bout was eventually arrested in 2008, while on holiday in Thailand, after allegedly trying to sell weapons to US agents posing as Colombian rebels. He was extradited to the United States in 2010 where he has been charged with conspiracy to kill US nationals and government officers, conspiracy to use an anti-aircraft missile and conspiracy to provide material support to a designated foreign terrorist organisation (BBC News 2011b).In November 2011, Bout was found guilty of trying to sell 20,000 machine guns, other heavy weapons and 10 million rounds of ammunition to Colombian Farc rebels and could now be sentenced to life in prison (Harris and McVeigh 2011).

For more information about Viktor Bout, read the interview with the New York Times: Landesman (2003).

But it is not only individual criminals, corrupt companies and public officials that are engaged in the illicit trade; historically even whole governments can be involved. During the Cold War, both the US and Soviet Union covertly trafficked arms to client states or none-state actors, such as allied insurgents, to help fight the enemy side. These secret weapon transfers were seen as a foreign policy resource, but often had devastating legacies long after the Cold War ended. Two prominent examples involving the US were arms deliveries to the anti-Soviet mujahedeen in Afghanistan and the infamous Iran–Contra scandal, both in the 1980s (Stohl and Grillot 2007: 102–106).

3 Corruption and Money Laundering

Money laundering is a process that conceals the unlawful origins of proceeds, such as transnational organised crime and corruption, to make them appear legal (Reed and Fontana 2011: 7). Money made in the sale of illicit arms and drugs and from human trafficking needs to be protected from confiscation by the authorities and cleaned before it can be reintroduced into the formal economy. Corruption often enables the money-laundering process and can also prevent its detection through bribery and collusion with the financial sector and law enforcement.

Money is usually laundered in three stages: *placement* (criminal proceeds are placed into the financial system), *layering* (funds are camouflaged in a range of transactions across multiple jurisdictions to hide their source) and *integration* (funds are redistributed to the mainstream banking system and now appear legitimate). The placement stage is most at risk of detection and during the second stage of the layering, offshore accounts or fictitious ghost companies are opened with false identities or by associates to disguise the money (ibid.: 12–14).

Simple wire transfers to foreign accounts are still common, but at the same time the use of more elaborate money-laundering methods, such as creating shell banks, trusts or hedge funds or using real estate purchases and investments in businesses that generate large cash flows – for example, casinos, hotels, travel agents, restaurants and financial firms – is growing (Levi *et al.* 2007; Reed and Fontana 2011). Another layering method, called 'smurfing', involves splitting large transactions into several smaller, less suspicious transfers (Scott-Joynt 2002).

Chaikin and Sharman (2009: 1) point out the close relationship between corruption and money laundering:

> *Corruption and money laundering are symbiotic: not only do they tend to co-occur, but more importantly the presence of one tends to create and reciprocally reinforce the incidence of the other. Corruption produces enormous profits to be laundered, estimated at more than $1*

trillion of illicit funds annually, funds that are increasingly laundered in the international system. At the same time, bribery, trading in influence and embezzlement can compromise the working of Anti-Money Laundering systems.

Another linkage is highlighted by Levi *et al.* (2007: 392): 'Very few people pay large bribes using their own legitimately acquired funds. In most cases of bribery ... the money that is generated to pay the bribes comes from some form of unlawful activity.'

3.1 POLITICALLY EXPOSED PERSONS (PEPS)

Politically exposed persons (PEPs) are seen as 'a particular Anti-Money Laundering risk because of their perceived connection with corrupt ... regimes' (TI Australia 2008: 4). It is important to note, however, that it is not the case that any prominent public person, politician or public official is automatically defined as a PEP. The term applies only to those who are perceived to have gained their wealth through illicit means, such as corruption, stealing from state funds or involvement in transnational organised crime.

PEPs often have not only their ill-gotten gains to hide but also their identity, and therefore use non-family members as intermediaries, to disguise their money and open bank accounts. A common practice is that less well-known or totally unknown persons open accounts on behalf of a PEP, who then has signing rights and credit cards on the account.

The United Nations Convention Against Corruption (UNODC 2004a: 42) defines PEPs as 'individuals who are, or have been, entrusted with prominent public functions, and their family members and close associates ...'. This can be current or former heads of state, prominent senior public officials from government, judiciary, military or parliament, but also political party officials or senior corporate executives. Fenner (2009: 143) describes PEPs as 'individuals who are active and visible in the political arena or who hold high public office, and thus are highly exposed to corruption risks'.

Having identified a PEP, financial institutions should ensure that decisions to take them on as clients are made at a senior level, as they require ongoing and enhanced due diligence throughout the business relationship in relation to the source of their wealth, their businesses and transactions. Most leading banks have what they refer to as a PEP Desk, which is a department of private bankers who are specifically trained to question the assets, transactions and source of funds from PEPs. A rising number of financial institutions have realised that they need to carry out effective PEP due diligence simply to prevent reputational damage. It is not the stricter international regulations or fines that ensure increasing compliance, but the fear of featuring on the media's front pages in relation to an account of a corrupt head of state, demonstrating to the public and their clients that their bank conducted business with criminals.

For more information about PEPs read Greenberg and Gray (2010).

FAMOUS POLITICALLY EXPOSED PERSONS

The following list illustrates famous cases (some have already been covered in Chapter 6) of PEPs involved in grand corruption, which have been important in shaping regulatory Anti-Money Laundering and asset recovery efforts:

- **Sani Abacha**: Former dictator of Nigeria, who embezzled $2bn–$5bn during his time as head of state during the 1990s. By 2008, $1.2bn had been recovered from bank accounts around the world, with $700m alone from Swiss accounts. (Fenner 2009; Swissinfo 2009)
- **Ferdinand Marcos**: Former dictator of the Philippines, who is said to have looted billions during his 20-year reign and deposited it in Swiss bank accounts. In 1997, Switzerland's highest court ordered that over $650 million held in Marcos's accounts should be returned to the Philippines. (Swissinfo 2009)
- **Raul Salinas**: Brother of former Mexican president Salinas, was sentenced for laundering millions of dollars of drugs money. He secretly transferred $87 million out of Mexico between 1992 and 1994 using Citigroup banks in the US. (BBC News 1999)
- **Jean-Claude Duvalier**: Haiti's ex-dictator, whose assets in France and the US were frozen. The dictator and his family allegedly paid off Haitian officials to drop their attempts to repatriate the money. (*The New York Times* 2003)
- **Mobutu Sese Seko**: Late dictator of Zaire (now Democratic Republic of Congo), whose looted state assets were frozen by Switzerland in 1997, when he was booted from power. In 2008, the Swiss government tried to recover the frozen assets, but this has not yet been successful. (Swissinfo 2009)

- **Charles Taylor**: During his six years as president of Liberia, Taylor stole $100 million of his nation's wealth. Since 2007, he has been on trial for war crimes at the Special Court for Sierra Leone at the Hague. He is accused of having used child soldiers, terrorised civilians for 10 years with his rebel army and controlled the trade of conflict diamonds. (Weiner, 2003)

The International Centre for Asset Recovery of the Basel Institute for Governance in Switzerland was established in 2006 as a knowledge centre for asset recovery which assists and trains countries in implementing UNCAC provisions on repatriating proceeds of corruption, money laundering and other crimes. The centre also compiles an overview of precedent-setting recovery case studies. Visit the centre's website at:

www.assetrecovery.org

3.2 OFFSHORE FINANCIAL CENTRES

One of the main motivations of corrupt heads of state to deposit money abroad is the concern that if funds are stored 'onshore' they might be detected by successor regimes, political opponents or prosecutors (Levi *et al.* 2007: 408).

Offshore financial centres offer the advantages of little regulation or taxation and stricter secrecy laws. They attract mainly non-resident clients and are renowned as tax havens. The income from offshore activities is often one of the few main sources of wealth for offshore havens, which are mainly small Caribbean and Pacific island states and former colonies. Tax havens also exist in Europe and include Liechtenstein, Monaco, Andorra, the Isle of Man, Jersey and Gibraltar. However, they are also being used for money laundering and terrorist financing as companies can be set up easily and ownership is usually not disclosed.

The stigma of financial crime along with growing international pressure to conform to international financial standards has led to many reforms in this sector (Houlder 2008). In 2008, the International Monetary Fund dropped the distinction between onshore and offshore financial centres as the distinction had been blurred over time and progress had been made in terms of meeting minimum international compliance standards (Houlder 2008).

4 Anti-Money Laundering (AML) Regimes

Anti-Money Laundering (AML) regimes or systems are designed to track, investigate and recover the proceeds of serious organised crime, such as drug trafficking, terrorist financing, arms smuggling and fraud and corruption. AML standards aim to make the seizure and freezing of crime proceeds easier and the exchange of financial data more effective internationally. They also introduced rules for banks to know the beneficial owner of accounts and to report any suspicious transactions (Levi *et al.* 2007: 395).

Deregulated financial markets have made money laundering much easier and at the same time tackling illicit flows much harder as proceeds from organised crime are now moved across borders. With the integration of global financial markets, the 1990s saw the creation of AML regimes across the world and a general rise in international standards and financial monitoring systems (Chaikin 2010; Reed and Fontana 2011). A decade later, the terrorist attacks on 11 September 2001 against the US have given the debate around AML regimes even more urgency and the issue of tracking terrorist financing has moved into the spotlight (more on this in Section 4.4). The pressure to control money laundering has led to an increased number of regulations and investigations which, in return, have considerably increased the prices for money laundering services as the risks of being detected are higher than ever before. This can act as a deterrent to corrupt acts in the first place.

At one point 'one third of the world's illegal wealth was estimated … to have been secreted with Swiss banks' (Pujas 2009: 100). However, Switzerland has changed its legal climate and is now, along with the US, at the forefront of AML legislation, while other countries are still lagging behind and need to improve their AML systems. 'In the absence of a level playing field in AML, money laundering will exploit differences in national laws and implementation to conceal their illicit assets' (Chaikin 2010: 5).

4.1 FINANCIAL ACTION TASK FORCE (FATF)

Established in 1989 by Western governments in Paris, the Financial Action Task Force (FATF – or GAFI in French) is an international 'policy making body' for legislative regulatory reforms to combat money laundering and terrorist financing (FATF n.d.). FATF has 35 member states and monitors their progress in implementing its recommendations. Its main body of work has been the highly influential 'FATF 40 Recommendations' on money laundering, which was the first set of global AML standards published at the time. FATF has since added '9 Special Recommendations on Terrorist Financing' in 2001 and 2003. The full set of recommendations is now known as FATF 40+9 and more than 100 countries have adopted it (Levi et al. 2007: 396).

The recommendations were originally introduced to fight the proceeds from international drugs trade, 'but have now become the main set of global standards for the fight against laundering of proceeds of crime in general' (Reed and Fontana 2011: 23).

FATF standards are not legally binding but are extremely influential, as they criminalise money laundering and require banks to keep records of all transactions for at least five years (Chaikin 2010: 3). Any suspicious transactions need to be reported to Financial Intelligence Units. One of the most important provisions is the 'Know Your Customer' (KYC) rule, to prevent banks from unwittingly laundering illicit funds and force them to examine their customers' risk level in relation to AML and terrorist financing (Chaikin 2010: 3).

In addition, FATF requires banks to introduce increased risk management to detect PEPs and the need for senior management to approve opening accounts for PEPs. Banks need to determine the origins of funds and monitor the ongoing business relationship.

Intensive worldwide peer pressure through 'blacklisting' or 'name and shame' initiatives against the so called 'Non-Cooperative Countries and Territories' led to countries with no AML measures in place adopting the FATF standards. Before 2006 there were 23 countries on the black list; however, the list is now defunct and has no more entries. Despite this, some jurisdictions have now made it illegal for public officials not to declare foreign accounts (Levi *et al.* 2007: 399).

Another example of the global adoption of AMLs is the World Bank, which has made it one of its requirements when lending money that recipient countries commit to fighting money laundering.

4.2 FINANCIAL INTELLIGENCE UNITS (FIUS)

FATF standards have been very effective in creating a network of independent national Financial Intelligence Units (FIUs) which have been set up worldwide to promote AML and to combat the financing of terrorism. It is believed that 'more than 100 countries have established national FIUs whose job is to receive, analyze, and process suspicious transaction reports submitted by regulated institutions' (Levi *et al.* 2007: 401).

FIUs establish links between clients and businesses and try to identify the beneficiaries of illicit funds. In order to be effective, it is essential that FIUs and anti-corruption agencies collaborate with each other and that national and international AML laws are harmonised.

The Egmont Group of Financial Intelligence Units, established in 1995 in Brussels, has been set up as an informal working group to develop international cooperation between FIUs around the world in the fight against money laundering and terrorist financing. Members of this group meet regularly to share best practice and to foster the implementation of domestic initiatives in this field (The Egmont Group 2011).

For more information on the Egmont Group and access to 100 case studies outlining the work of various FIUs, visit:

www.egmontgroup.org

4.3 LIMITATIONS OF AML REGIMES

Very little evidence is available on the effectiveness and impact of AML systems and it is believed that they may not have had a great impact on reducing global corruption and looting of state assets (Reed and Fontana 2011: 30). The following issues have been identified as the main obstacles:

Immunity laws

Politicians sometimes have immunity in relation not only to the office that they hold but also to the time before they were elected, or even lifelong immunity. An allegation of corruption therefore only rarely translates into prosecution and conviction of the politician involved (Pujas 2009: 90). An existing head of state who is being investigated in a foreign country for money laundering can be protected by domestic immunity laws. Often the confiscation of assets abroad requires a criminal conviction, from which it is hard to achieve immunity. However, national immunity is not always recognised abroad and when political leaders depart office they are more vulnerable to being persecuted (Chaikin 2010: 4). There have been several successful cases of looted national assets being repatriated, but rarely has a former corrupt head of state been made to stand trial.

Bank secrecy

Another obstacle to international cooperation is banking secrecy; in particular, until recently, Caribbean and Pacific offshore havens had very strict privacy laws which held the identity of bank accounts or company owners hidden from investigators (Scott-Joynt 2002).

However, with the terrorist attacks of 11 September 2001, international pressure has increased. This, together with the introduction of FATF blacklisting, has led to almost all states having now introduced AML measures. Even Switzerland, once a renowned haven for secret accounts, reformed its banking sector over the last decade and made it easier for funds to be disclosed or frozen. A major turning point was the joined lawsuits brought by Holocaust victims in the late 1990s which forced Switzerland to take action to improve its global image (Pujas 2009: 100). However, secrecy laws still need to be further reformed so that it becomes easier to trace the real owner of funds.

Ineffective PEP monitoring

Customer due diligence is often not strictly followed and suspicious transactions are not always reported. It is necessary to provide training to bank staff and FIUs to detect and report connections between financial transactions and a corrupt act (Levi *et al.* 2007: 411; Reed and Fontana 2011: 32). Another issue is that money can also be laundered via extended family, friends or business associates, which some AML laws do not take into account. 'However, a fundamental weakness of the FATF Standards is that they only require enhanced due diligence obligations where *foreign* PEPs open accounts; they do not impose enhanced due diligence obligations on domestic PEPs. This loophole has allowed corrupt governments to enact PEPs laws that do not apply to local politicians' (Chaikin 2010: 4). The UN Convention Against Corruption (UNCAC), makes however no distinction between domestic and foreign PEPs and stresses that due diligence also should apply to families and associates of PEPs.

FIUs and banks vulnerable to corruption and influencing

There is a risk of collusion for banks and FIUs. FIUs are able to trace back who reported a suspicious transaction, which can lead to reprisals (Levi *et al.*

2007: 401; Reed and Fontana 2011: 32). Another weak point in the fight against money laundering is the fact that, on many occasions, banks are simply greedy or under pressure to meet targets, which can lead to PEP accounts being opened by the banker 'turning a blind eye'. AML regimes have created initiatives for money launderers to try to bribe financial institutions to accept their funds (Levi *et al*. 2007: 406).

Another observation is that corrupt regimes sometimes abuse AML laws to freeze the funds of political opponents or government-critical NGOs (Reed and Fontana 2011: 34). This point links to the fact that PEPs are often entrusted with authority, which allows them, through their influence on the judiciary, legislative and the military, to undermine or steer AML or corruption investigations. International investigations into money laundering often require evidence from the home country of the accused, which corrupt public officials can prevent (Chaikin 2010: 3). For example, 'In June 2003 the Italian government pushed through legislation to expand immunity for a handful of senior political figures, including the prime minister, who was at the time facing trial for corruption' (Pujas 2009: 90).

In terms of reducing corruption, AML systems are not designed to detect and fight corruption specifically, but to tackle a wide range of crimes such as drug trafficking and terrorist financing. Corruption is very costly to investigate and can be a drain on public funds. Therefore corruption cases are often still not seen as important enough to investigate and use limited resources on, except perhaps for cases of grand corruption. There is a 'preoccupation of rich countries with using AML to tackle drug crime and terrorist financing, and insufficient priority attached to corruption as a major source of money to be laundered from the developing world' (Reed and Fontana 2011: 30).

Reed and Fontana (2011: 36–37) also criticise the cost of setting up FIUs in developing countries. They argue that AML systems are better suited to advanced financial economies in wealthy states; while in poorer states financial transactions still mostly take place in cash, introducing elaborate AML regimes is expensive for developing countries and the benefits not proportionate to the costs. 'The strictness with which AML regimes have been forced onto developing countries contrasts with the leniency shown towards secrecy jurisdictions in advanced market economies …' (ibid.: 16). This is perceived as a double standard by some developing countries, which complain that AML measures seem mainly to focus on them, whereas most bribes come from OECD countries and most proceeds are laundered there as well (Levi *et al.* 2007: 407).

4.4 AML AND TERRORIST FINANCING

Before the terrorist attacks on 11 September 2001 against the US, terrorism, organised crime and corruption had not been linked in international law making. However, in response to the attacks and the resulting 'War on Terror' with further high-profile attacks in Madrid (2003), Bali (2002 and 2005) and London (2005), international organisations responded fast by including counter financing of terrorism (CFT) regulations on their agenda and recognising the close links with corruption and money laundering. One example is FATF, which added '9 Special Recommendations on Terrorist Financing' in 2001 and 2003 to its existing recommendations on money laundering. And in 2005, the Council of Europe adapted the Convention on Laundering, Search, Seizure and Confiscation of the Proceeds from Crime and on the Financing on Terrorism, the first international treaty covering both AML and CFT (COE 2005). The implementation of the convention is monitored by the 2010-created Committee of Experts on the Evaluation of Anti-Money Laundering Measures and the Financing of Terrorism (MONEYVAL), which publishes country assessments and progress reports on how Council of Europe member states implement AML and CFT systems and comply with international standards such as FATF 40+9 . The country evaluation reports are available on the Committee's website: www.coe.int/moneyval.

The Council of Europe warned in 2005 that organised terrorist groups 'misuse the world's financial system to fund their illegal operations, thus posing a serious risk to financial institutions of being used for hiding terrorist money' (COE 2005). While in cases of money laundering where the funds are of illicit origin and an attempt is made to conceal them, funds from terrorist financing can stem from both legal and illegal sources. For example, charities and businesses are sometimes used as a cover for terrorist funding. The diversion of charitable fund from legitimate organisations or the creation of bogus charities demonstrates the linkages between fraud and corruption and terrorist financing (FATF n.d.). Terrorist groups also often engage in transnational organised crime, such as the illegal drugs trade, to finance their activities (FATF n.d.).

The primary goal of terrorists is not necessarily to conceal the sources of the money, but to hide the nature of the funded activity. Despite these differences, similar methods are used for money laundering and terrorist financing. In both cases, the actor makes an illegitimate use of the financial sector. It makes sense, therefore, to put combined measures into place that address both AML and CFT.

However, as terrorist attacks often require only small amounts of funds, transnational terrorist networks often prefer using informal money exchanges – so-called 'hawala' ('hundi' in Pakistan and Afghanistan). These systems don't involve records and are therefore harder to trace (Scott-Joynt 2002).

> *The whole system relies on trust between brokers, rather than paper records or third party guarantees, with any shortfalls between what goes out and what comes in settled periodically. The systems are hundreds of years old, and are used entirely legitimately by, say, people working abroad and sending money home to relatives who may not have a bank account (Ibid. 2002).*

 For more background information on 'hawala' and its links to money laundering and terrorist financing, read Bowers (2009).

FATF 2008 report on 'Terrorist Financing', available at:

www.fatf-gafi.org

The Terrorism, Transnational Crime and Corruption Centre (TraCCC) at George Mason University in the US, founded in 1998, researches the linkages between the three areas. Visit the centre's website at:

http://policy-traccc.gmu.edu/

5 Case Study: General Pinochet and US Bank Riggs

An interesting example of the issue of money laundering and PEPs, and the associated reputational and financial risks for any bank, is the case of General Pinochet and former US bank Riggs. While Chile's General Pinochet was in London for medical treatment in 1998, Spain requested his extradition on torture charges and ordered financial institutions around the world to freeze his assets.

Pinochet's brutal regime ran from 1973 to 1990, in which time it is estimated that 3,000 Chileans were killed, tortured or disappeared (O'Hara 2005). Under

Spanish law, perpetrators of human rights abuses, torture and genocide worldwide can be charged in Spain if Spanish citizens have been victims.

General Pinochet's assets were frozen by a UK court as the charges of crimes against humanity were brought against him. In 2004, a US Senate report alleged that former Washington bank Riggs, a bank with a large client base in the diplomatic community and mainly involved international business, set up several accounts for Pinochet while he was under UK house arrest in that year (BBC News 2004). The bank was accused of assisting Pinochet in moving money (up to $8m) from London to the Bahamas to evade his assets being seized. Riggs set up two pseudo companies, Ashburton Co. Ltd and Althorp Investment Co. Ltd, which held most of the Pinochet money (O'Hara and Day 2004).

It is claimed that between 1994 and 2002 the bank helped Pinochet to set up offshore front companies and open accounts held under aliases to hide the dictator's identity. Riggs was allegedly hiding these accounts from investigators and therefore made itself complicit in money laundering and corruption (BBC News 2004).

'In documents required by federal regulators, for example, the bank referred to Pinochet not by name, but as "a retired professional" who held a "high paying position in public sector for many years"' (O'Hara and Day 2004).

The BBC reported in 2004 that 'in 2000, when the Office of the Controller of the Currency [OCC] asked for a list of clients' accounts controlled by foreign political figures, Pinochet was not on the list. Not until spring did the OCC discover the Pinochet accounts, when an examiner demanded an explanation for coded references to cashier's checks that had been mailed or delivered to Pinochet' (BBC News 2004).

US Senate investigators also found that the top federal bank examiner, Ashley Lee, in charge of supervising Riggs at the time, kept details of the bank's relationship with the dictator hidden in his file about the bank and recommended that Riggs should not be punished for its money laundering compliance failings (O'Hara and Day 2004). Lee retired from government to join Riggs as senior executive, prompting accusations that he had become 'too close' to the bank to monitor its dealings effectively from 1998–2002 (ibid.).

In 2000, a UK court ruled that Pinochet was too ill to stand trial and he was allowed to return to Chile. Two years later, he was declared mentally unfit by Chile's Supreme Court and never tried for the alleged crimes against humanity. In May 2004, Riggs was fined $25m in civil penalties for AML breaches in its dealings with Saudi Arabia and Equatorial Guinea in a federal investigation. A year later, in March 2005, the bank was fined another $16m for helping Pinochet and corrupt leaders of Equatorial Guinea to hide hundreds of millions of dollars in secret accounts (Rowley 2005).

The judge in the case, Ricardo Urbina, said, 'There is no way of measuring the amount of harm and atrocities and human rights violations perpetrated by Pinochet and Equatorial Guinea as a result of the enabling criminal activity by Riggs bank. [The bank] now stands disclosed before this court as a greedy corporate henchman of dictators and their corporate regimes' (ibid.).

In the same year, the Spanish court dropped its charges against the bank's controlling family, Riggs's director and the former account manager in charge of Pinochet's accounts, in return for an $8m donation to the charity of Pinochet's victims (O'Hara 2005). However, the bank had already suffered irreversible reputational damage and after Riggs's head of board stepped down, the bank was eventually sold in 2005.

Study Questions

- What are the main stages in the money laundering process and what role do PEPs play?

- In what ways is corruption linked to money laundering and other forms of transnational organised crime?

- Critically examine the response of the international community to money laundering.

10

Corruption and International Aid

1 Introduction

There is an increased awareness today in the development community (in both donor and recipient countries) that aid is in danger of not reaching the poor due to corruption. With development assistance steadily rising over the last 50 years, it was estimated that in 2010, leading donor countries gave $126bn in development aid to lower-income countries (OECD n.d.c.). The potential for corruption with figures as high as this is immense. For example, in several of the top-ten aid recipient countries, such as Iraq, the Democratic Republic of Congo, Indonesia, Pakistan and Vietnam, corruption is believed to be widespread (TI 2007: 3).

Corruption can seriously undermine the intended results of development aid by diverting money from purposes or beneficiaries. When it comes to emergency aid for natural disasters or violent conflicts, corruption can have an even more dramatic consequence: 'the cost of corruption in humanitarian relief effectively mean lives lost, not just loss of profits or lower growth' (Ewins *et al.* 2006: 3).

Many donor organisations have in the past preferred to keep quiet about incidents of internal or external corruption in order not to lose donations from the public and fuel aid fatigue. Corruption 'is a particularly sensitive issue within emergency relief because reports of corruption could undermine public trust in the work of aid agencies, as a result, a veil of silence has been drawn over public discussion of the issue. This silence is itself potentially damaging …' as it inhibits the sharing of good practice in minimising corruption (Willitts-King and Harvey 2005: 6).

Corruption in the context of aid can range from NGOs defrauding donors through false accounting at headquarters to field staff demanding payment from the local population in exchange for relief goods or government officials requesting bribes to speed up paperwork. However, corruption does not always involve financial gains; rather, in the context of development aid and humanitarian aid, it can involve 'the abuse of power to enhance personal reputations or for political purposes, access to physical services such as connection to a water supply or preferential treatment in recruitment, training or medical care, or, of recent note, gain in terms of sexual exploitation' (Ewins *et al.* 2006: 20).

In relief contexts, money or assets may not be the commodity that is most highly valued. People may also be forced into corrupt actions by those who threaten them or their families. 'This illustrates the importance of an understanding of the local context when trying to prevent corruption, and highlights the many factors that need to be understood and considered when evaluating corruption risks' (ibid.: 8).

2 Humanitarian Aid

Humanitarian aid (also often referred to as humanitarian relief, relief aid or emergency aid) can be understood as assistance to those affected by natural disasters, human conflict or other forms of severe political, economic or social breakdown. It aims to prevent human suffering through the short-term provision of food, water, shelter and emergency services to affected areas, though it often evolves into longer-term reconstruction and rehabilitation efforts.

> *Corruption in humanitarian aid undermines the fundamental purpose of humanitarian action. Its effects include the diversion of relief supplies away from affected communities, inequitable distribution of aid and sub-standard or inappropriately located infrastructure. Such outcomes ignore the needs of the intended beneficiaries of aid, often further marginalising those from the poorest sections of society and deepening existing social conflicts. Tackling corruption in humanitarian aid is therefore key to ensuring effective and equitable humanitarian assistance to those in greatest need (TI 2006b).*

The issue of corruption in humanitarian relief operations is worth exploring as in this context large sums of money have to be spent quickly in often instable and difficult situations. For example, by October 2011 the United Nations

Office for the Coordination of Humanitarian Affairs (OCHA) recorded US$720 million in relief funds for Japan (OCHA 2011a), while Pakistan's humanitarian funding situation was US$1.3 billion after the disastrous floods of 2010 (OCHA 2011b) and Haiti was given US$1.1 billion after the devastating earthquake in the same year (OCHA 2011c). One of the leading global recipients of aid is Sudan, which for example received US$1.3bn of humanitarian aid in 2009. (Global Humanitarian Assistance 2011). Humanitarian agencies are facing immense public pressure to spend these large sums effectively and to deliver aid rapidly to the suffering populations. These challenges pose great risks of corruption.

2.1 CHARACTERISTICS FUELLING CORRUPTION

The process of deciding who gets assistance in emergencies offers immense opportunity for corruption. The recipients of aid are often particularly vulnerable to abuse, such as demands for payment to be included on registration lists for food or shelter. In addition to the time pressures of emergencies, the large scale of procurement processes, rapid recruitment and dramatically expanding budgets all contribute to further increase the risks of corruption (Willitts-King and Harvey 2005). Humanitarian agencies are often under great pressure to disburse aid rapidly due to the scale and urgency of need as well as the media interest that is typically generated by disasters. As mentioned in the introduction, countries in which humanitarian relief is delivered are often some of the most corrupt in the world.

Both the conditions inherent in humanitarian emergencies and the characteristics of the humanitarian relief system contribute to the risk of corruption (TI 2006b). Ewins *et al.* (2006: 13) describe the three particular characteristics of humanitarian relief that fuel opportunities for corruption. The first factor is the asymmetrical power relationship between the beneficiaries, the agencies and donors. This one-sided transfer of resources affects transparency and accountability levels in the humanitarian aid system (TI: 2006b). Another factor is the short response time to a crisis which often does not allow for elaborate corruption- or fraud-proofing of procedures. Lastly, emergency aid tends to be either 'high-profile, with a proliferation of organisations, large amounts of funding and huge coordination challenges, or "forgotten", with extremely limited resources and capacity' (Ewins *et al.* 2006: 13).

Table 10.1   Sector-specific risks of corruption in humanitarian relief work

Sector	Examples
Shelter	Especially where there are disputed land titles and these are of commercial value, officials may be bribed or influenced to decide in the favour of non-beneficiaries.
Food aid	Diversion, luxuries, keeping livestock, skimming. National programmes will involve particular management challenges throughout the programme cycle.
Health care	Privatisation as a result of deterioration results in charging fees for medical services or supplies. The practice of charging fees makes it more difficult for beneficiaries to know what they are really required to pay for, increasing the risk of corruption. The unauthorised use of medical equipment is also a result of this deterioration.
Water and sanitation	Often involves outsourcing, boreholes, agency capacity to monitor contract terms and conditions. Water points by definition must be located on someone's land. This lends itself to beneficiaries being denied access, given restricted access and/or being charged for it.
Refugees and internally displaced persons	Regulations at camps, gaining access, temporary leave and re-entry, bribes from outside the camp to people within it.
Protection	Forced repatriation, violence not investigated.

Source: Reprinted from In Focus 2006 edition, ODI Risk Maps, Table: Sector-Specific Risks (TI 2006a). Copyright 24 March 2011 Transparency International: the global coalition against corruption. Used with permission. For more information visit http://www.transparency.org.

The corruption risks can also be divided into internal and external factors. First, emergency aid usually gets distributed in a challenging environment, characterised by weakened state capacity, destroyed infrastructure, mass movement of people and potential outbreaks of diseases or conflicts. These circumstances result in absence of rule of law and the creation of parallel illegal structures which pose great incentives for corruption (TI 2006b: 1–2). Another external risk lies in the difficulty to judge demand and supply in the affected region: 'In the case of undersupply, individuals and communities may be forced to engage in corrupt activities in a desperate bid to survive. Where there is oversupply, aid not needed for survival may become available for illegitimate purposes' (TI 2006b: 2).

Humanitarian aid is also vulnerable to various internal threats of corruption, and embezzlement can take place at every stage of the aid cycle; when relief goods are ordered there is the risk of inflated prices or delivery of poorer quality which involve kickbacks to the procurement employee. Staff might be tempted to sell relief goods to dealers or to distribute them to persons not entitled to receive them in return for bribes (Cremer 1998). Another method is to delay the spending of funds and invest them in the meantime to make a profit. Staff might also try to take advantage of differences between the official rate of exchange and that on the black market to forge account statements (ibid.).

Table 10.2   Examples of corruption risk for each stage of the relief project cycle

1   Initial assessment, decision to respond and programme design: • Bribery of those conducting the assessment to inflate needs or to favour specific groups. • Coercion to influence the shape, size or location of programme.
2   Fundraising and allocation of funding: • Bogus NGOs are set up internationally or locally to raise funds from the public. • Double funding: allocating the same overhead expenditure to two or more projects.
3   Scale-up of local offices/working with partners: • Bribes demanded for expediting permits, licences, leases, essential public services (for example: communications, electricity), for local offices. • Agency staff invent partners or demand kickbacks.
4   Procurement and logistics: • Inclusion in a tender list as a result of a bribe. • Bribes to accept sub-standard relief goods. • Unauthorised use of agency vehicles or other modes of transport for private gain. For example: transporting commercial goods, taxi services or social purposes.
5   Targeting and registration: • Illegitimate inclusion on distribution lists. • Powerful individuals within the community manipulate the beneficiary lists.
6   Implementation and distribution: • Those involved in the distribution divert assistance for private gain. • Extortion of beneficiaries. • 'Taxation' of relief goods.
7   Monitoring, reporting, evaluation and project closure: • False or exaggerated reporting by project managers. • Favourable reports that hide financial problems.
8   Finance, Administration and Personnel: • Staff divert funds being paid to the agency or partner. • Coercion to select key people for jobs. • Payroll fraud, for example: non-existent employees, salary higher than authorised salary.

Source: Adapted from In Focus 2006 edition, ODI Risk Maps: examples of corruption risk for each stage of relief (TI 2006a). Copyright 24 March 2011 Transparency International: the global coalition against corruption. Used with permission. For more information, visit http://www.transparency.org.

For more detailed information on the risks of corruption affecting humanitarian aid, read the Overseas Development Institute report by Ewins *et al.* (2006).

2.2 CORRUPTION AND EXPLOITATION IN REFUGEE CAMPS

As mentioned earlier in this chapter, corruption does not necessarily involve financial gains. For example, in the context of humanitarian relief, corruption can involve the abuse of power to sexually exploit those in desperate need of humanitarian aid. This is one of the most shocking practices; unfortunately, such cases are not isolated but are commonplace in many refugee camps.

In 2002, it was revealed that aid workers for more than 40 development agencies and NGOs in West Africa had been involved in 'extensive sexual exploitation of refugee children, offering food rations in return for favours' (*The Guardian* 2002). More than 1,500 children were interviewed over six weeks by a team from the United Nations High Commission for Refugees (UNHCR) and the British-based charity Save the Children in refugee camps in Liberia, Guinea and Sierra Leone. The report commissioned by the two agencies in response to growing concerns over numerous reports of child abuse by aid workers found that not just aid workers were accused of sexual exploitation, but also UN peacekeepers and community leaders. The report states that 'most of the ... exploiters were male national staff who traded humanitarian commodities and services for sex with girls under 18' (*The Guardian* 2002). A victim described to the investigators that she was 'continually sent to the back of the queue for aid because she had refused to have sex with one aid worker' (BBC News 2002b). Aid agencies were shocked to find some of their own hired local staff used 'the very humanitarian aid and services intended to benefit the refugee population as a tool of exploitation' (*The Guardian* 2002).

The scale of the problem has surprised relief personnel as 'the very people who are meant to be providing services are the exploiters themselves' (BBC News 2002b). In response to its findings, Save the Children has sacked one of its employees and two of its volunteers and has promised to put a stop to the practices. UNHCR started to investigate aid workers who are demanding sex from refugee children in return for the aid they are supposed to give. 'Accused of turning a blind eye for decades to cases of abuse by its peacekeepers, the UN recommended in 2005 that guilty soldiers be punished, their salaries frozen and a fund set up to help any women or girls made pregnant' (*The Times* 2008).

The following areas were identified as the main factors contributing to the occurrence of exploitation in relief projects: there is a largely unregulated national staff; abuses of power are going unpunished; and there is a clear absence of international and, most importantly, female staff at refugee camps (BBC News 2002b). In response to this, UNHCR has increased security and the international presence in camps and deployed more female staff. Furthermore, the agency established for refugees a secure channel for raising complaints with senior UNHCR staff (BBC News 2002b). UNHCR also drafted a new code of conduct, which explicitly prohibits the abuse of power and sexual exploitation. 'The "zero tolerance" policy towards sexual misconduct includes a "non-fraternisation" rule barring [staff] from sex with locals' (*The Times* 2008).

In 2006, Save the Children conducted another study to assess whether any progress had been made since the 2002 allegations of exploitation and UNHCR's investigations into the matter. Researchers visited temporary camps for civil war refugees in Liberia and found a similar situation; children were still being exploited and men abusing positions of power. The study identifies humanitarian workers, peacekeeping soldiers, businessmen, camp management officials, government officials, police officers, ex-combatants and even teachers (who ask for sexual favours instead of school fees) as those being involved in the exploitation (Save the Children 2006: 11).

The study describes how NGO and UN staff are seen as men with status and money who offer underage girls money, clothing, food, beer or watching a video in exchange for sex (ibid.: 12). Interviewees said they felt that attitudes had changed since the war and reported that children had not been involved in prostitution before living in the camps, which are characterised by overcrowding, poverty, unemployment, bad sanitation and no recreational activities for children (ibid.: 14). The study showed that many parents turned a blind eye and 'accepted it because of poverty and the dire situation in the camps' (*The Independent* 2006). Most were afraid to report it because implicating NGO staff could lead to that organisation or aid delivery being withdrawn. Victims often would not know where to report abuse as the Camp Management Committee and block leaders were themselves involved in it (Save the Children 2006: 14).

Only a year later, new allegations were made when the UN's children's aid organisation, UNICEF, published an internal report in 2007 documenting cases of sexual exploitation by the 10,000 UN police, peacekeepers and staff from over 70 countries in southern Sudan. In addition, Save the Children's research in the Ivory Coast, Southern Sudan and Haiti found that hundreds of starving and desperate youngsters as young as six were being coerced to 'sell sex for food and soap ... in war zones and disaster areas' (*The Times* 2008).

3 Development Aid

'For a long time corruption has been a taboo subject among institutions of development cooperation, in particular corruption occurring within their very own work' (Cremer 2008: 1). Until the mid-1990s, corruption in development aid (also called development assistance, overseas aid or international aid) was largely regarded as a domestic political problem and not the responsibility of the donor organisation. Even though development professionals were well aware of the extent and impact of corruption, many multilateral donor agencies, such as the World Bank, regarded corruption as a political issue that would go against their own rules not to involve political considerations in the decision making on loans. Bilateral government donors were also reluctant to address the issue of corruption in their aid projects for diplomatic reasons (Cremer 2008: 3).

However, after the end of the Cold War, the priorities of the international aid community shifted and the former dogma of winning strategic allies became less important. Instead, aid effectiveness became the focus of debates on aid budgets (Eigen and Eigen-Zucchi 2003: 588).

While humanitarian aid is primarily used for short-term emergency relief, development aid aims to create long-term sustainable economic growth and social development in developing countries. It is distinguished from humanitarian aid as being aimed at alleviating poverty in the long term, rather than alleviating suffering in the short term.

Development aid is intended to reduce poverty and strengthen sustainable social, governmental and economic development. It consists of a multi-layered aid system with several levels of actors, for example, bilateral and multilateral donors. Bilateral donors are government agencies (for example, the US's USAID, the United Kingdom's DFID, Canada's CIDA, Germany's

GTZ, Norway's NORAD etc.) which give aid directly to recipient countries on a state-to-state basis, whereas multilateral donors give aid through intergovernmental organisations. Multilateral donors include UN agencies and funds (UN Development Programme or World Food Programme), the European Commission or multilateral development banks, such as the World Bank, and regional counterparts such as the Asian Development Bank or European Bank for Reconstruction and Development. The main traditional bilateral donors are the 23 member countries of the OECD Development Assistance Committee (DAC), the so-called DAC donors. However, recently a growing number of new donors from emerging markets such as China and Brazil have joined the traditional cartel of donors (Reisen 2009).

In addition, donor agencies have started to channel increasing funds through local and international NGOs (for example, Oxfam, ActionAid and International Alert) and private–public partnerships, such as The Global Fund. This multi-layered system of aid delivery can pose extra challenges in terms of corruption and accountability.

Involving NGOs can have advantages and disadvantages. The downside is that many smaller and inexperienced organisations do not have even rudimentary financial controlling systems in place to prevent corruption and self-enrichment (Cremer 2008: 81). Corruption can also become an internal problem for NGOs, when staff hold positions similar to those of public officials, which makes them susceptible to bribes (ibid.: 79).

In contrast, however, development assistance provided through NGOs can help to control misuse because it creates competition in the field of international development. This bidding for funds among NGOs active in developing countries also means that donors can withhold aid if they believe that their funds are being misused and select a different implementing partner. Unlike government bodies, NGOs do not hold monopolies over regions or sectors and can therefore be exchanged when misuse is detected. If dealing with government officials instead, donors would have to discontinue their work in that region or sector due to a lack of alternatives (ibid.: 83).

Often, a variety of sub-contracting agreements are made, both with donor organisations directly funding NGOs and with UN agencies that, in turn, sub-contract NGOs. Donors, international NGOs and UN agencies often develop partnerships with local NGOs and community-based organisations or work with national or local authorities in developing countries. In the case of emergency aid, private for-profit companies and militaries are also becoming increasingly involved (Ewins *et al.* 2006).

It is impossible to say which of these implementation models is more or less prone to corruption as each of them raises different types of fraud and corruption risks.

> *Having more steps in a contracting chain by, for instance, working with local partners creates additional layers of administration and reporting, where corruption might occur. However, it may also lessen risks by adding extra layers of accountability and reporting mechanisms, or by increasing the degree of accountability to and acceptance by local populations (Ewins et al. 2006: 25).*

Providing aid through multiple layers (from donor to international NGO to local NGO to beneficiary) and providing it more directly (from donor straight to government or to local NGO) involves different corruption risks, but also different levels of efficiency that need to be considered. Reducing the number of actors involved in the process, to minimise corruption risks, may cause deficiencies in accountability and effectiveness. Willitts-King and Harvey (2005) stress that the costs of minimising corruption need to be seen within the context of wider calculations about how assistance can be delivered most cost-effectively, efficiently and accountably. While larger agencies usually invest more resources in management and systems, smaller organisations may be more responsive and locally accountable.

3.1 PROJECT AID AND BUDGET SUPPORT

Two of the main aid instruments used by donors, project aid and budget support, are particularly vulnerable to corruption. An overview of corruption risks for each of these two aid modalities is outlined below:

Project aid

Project aid supports a specific project, such as building a local school or providing vaccinations. The risk of corruption depends on the nature of the project undertaken (size, sector, stakeholders and internal process etc.) (Fritz and Kolstad 2008: 14). One of the biggest problems is the leakage of funds in developing projects which reduces the overall effectiveness of aid and sometimes even prevents projects from having a positive impact on the ground.

When using project aid in countries with high levels of corruption, Fritz and Kolstad (2008: 20) advise that it is essential for donors to have effective risk management mechanisms and controls in place, because corruption is a constant risk throughout the project cycle:

- *Design stage*: Corruption in the assessment phase that decides the scale, form and location of a project leads to inflated needs that favour specific companies, contractors or recipient groups in return for kickbacks (TI n.d.g). In the procurement and bidding phase, there is the risk of bid rigging and collusive bidding between companies and public officials or local project staff, which can inflate prices or lead to the appointment of incompetent contractors (Teggemann n.d.).

- *Implementation phase*: Bribes might be requested by local partners and public officials to release funds, granting permits or licences and general services. Kickbacks might also be paid by contractors to public officials or local aid partners to ignore unfinished or sub-standard work (for example, school buildings, hospitals, roads and sanitation projects). Another risk is that the actual aid deliverables are misappropriated and end up in the hands of privileged elites (agricultural equipment, medical supplies, livestock, and so on) (ibid.).

- *Monitoring and evaluation stage*: Local partners producing forged financial reports, bills or payroll lists and exaggerating or hiding facts from donors. Again, bribes play a significant role in this phase as they can produce favourable audits and evaluation reports (TI n.d.g, Teggemann n.d.).

 For more information on corruption and fraud in international aid projects, read Kramer (2007).

Budget support

Budget support is aid that flows directly to the recipient government's budget or national treasury. Generally, it is untied aid and can be disbursed according to the recipient's own allocation system. Sector budget support (also called programme-based assistance) is similar, except that it is directed for a specific sector, such as health or education. Both national and sector budget support have been increasingly used as a policy-based form of aid by the European Commission and some bilateral donors, such as the United Kingdom. It is believed that this form of assistance has the benefit of increasing the recipient country's ownership and long-term planning abilities, strengthening its institutions and reducing transaction costs for donors (Fritz and Kolstad 2008: 10).

However, other bilateral donors, such as Germany, Japan and the US, have been more wary and prefer to have greater control over their aid, directing it to more specific activities (Fritz and Kolstad 2008: 9). The concern is that budget support in countries with autocratic governments and high levels of corruption is risky. Funds also risk becoming less transparent due to weak budget reporting and being easily diverted or pocketed for private gain. This aid modality has the highest risk of corruption and therefore also greater reputational risks for donors who have an interest in avoiding being seen directly supporting a corrupt leadership (ibid.). For this reason, budget support is more prone to suspension than aid projects and can only be an effective form of development assistance when the recipient country has reasonable governance, administration and budgeting systems in place.

3.2 THE GLOBAL FUND AND UGANDA

The Global Fund to fight AIDS, Tuberculosis and Malaria is a private–public partnership founded in 2002 and based in Switzerland. The Fund describes itself as 'a new approach in international health financing' as it consists of a coalition of governments, civil society, private sector and affected communities (The Global Fund 2011).

Working in collaboration with other bilateral and multilateral aid organisations, the Global Fund has so far funded $21.7bn for more than 600 programmes in 150 countries. The organisation has provided AIDS treatment for three million people, anti-tuberculosis treatment for 7.7 million people and the distribution of 160 million insecticide-treated bed nets for the prevention of malaria (ibid.).

Its original mandate was limited to that of a supplier of additional funds to national programmes and institutions in countries where adequate capacity already exists at the local level and only the additional finance is missing to scale up the work. The Fund provides no technical support to implement the funded programmes or field offices in the recipient countries and operates from its headquarters in Geneva (Kasper 2006: 108).

The Global Fund tries to increase transparency by making its disbursement amounts publicly available, in the hope that partners will use the information to hold recipient governments to account (ibid.: 109). The partnership model was designed with the aim that stakeholders act as pressure groups to monitor that there is no diversion of funds and that the money is used effectively. However, this can only work in countries with a strong civil society already in place and the Global Fund found that it subsequently had to take on more responsibilities itself: '… because partners have tended to view the Global Fund as yet another external body coming in to finance its own projects, rather than one that simply provides additional resources to a national response that all parties would support' (ibid.: 109).

The Global Fund is one of Uganda's key health partners and has provided over $164m in grants to the country to fight the three diseases between 2003 and 2009 (The Global Fund 2009).

However, in 2005, the Fund's engagement with the country was seriously undermined by the discovery of large-scale embezzlement of grants. PriceWaterhouseCoopers, hired by the Global Fund to audit the funding, discovered serious mismanagement and corruption in one of the five grants that had been disbursed, with over $1.6m unaccounted for, mishandled or embezzled.

Responsible for administrating, implementing and overseeing the allocation of the grants was a designated project management unit (PMU) in the Ministry of Health for which the Fund had provided project support (Fritz and Kolstad 2008: 14). Implicated in the scandal were Uganda's Health Minister, Jim Muhwezi, and his two deputies, Alex Kamugisha and Mike Mukula. All three subsequently had to depart the cabinet in 2006, but were never charged.

The money for fighting the diseases had been diverted from its intended beneficiaries by a variety of means. For example, investigators discovered discrepancies in exchange rates when converting the grants from US dollars into Ugandan shillings, irregularities in the procurement process and inflated prices. In other instances, money had been siphoned off through generous allowances for attending meetings and false receipts had been issued. Funds had also been lost through misallocation of the money to unrelated purposes (IRIN 2006; Bass 2005: 1840). The Ugandan public and civil society organisations in the country were outraged by the findings and Uganda's President, Yoweri Museveni, promised a judicial inquiry into the affair (IRIN 2006).

The Global Fund had committed more than $200m over a two-year period to Uganda as part of five grants (two each for HIV/AIDS and malaria and one for tuberculosis), of which $45.4m had already been disbursed by the time the scandal broke in 2005. Table 10.3 below provides an overview of the grants and amounts involved.

Table 10.3   Total of Global Fund grants in Uganda 2003–2004

Disease	Start date	2-year amount (US$ millions)	Total lifespan amount (US$ millions)	Disbursed (US$ millions)
HIV/AIDS (Round 1)	15 June 2003	36.3	48.8	26.1
HIV/AIDS (Round 2)	1 Nov 2004	70.3	118.5	7.5
Malaria (Round 2)	15 March 2004	23.2	35.7	9.7
Malaria (Round 4)	1 May 2005	66.4	158	0
Tuberculosis (Round 2)	15 March 2004	4.7	5.7	2

Source: The Global Fund to Fight AIDS, Tuberculosis and Malaria 2005.

In response to the revelations, the Global Fund suspended its five grants worth $367m (in total lifespan) in August 2005, only to lift the suspension and release the funds again a few months later, in November 2005, after assurances from the Ugandan government of a thorough criminal inquiry. The Global Fund explained the speedy lifting of the suspension with its commitment to a long-term partnership with Uganda and expressed its renewed confidence in the country (The Global Fund 2009). The main motivation for the Fund was 'to ensure continuality of life-saving treatment for the ultimate beneficiaries of funded programs in Uganda' (The Global Fund 2005). The case demonstrates the moral dilemma donors can find themselves in when contemplating whether to withhold aid when dealing with corrupt structures in the face of people dying. In Uganda, only 170,000 of the 300,000 people living with HIV/AIDS are able to access antiretroviral drug treatment and thousands die every year even from malaria, a curable disease (Bogere 2009).

In March 2007, The Global Fund turned down Uganda's grant application for $16m over frustration about the slow progress of the inquiry that in two years had failed to prosecute a single individual over the corruption. Alarmed by the refusal, the Ugandan police finally conducted their investigations with more urgency and the Fund resumed its funding shortly afterwards (PlusNews 2009). After negotiations, both sides agreed to change the way the grants were managed to restore confidence. The Fund requested the dissolving of the PMU and also asked for a third-party procurement agent. Before the corruption case, the Fund had paid the five grants to the Ugandan Ministry of Finance, which funnelled the money to the Ministry of Health, where it was administrated by the PMU. Under the restructure of the grants, the Ministry of Finance now plays a more active role and retains control over the funding (Bass 2005: 1840).

The Fund effectively changed the aid modality to sector budget support through government systems rather than a PMU (Fritz and Kolstad 2008: 14). 'Thus the responsibility for the funds and for accounting and auditing was shifted from mixed – and blurred – ownership to full government ownership, which now becomes responsible for accounting for the use of these resources in the health sector' (ibid.: 14).

However, it remains to be seen whether the embezzlement really only occurred because of the PMU and whether there will be more government scrutiny in the future. It was believed that the political environment in Uganda at the time had also played a large role in the case. The Global Fund embezzlement had happened during a time when President Museveni had rallied for support to change the constitution and to become re-elected for an unprecedented third term. This created a futile environment for corruption because increased funding for political activities was needed and government scrutiny was lacking (Bass 2005).

The Ugandan probe into the mismanagement of the grants resulted in the prosecution of four people, who were jailed, and the recovery of $1m of the stolen funds. In another show of commitment, the government set up a dedicated Anti-Corruption Court in 2008 to handle the investigations (Bogere 2009). However, causing further embarrassment for the Ugandan government were reports in 2009 that funds meant for the ongoing investigations of the Global Fund embezzlement had vanished from the Bank of Uganda and could not be traced (Karugaba 2009).

The first person charged in the case was Teddy Seezi Cheeye, CEO of the NGO Uganda Centre for Accountability, which had been paid $60,000 to monitor the Fund's grants. Cheeye was found guilty of having spent half that money on a private trip to China and was convicted for forgery and embezzlement to ten years in prison in 2008. A former TV producer, Fred Kavuma, was sentenced in 2009 to five years for obtaining $19,000 of the grants under false pretences for private gain and submitting forged receipts. In the same year, the two directors of the Ugandan NGO Value Health, Analiza Mondon and Elizabeth Ngororano, were also each sentenced to five years for mismanaging funds and producing false documents (PlusNews 2009). The High Court judge in the cases, James Ogoola, stated that 'the greatest losers have been the people of Uganda. As the sick lay dying, the greedy middlemen dived for the kill' (PlusNews 2009).

Apart from Uganda, there had only ever been two other suspensions by the Global Fund so far, which were in Burma and Ukraine (Bass 2005). 'Uganda is the only country which has been allowed to remain at the helm during and after the suspension process. Now that its accounts are unfrozen, it has become a test case for the feasibility of country-driven reform' (ibid.: 1839).

4 Corruption and the World Bank

The World Bank, which provides financial and technical assistance to developing countries for development programmes (such as infrastructure, education, healthcare and civil service reform) with the goal of reducing global poverty, is the financially strongest multilateral donor organisation. Since 1946, the World Bank has lent around $525bn, of which, it was estimated, between $26bn and $130bn has been lost to corruption (Cremer 2008: 2).

Unfortunately, until well into the end of the 1990s, the bank (as well as the International Monetary Fund, another multilateral development agency) largely ignored the issue of corruption, afraid of borrower sensitivity and being accused of domestic interfering (Cremer 2008: 3). Before James D. Wolfensohn became World Bank President in 1995, the bank considered corruption simply an issue of politics, rather than one of economic development.

Under Wolfensohn, the bank finally started participating in international efforts to fight corruption and developed internal controls to audit its projects. With the bank pushing the issue of corruption into the spotlight, there was a knock-on effect on other donor organisations, which could no longer ignore the risk and started examining their own projects (Cremer 2008: 6).

TWO EXAMPLES OF FRAUD AND CORRUPTION AFFECTING WORLD BANK PROJECTS

- It is estimated that at least 20–30 per cent of the $30 billion of World Bank loans to Indonesia during the General Suharto regime from 1967–1998 were diverted from the country's development budget funds. That amounts to approximately $9 billion of international aid loans wasted (Hawley 2000).
- In 2008, the World Bank discovered that five of its health projects in India involving HIV/AIDS, malaria and tuberculosis, worth millions of US dollars, were affected by incidents of fraud and corruption (BBC News 2008e).

To counter corruption in international development with a coordinated approach, a group of five international financial institutions (World Bank, African Development Bank, Asian Development Bank, European Bank for Reconstruction and Development and European Investment Bank Group) set up the International Financial Institution (IFI) Anti-Corruption Task Force in 2006. The banks agreed to standardise their definition of corruption and introduce a uniform framework to fight fraud and corruption, the so-called 'IFI Anti Corruption Task Force Uniform Framework'.

 For more detailed information on the work of the Anti-Corruption Task Force and the framework, read International Financial Institution Task Force (2006).

The World Bank itself improved its internal anti-corruption procedures by training staff in corruption awareness and setting up a 24-hour hotline to allow staff and members of the public to report allegations. The bank also formed the Department of Institutional Integrity and Sanctions Committee to investigate allegations of corruption in the execution of contracts.

The committee has the authority to ban companies and individuals found guilty of bribery, theft and corruption, by placing them on a blacklist of ineligible firms, effectively debarring them from future projects worldwide. This list currently holds over 200 firms debarred by the World Bank and is a powerful deterrent for companies in the development sector (World Bank n.d.a.; Cremer 2008: 115). Under pressure from development NGOs who were lobbying the bank for years to publicise internal fraud and corruption investigations involving their own projects, the World Bank recently started to publish annual integrity reports outlining the results of its investigations (World Bank n.d.b.).

Another of the World Bank's anti-corruption measures was to include a clause on fraud and corruption in its procurement guidelines which threatens to withdraw any loan if there was any bid rigging or bribery involved (Cremer 2008: 113). This sanction instrument has become something of a controversy for the bank, which was criticised for not breaking off cooperation with corrupt firms or governments completely. However, as Cremer (2008: 123) explains:

> ... breaking off one single project or recalling part of a loan represents measures that can be precisely steered and effectively implemented. Donors can send a clear signal that they have seriously committed themselves to corruption control and that they expect borrowing countries to take further steps to reform the public sector. In the end, a gradual approach is more appropriate than a radical threat without consequences.

The World Bank's sanction policy came under particular fire over the high-profile scandal involving several leading global construction companies in the Lesotho Highlands Water Project. The bank was heavily criticised for acting slowly and taking years to suspend or ban firms under investigation for bribery in this project (Mekay 2006). The Lesotho case is described in more detail in the next section of this chapter.

For more information on the World Bank's anti-corruption and integrity work, visit:

www.worldbank.org/integrity

For more background information on the role of the World Bank in development assistance and its fight against corruption, read Marquette (2003).

4.1 THE LESOTHO HIGHLANDS WATER PROJECT

The World Bank funds several large-scale infrastructure programmes around the world, financing power plants, harbours and airports, road and rail networks and water supply infrastructure. The Lesotho Highlands Water Project (LHWP) is a multi-billion dollar World Bank-funded hydropower project between the Lesotho and South African governments to transfer water from the Lesotho Highlands to an industrial region in South Africa. The World Bank gave Lesotho a $160m loan as part of the dam and tunnel project for the LHWP, which Lesotho's government hoped would allow the country to sell water to South Africa and gain hydropower at the same time (Lugar 2005).

However the project was soon marred with scandals and the World Bank had to ban several European, Canadian and South African construction companies for corruption in the project; overall, 12 of the world's major construction companies were implicated in the scandal (Mekay 2006). The firms involved were accused of paying the bribes to Lesotho officials to win the lucrative contracts for the project (Lugar 2005). The bribes were paid to the Lesotho Highlands Development Authority's Chief Executive, Masupha Sole, who in 2002 was convicted of 13 counts of bribery and sentenced to 18 years in prison. Sole had made more than $2m in bribes over 10 years from agents of 12 global engineering companies (Mekay 2006). Most of these companies came from countries that had signed the OECD Anti-Bribery Convention, which makes bribery of a foreign public official a crime.

In 2002, one of the accused companies, Canadian firm Acres International, was found guilty of paying bribes and ordered to pay a criminal fine by the Lesotho High Court. The firm had received lucrative contracts worth $17m in 1987 and 1991 on the LHWP and was found guilty of two counts of bribery. In 2004, Acres was barred by the bank for three years from bidding for its projects (World Bank 2004).

In another case involving German firm Lahmeyer International, it took the World Bank over five years to finally blacklist the company in 2006, having started investigations into the company's conduct in 2001. The Lesotho government had even announced criminal investigations as early as 1999. The bank's sanctions committee did not feel that the evidence was sufficient in 2001 and decided to wait for the outcome of the Lesotho criminal trial (World Bank 2006).

In 2003, Lahmeyer was eventually convicted by a Lesotho court of six counts of bribery, which resulted in the bank reopening the case against the company in 2005. However, in the meantime, Lahmeyer had been allowed to bid for World Bank projects for over five years since the first allegations. Even during the 2005 investigation, the firm was not suspended and allocated four contracts worth $1.4m before the 2006 ban (Mekay 2006).

In 2006, Lahmeyer was eventually banned by the bank for seven years from any World Bank-financed contracts, but with the option of a four-year reduction if the company met compliance standards (World Bank 2006). The bank required Lahmeyer to put corporate compliance and ethics programmes in place and disclose any past misconduct.

Civil society organisations, monitoring the project and acting as whistleblowers, criticised this voluntary disclosure programme, which offers companies the opportunity to confess to malpractice and corruption in exchange for confidentiality and not being banned. Critics point out that this confidentiality conveniently also allows the bank to cover up its own negligence or complicity (Mekay 2006).

As a result of the described corruption, the costs for the LHWP project became inflated (the first phase alone had cost an estimated $2.6bn; the second cost an additional $1.1bn) and questions were raised over its original assessment in 1986. Companies involved in the corruption such as Lahmeyer International had also been part of the consortium that had carried out the LHWP feasibility study and its environmental impact assessment (ibid.). The LHWP had long raised concerns among environmental groups about its impact on the environment and the local population – of around 27,000 living in the affected area in Lesotho – as it needed to dispossess and relocate hundreds of people and farmlands, making it harder for them to access fresh water (ibid.).

As well as Sole, Reatile Mochebelele – CEO of the LHWP and chief delegate on the Lesotho Highlands Water Commission – was eventually charged in 2006 with taking bribes in relation to the project (Rickard 2006). Investigating the LHWP corruption case took several years and was very costly, almost bankrupting impoverished Lesotho (Luger 2005). The Lesotho government was heralded at the time for taking on the big international companies in court and setting legal precedents (Nussbaum 2005). The World Bank, however, was criticised for not sufficiently supporting the criminal investigations in Lesotho. It also faced questions over the performance of its own scrutiny mechanisms, which had failed to detect the cases of corruption in its own funded project. Instead, it was local action on the ground in Lesotho that brought the world's spotlight onto the scandal (Muller 2004).

5 Does Aid Increase Corruption?

There is currently no consistent empirical evidence to suggest that aid causes corruption *per se*. However, evidence does suggest that in non-democratic countries with low governance standards, certain aid instruments (for example, humanitarian aid or budget support) and specific donor practices (for example, promotion of public sector privatisation) bear higher risks than others and can more easily lead to corruption (Fritz and Kolstad 2008: 8). When governments in developing countries become used to receiving long-term budget support or programme assistance, it can discourage them from reforming inefficient government bodies and policies (Teggemann n.d.).

High levels of aid can encourage rent-seeking behaviour and corruption. 'Aid inflow much like natural resources provides opportunities for wealth' (ibid.). It can cause struggle over the control of aid and increase corruption and instability. In particular, budget support and government programme assistance, which through their fungible characteristics pose high corruption risks, are two aid instruments that are criticised for enabling corrupt governments to enrich themselves (Teggemann n.d.; Fritz and Kolstad 2008). Public officials in recipient countries can divert them into their own pockets instead of spending them for their designed purposes. Corrupt elites in developing countries might also use aid for their own prestige projects, for rent-seeking or to fund the military instead of basic needs programmes such as education, health or infrastructure for local communities (Teggemann n.d.). However, it is also important to bear in mind that direct budget support accounts for only around 20 per cent of all aid (Fritz and Kolstad 2008: 9).

It has long been debated in the international development community whether highly corrupt governments should continue to receive aid or if mainly those that show willingness to reform and good governance standards should receive it. It is hoped that this would work as an incentive for aid-dependent countries to improve the levels of transparency and accountability in public administration and financial management. So far, this idea has not been widely implemented by donors, mainly because aid is often also linked with strategic interests – in particular, funds from bilateral donors. This means that aid is more often directed to former colonies or political allies, rather than based on conditions such as democracy, human rights or low levels of corruption (Teggemann n.d.).

In contrast, multilateral aid is less guided by strategic or political interests: 'Here, aid allocation has been targeted towards lower income countries with good management, which receive 30 per cent more than poorly managed countries in the same income and population group' (ibid.).

6 The Problem of Accountability

Accountability in development or emergency aid has been low due to the overseas nature of aid, which is delivered not only on a state-to-state basis through bilateral aid agencies but also through multilateral donors and NGOs. Beneficiaries in recipient countries, which are often poor and marginalised populations, are not in a position to hold their governments or overseas donors to account (TI 2007: 11–12). At the same time, it is also difficult for tax payers in donor countries to scrutinise the delivery of aid in this multi-layered system.

Both development and relief agencies need urgently to improve the quality of their accountability to beneficiaries and donors. 'In the context of corruption, accountability to beneficiaries and their representatives is particularly important because they are often best placed to recognise and fight corruption at the local level' (Ewins *et al.* 2006: 27). Humanitarian assistance as it is currently delivered is often lacking local accountability, and therefore viewed by the local population as entirely external. For instance, in Sudan, Duffield *et al.* (2000: 182) found that:

> *Relief items are generally regarded as not belonging to anybody and stealing from them is not as disgraceful as stealing local grain from someone's house. The local legal system does not contain mechanisms*

to deal with theft of relief goods. Theft of relief items therefore falls into a different moral category from other types of theft and traditional methods of social punishment do not apply in the same way. When someone is accused of stealing relief items, they may respond according to the following logic: So what, did I steal from your mother's house?

This illustrates the problem that the current international aid system is often seen as a Western endeavour, and even one with imperial overtones. Corruption might be fuelled by the notion of humanitarian relief and international aid largely funded and provided by agencies that are perceived as 'Western' (Ewins *et al.* 2006).

Despite the efforts of development and humanitarian agencies to improve procedures for accounting, procurement, asset management and their own monitoring, evaluation and audit functions, 'these systems of accountability have largely flowed upwards, with aid agencies justifying expenditure to the donors that fund them. Progress on downwards accountability, of aid agencies to the people they are trying to help, has been far slower. Downward accountability is promoted through providing information about entitlements, and effective complaints mechanisms to respond to grievances' (Willitts-King and Harvey 2005: 6).

Upward accountability to donor administrations has demonstrated its serious limitations in terms of relevance as well as in its ability to detect corruption. Strengthening the [downward] accountability of aid toward intended beneficiaries is the most effective way of limiting corruption (TI 2007: 9).

Willitts-King and Harvey (2005) believe it is crucial to tackle corruption at field level. This can be achieved by, for example, letting beneficiaries participate in decision-making forums and implementation processes. 'The design, implementation and monitoring of aid should support transparent and inclusive processes that strengthen domestic accountability mechanisms' (TI 2007: 21).

Aid deliverers may well be able to report that the right amount of food was distributed to the right number of people, but this says little about whether kickbacks were paid to ensure registration, what proportion of the food went to the local government official at the distribution site, or what bribes local militias demanded so that beneficiaries could get

> *the food home. These problems remain largely unseen and certainly unreported, in part because of the weakness of downward accountability (Willitts-King and Harvey 2005: 7).*

Aid beneficiaries need to have a clear understanding of what aid they are entitled to, and what the criteria for targeting and selection are. Ideally, they should also be involved in the management and decision-making process, which could greatly reduce the risk of corruption. The ability of agency staff or local authorities and elites to abuse relief systems depends on a lack of transparency and understanding about how the aid distribution works among those receiving it. The promotion of transparency should therefore be part of any anti-corruption strategy (Willitts-King and Harvey 2005).

Another way of strengthening accountability was explored at the OECD Paris High Level Forum in 2005, which was attended by development officials and ministers from 91 countries, 26 donor organisations and partner countries, and representatives of civil society organisations and the private sector. Participants issued the Paris Declaration on Aid Effectiveness, in which they stressed the benefits of mutual accountability and introduced the concept of mutual accountability frameworks and joint aid effectiveness reviews. 'Mutual accountability aims to place the aid relationship on a two-way contractual basis, where donors commit to providing effective aid and recipients commit to using aid well' (TI 2007: 12). Mutual accountability also includes civil society, media and businesses in the monitoring of aid effectiveness and accountability.

Read the full text of the Paris Declaration on Aid Effectiveness at the OECD's website:

www.oecd.org

7 Efforts to Reduce the Risks of Corruption

The last couple of years has seen a move by many donors to take corruption more seriously and improve the mechanisms through which aid is delivered by increasing the number of governance reform projects in their portfolio (Teggemann n.d.). Donors are trying to fight corruption with projects designed to reform government structures and institutions and to raise awareness about corruption in the recipient country. The number of capacity building projects in the areas of institutional reform, financial management and public administration on both the local and national level has increased dramatically and donors are hoping that this will have positive knock-on effects on corruption levels and overall aid effectiveness (ibid.).

One of the most targeted areas is public financial management in developing countries. 'Public financial management is seen as the heart of these efforts to build financial integrity and prevent corruption' (TI 2007: 14). Improving transparency in budget planning and reporting is a key aspect in reducing corruption and increasing accountability.

Preventive mechanisms for tackling corruption in humanitarian aid include corruption risk assessments to identify potential perpetrators and areas of risk. Another approach is to have strong financial and administrative managements systems in place to keep track of high-value relief goods, such as fuel vehicles and medical equipment (TI 2006a: 3). Accurate targeting and effective distribution of relief can also help to prevent corruption. And lastly, better coordination among donors by adopting consistent policies and procedures and sharing best practice could also assist (TI 2006a: 3).

Examples are the introduction of sanctions and blacklisting of corrupt partners. 'Almost all donors today have integrated anti-corruption clauses into their agreements with project partners and contractors. … Sanctions in cases of breach of such agreements include revoking contracts, penalties or debarment from future contracts' (Huber-Grabenwarter and Boehm 2009: 51).

Reporting, monitoring and audit approaches have become increasingly professional in how they demonstrate accountability to their donors. So-called 'fraud audits' have been introduced which involve tracing suspicious transactions, checking prices, testing deliverables and conducting interviews (Kramer 2007: 4). Effective monitoring and evaluation of aid allocated and received by beneficiaries can also be a useful tool to detect diversion of funds and misappropriation. However, there are a number of challenges:

> *Monitoring and evaluation often have a mix of objectives; exposing malpractice may not be a primary aim. Aid agencies sometimes have to make trade-offs between monitoring and implementation, and the capacity to monitor and evaluate often gets squeezed (Willitts-King and Harvey 2005: 33).*

Furthermore, often the same programme staff are responsible for implementing a project as well as for monitoring it, which makes it less likely that potential abuse will be detected as staff involved in corrupt practices are unlikely to report on themselves. To tackle this issue, donors have introduced measures such as external auditors, whistleblower protection, confidential hotlines, ombudspersons and voluntary disclosure programmes (Kramer 2007: 4). Some aid agencies have even called for the establishment of an international humanitarian ombudsperson to strengthen accountability. The ombudsperson would have specific legal or administrative powers to investigate incidents of fraud and corruption in humanitarian relief work (TI 2006a).

As already mentioned, ownership-based mechanisms can reduce corruption risks and increase accountability at a very low cost. For example, by ensuring access to information by publicising aid targets, entitlements, mechanisms and intended recipients, beneficiaries become aware of their entitlements (ibid.: 4). Another ownership mechanism is aimed at active participation of beneficiaries in the design and implementation of projects to make them more responsive to their actual needs and avoid over- or undersupplies of aid. 'A lack of participation can also limit aid agencies' understanding of the context in which aid is given, potentially leading them to ignore important social, political and economic relations, in turn increasing opportunities for corruption' (ibid.).

In this context, aid agencies have started to introduce more participatory processes at the sub-national and local level to improve accountability. Involving the beneficiaries in all project stages can be complemented by including civil society organizations and local media in the recipient countries to increase awareness about corruption and empower stakeholders and the local population (Teggemann n.d.). As Cremer (2008: 136) argues: 'A coalition of civil society organizations can attack systemic and organized corruption by disseminating information on the corrupt system, uncovering conspicuous consumption by those who have grown rich through corruption, and increasing political pressure for change.' Transparency International's 'integrity pacts' are an example of this kind of civil society coalition. Engaging with civil society and domestic media as partners in the fight against corruption of public resources is also an approach promoted by Transparency International through the concept of National Integrity Systems (NIS) (TI 2007: 19–20).

To access over 70 NIS country assessment reports conducted since 2001, visit Transparency International's website:

www.transparency.org/policy_research/nis/nis_reports_by_country

By introducing conditionality, some donors have tried to link aid to specific demands – for example, only to give aid once a country has implemented governance reforms, or not to provide aid until an absolute standard, such as respect for human rights or democratic freedoms, is met (Fritz and Kolstad 2008: 13). However, threats to withhold aid have not usually proven to be very feasible and aid was in most cases continued, either out of strategic interest or in the context of humanitarian emergencies. 'The challenge facing donors is to draw a line between countries that are considered "too corrupt" and those that have "acceptable" levels of corruption' (ibid.: 20).

For various worldwide examples and case studies of anti-corruption campaigns in relation to development aid, read Bracking (2007).

8 Case Study: Public Expenditure-tracking Surveys

Public expenditure-tracking surveys (PETS) are quantitative data collections on the supply side of public frontline services coupled with qualitative interviews on the perceptions of the service facility's users. The surveys gather information from a service facility such as a local government, school or hospital by focusing on financial flows and services delivered. PETS are powerful diagnostic tools to examine the use and abuse of public funds and give insight on issues such as decentralization, cost efficiency and accountability (World Bank n.d.c.). Most of the time, developing countries do not collect or monitor financial flows and public expenditure closely and in the absence of reliable data on public budget allocations and its use, PETS are able to trace flow of public money from its origin to allocated destination and calculate the scale of anomaly in specific sectors such as health or education.

Uganda was first country to pilot PETS and the surveys were initiated because, despite a large increase in public spending on education in Uganda, this had not been translated into an increase in enrolment in primary schools (Reinikka and Smith n.d.: 69). From 1991–1995 independent research teams sponsored by the World Bank surveyed 250 primary schools in 19 of Uganda's 39 districts for the public expenditure-tracking surveys and found that, on average, only 13 per cent of central funds reached local schools during that period of time (Wagle and Shah 2003: 2). The district government had retained around 87 per cent of the public funds for non-education purposes and it was believed that these missing funds were used for political activities and patronage (Reinikka and Smith n.d.: 75).

A breakdown of the figures showed that, in 1991, the schools had received on average only 2 per cent of the allocated funds, while in 1995 this increased to 26 per cent. However, this was unevenly spread among the schools, with some schools receiving nothing on average and others 25 per cent in a good year (Wagle and Shah 2003: 2). The local government had withheld the money, arguing that children had not paid their school fees. However, further research discovered that the schools had indeed sent the fees and the district governments had pocketed both the central government funds and the school fees, while the schools stayed under-funded (ibid.: 2).

The surveys' findings also highlighted that decentralisation had not been entirely successful in Uganda's education sector as those schools that still received their funds directly from the central government had not suffered as much leakage as those receiving money from the district administrations (ibid.: 3).

In response to the surveys' findings, the Ugandan government decided to launch a public information campaign on radio and in newspapers, targeting the schools. A second measure was that schools and district administrations had to put up public notices on all funds they had received from the central government. This gave parents and schools access to vital information and empowered them (Reinikka and Svensson 2004: 326). Before the campaign, parents and schools had no knowledge of their entitlements and disbursement of public money wasn't routinely monitored.

When the information campaign was evaluated in 2001, it showed that large improvements had been made and the leakage had reduced dramatically from 80 per cent to 20 per cent in six years (ibid.: 326). The research also proved that this was really the result of the information drive as schools with access to newspapers reduced their leakage more than those without such access, even though before the information campaign there was no difference between the leakages (ibid.). It was estimated that around 75 per cent of the increase in funds which finally reached their destination was due to the government's mass information campaign (Reinikka and Smith n.d.: 69).

The Ugandan case is an example of a cost-effective survey that demystified a governmental process, prompting a smoother flow of information to enhance transparency in budget allocation and use that resulted in capitation grants the schools were supposed to be receiving going up from almost 0% in 1991 to nearly 100% in 1999 (Wagle and Shah 2003: 3).

Public expenditure-tracking surveys have been influential in highlighting public fund leakages and the Ugandan case particularly has received a lot of attention due to its surprising findings. The case shows that increased transparency of financial flows can strengthen accountability, empower local populations and reduce the capture of public funds – and that this can be achieved through inexpensive initiatives, such as mass information campaigns. 'This not only made information available to parents but also signalled that the centre had resumed its oversight function' (Reinikka and Smith n.d.: 76).

The first public expenditure-tracking service in Uganda stimulated health and education surveys in other developing countries; however, Uganda was the most extreme case in comparison with other PETS' findings. Evidence from other PETS in the primary education sector conducted between 1999 and 2002 have shown interesting findings: the non-wage leakage of funds was 60 per cent in Zambia, 57 per cent in Tanzania and 50 per cent in Ghana (Reinikka and Svensson 2004: 328). PETS have since been conducted in several countries, among them Peru, Honduras, Madagascar, Papua New Guinea, Rwanda, Senegal, Mozambique, Kenya and Bangladesh (Reinikka and Smith n.d.: 67).

Study Questions

- In what ways is humanitarian aid particularly vulnerable to corruption?

- Why is accountability a major problem in international aid and how can it be improved?

- Describe some of the measures development agencies have used to minimise the risk of fraud and corruption in their aid programmes and projects.

- Consider if aid actually contributes to the problem of corruption in developing countries.

11

Corruption and World Health

1 Introduction

Corruption in the health sector affects people all over the world. 'Money that should be spent on alleviating poverty and illness ends up instead in private pockets. In this way, corruption violates human rights, as people are denied the care that their governments are obliged to provide' (Robinson 2006: xiv).

In developing countries, where access to healthcare is already limited and resources are scarce, the impact of corruption in the health sector can be particularly devastating. 'The poor are disproportionately affected by corruption in the health sector, as they are less able to afford small bribes for health services that are supposed to be free, or to pay for private alternatives where corruption has depleted public health services' (TI 2006c: xvi).

Corruption deprives people of access to healthcare and can lead to the wrong treatments being administered. For example, corruption can result in 'cases of water being substituted for life-saving adrenaline and active ingredients being diluted by counterfeiters, triggering drug-resistant strains of malaria, tuberculosis and HIV, the world's biggest killer' (TI 2006c: xvi).

The central element in a human rights approach to health is 'ensuring that essential medicines are available, accessible [on a non-discriminatory basis] and of good quality [scientifically and medically approved]. Corruption hampers compliance with each of these obligations' (Robinson 2006: xiv).

This chapter looks primarily at the dangerous effects that counterfeit drugs have, in particular with regard to developing countries. It also analyses the impact that corruption has on the prevention and treatment of HIV/AIDS. A case study illustrates the dangers of fake malaria drugs to Southeast Asia and Africa.

2 Vulnerabilities of the Health Sector

Spending on health ranges from only 5 per cent in low income countries to more than 15 per cent in OECD countries, with the global annual spending on health to be estimates at around $3 trillion (Hussman 2011: 5). With sums this large, the health sector attracts a lot of corruption, simply due to the large amounts of public money consumed (Savedoff and Hussman 2006: 4).

Corruption in the health sector is widespread and affecting every country and health system. The forms of corruption may vary across the different systems and actors involved due to their specific institutional structure and financing model (Savedoff and Hussman 2006: 11). 'It occurs in systems whether they are predominantly public or private, well funded or poorly funded, and technically simple or sophisticated. The extent of corruption is, in part, a reflection of the society in which it operates' (ibid.: 4). This type of corruption has no boundaries because 'regardless of country, the existence and roles of players within the healthcare continuum are the same' (Busch 2008: 9).

The health sector is particularly prone to corruption, due to its special nature:

- the imbalance of information in health systems between health professionals and patients;

- the uncertainty in health markets with regard to numbers of ill people and effectiveness of treatments; and

- the complexity of health systems due to the large numbers of parties involved.

(Savedoff and Hussmann 2006: 5–7)

Developing countries, which have integrated health systems where the public sector directly provides healthcare, often suffer from 'large scale diversion at ministerial level, bribes in procurement, illegally charging patients, diverting funds to private practice, and absenteeism' (Hussman 2011: 7). Middle and higher income countries with finance provider systems, where the provision of health and public financing are separated, are in contrast more prone to fraud in billing government or insurance agencies. Other problematic areas in this type of health system are unnecessary treatments, ghost patients, false invoices and overall corruption in the pharmaceutical supply chain and health service delivery.

With large proportions of health funding spent on hospital buildings, both types of system face the risk of hospitals providing a platform for illicit activities, 'given their size and complexity – hospitals provide many opportunities for corruption' (Vian 2006: 48). Areas at risk are, for example, corruption in procurement, construction and hospital administration, such as diversion of drugs and equipment or bribes for avoiding waiting lists.

Other common corruption risks that both health systems share are state capture and budget leakages, which play a significant role. The World Bank has financed several Public Expenditure Tracking Surveys (PETS), already mentioned in Chapter 10, which trace the flow of government health expenditure to frontline health services. Example studies using PETS to track resource flows have found in 2000 in Ghana that only 20 per cent of non-wage public sector health spending reached frontline services. In Tanzania 41 per cent leakage was measured in 1999. And in Peru the 'Glass of milk' food supplement programme saw a 71 per cent leakage on its way to beneficiaries (Lindelow *et al.* 2006: 31– 32; Nordberg and Vian 2008: 11–12). These results demonstrate that financial management and accountability is of vital importance in the health sector to prevent the diversion of funds.

In developing countries, informal payments are a large area of corruption in health and reduce access to care for the poor. Patients are made to pay unofficial fees or bribes in order to receive treatments that are supposed to be free of charge, to reduce waiting time, or to receive better quality of treatment and drugs (U4 n.d.c.). Another area is bribes, which are paid to avoid regulation and government monitoring of drugs, which leads to the rise in counterfeit medicines (Nordberg and Vian 2008: 8).

On short, corruption in health abuses the public's trust and goes against the medical principle of protecting peoples' health. Loss of trust in public health provision or the medical profession is one of the major consequences of corruption: 'Corruption in health erodes public trust in government institutions' (Hussman 2011: 5).

 To learn more about the challenges of corruption the health sector is facing, read the Nordberg and Vian (2008) and TI (2006c).

3 The Spread of Counterfeit Medicines

Counterfeit medicines represent an enormous and growing public health challenge – and a silent epidemic. Estimates by the London think tank, International Policy Network, in 2009 suggest about 700,000 people die each year from malaria and tuberculosis due to counterfeit medicines (Bennett 2010).

The production of sub-standard and counterfeit drugs is an under-reported problem that particularly affects low income countries. Counterfeit medicines are swamping developing countries, causing unnecessarily poor health and mortalities, and undermining public confidence in medicines and health structures. However, 'pharmaceutical companies and governments are reluctant to publicise the problem to health staff and the public, apparently to avoid any alarm that could prevent patients taking their genuine medicines' (Cockburn *et al.* 2005).

In industrialised countries (for example OECD states) with strong regulation, the incidence of counterfeit drugs is relatively low (around 1 per cent of market share), however, in Asian, African and Latin American markets, it can be up to 30 per cent of all medicines on sale (WHO 2010a). And when purchased over the internet, over 50 per cent of medicines sold online are fake and potentially harmful, with annual sales of counterfeit drugs on the Internet estimated at $12bn worldwide in 2008 (WHO 2010a; Parliamentary Office of Science and Technology 2010).

Table 11.1   Examples of counterfeit medicines

Counterfeit medicine	Country/Year	Report
Anti-diabetic traditional medicine (used to lower blood sugar)	China, 2009	Contained six times the normal dose of glibenclamide (two people died, nine people hospitalized)
Metakelfin (antimalarial)	United Republic of Tanzania, 2009	Discovered in 40 pharmacies: lacked sufficient active ingredient
Viagra & Cialis (for erectile dysfunction)	Thailand, 2008	Smuggled into Thailand from an unknown source in an unknown country
Xenical (for fighting obesity)	United States of America, 2007	Contained no active ingredient and sold via Internet sites operated outside the USA
Zyprexa (for treating bipolar disorder and schizophrenia)	United Kingdom, 2007	Detected in the legal supply chain: lacked sufficient active ingredient
Lipitor (for lowering cholesterol)	United Kingdom, 2006	Detected in the legal supply chain: lacked sufficient active ingredient

Source: 'Medicines: counterfeit medicines' – WHO fact sheet No 275, January 2010 http://www.who.int/mediacentre/factsheets/fs275/en (WHO 2010a)

3.1 HOW COUNTERFEIT DRUGS AFFECT THE HEALTH SECTOR

The manufacturing of counterfeit drugs is a global problem, but opinions on what constitutes counterfeiting vary from country to country, making it difficult to control. The World Health Organisation (WHO) describes counterfeit medicine as a medicine

> ... *that is deliberately and fraudulently mislabelled with respect to identity and/or source. Counterfeiting can apply to both branded and generic products, and counterfeit products may include products with the correct ingredients or with the wrong ingredients, without active ingredients, with insufficient active ingredients or with fake packaging (WHO 2006).*

This definition can also apply to drugs that have expired and been relabelled. Fake drugs can contain a variety of harmless or toxic ingredients, for example, talcum powder and rice flour, but also pesticides that can cause renal failure, boric acid, leaded road paint, floor polish or rat poison (Clark 2008). These substances can cause life threatening illness or death and one of the most deadly examples is Niger: In 1995 around 2,500 people died after receiving fake vaccines during a meningitis epidemic. The vaccines had been donated as a gift by another country which was unaware of the safety risk (WHO 2006).

Drug counterfeiting is different from the production of low-cost medicines. 'Some developing countries, as part of a principled stance in a broader public health debate, will allow their manufacturers to make certain generic medicines, for example, for HIV/AIDS patients, without paying license holders' (Kramer 2006). Counterfeiters, in contrast, operate illegally for profit, and the contents of the fake drugs can be different from the originals.

Estimates by the WHO reveal that the global market in counterfeit drugs is worth $32 billion (Taylor and Dickinson 2006: 106). 'All over the world counterfeit drugs sales account for almost 10 per cent of overall value' (Euromonitor 2008) and in developing countries alone this figure rises to 25 per cent. Cockburn *et al.* (2005) outline that in total '15 per cent of all sold drugs [worldwide] are fake, and in parts of Africa and Asia this figure exceeds 50 per cent'. The international counterfeit drugs industry is so large that it was estimated that by the year 2010, it will be a $75 billion dollar industry (Fairbairn *et al.* 2007).

Counterfeit drugs not only affect the health sector in terms of the economic loss but also have an impact on the personal health of consumers who end up taking them. Some of these fake drugs appear to be the same as the original drugs but, since they are made with cheap ingredients, they are less effective or even dangerous; as a result, they have been 'reported to be directly responsible for killing many people around the world each year' (ibid.: 19).

For more information on why counterfeit drugs pose a serious risk to public health, read the WHO factsheet 'Counterfeit medicines' (WHO 2010a), available at:

www.who.int

3.2 THE RISE OF COUNTERFEIT DRUGS IN DEVELOPING COUNTRIES

While corruption in the health sector exists in all countries, it is particularly of great concern in developing countries where public resources are already scarce and access to health is often limited for the most vulnerable in those societies. Corruption lowers not only the quality of healthcare that patients receive, it also increases the costs for healthcare provision and has a corrosive impact on the health level of the population (Nordberg and Vian 2008: 4).

Most counterfeit drugs are produced, traded and used in developing countries. China, for example, is a nation that has seen a boom in counterfeit drugs and according to a 2006 report by the London-based International Policy Network, between 200,000 and 300,000 Chinese people die each year from counterfeit or substandard medicine (Clark 2008).

While China's pharmaceutical industry is experiencing rapid growth, the boom in counterfeit drugs is costing human lives and eroding the public's confidence in medical products. 'It is estimated that China has become a major source of counterfeit drugs in the international market, along with India and Russia' (Jia 2007).

Despite frequent media stories in China reporting the success of the State Food and Drug Administration and its local branches in cracking down on counterfeit drug makers, fake drugs are expanding from rural markets to bigger drugstores in major Chinese cities. Commercial corruption and the poor performance of drug regulators are being blamed for the prevalence of fake drugs. However, the high price of medicines, particularly in developing countries, is a significant factor driving counterfeit drug making, since most counterfeiters target expensive drugs sold by international pharmaceutical firms (ibid.).

The lack of proper regulation and monitoring means that import licences are readily issued to non-professional pharmaceutical companies and drug regulations can be flouted with impunity. 'China needs to develop a system to accredit each of its 5,000 Chinese pharmaceutical manufacturers and 12,000 drug wholesalers to reduce the chances for fakes to enter the market' (Jia 2007). However, Western pharmaceutical manufacturers have been blamed for helping to increase the quality of the fakes by moving their production to China, where some factories have been 'caught out producing genuine articles during the day and knocking out illegal copies at night' (Calvert *et al.* 2007).

An alarming trend is that many forgers are switching to the more lucrative market of life-saving prescription medicines. Counterfeiting factories are preparing to move into the production of drugs for illnesses such as heart disease and cancer, in which the dosage is critically important (ibid.). Counterfeit drugs produced for developing countries are mainly medicines for HIV/AIDS, malaria and tuberculosis – the world's three most deadly diseases.

The swamping of Asia with fake drugs is a massive threat to health that is already spreading to Africa: high prices, soaring demand and a shortage of raw material mean that an epidemic of fake drugs in Africa is already taking hold. Two African nations that have already long been experiencing an epidemic of counterfeit drugs are Nigeria and Kenya. In Kenya, it has been reported that alongside the sale of counterfeit drugs, expired drugs are also sold, especially into rural and impoverished neighbourhoods where consumers are not aware of the risk they are taking (Fairbairn *et al.* 2007). In Nigeria, it was estimated in 2001 that 'up to 80 per cent of the drugs in the country's hospitals and pharmacies were fake' (Usborne 2005).

Though counterfeit drugs appear to be on the rise in Asia and Africa, measures are being taken by nations to stop these drugs from coming onto the market. For example, in Nigeria, the National Agency for Food and Drug Administration and Control (NAFDAC) has established mass education campaigns to deter potential users of counterfeit drugs. A study undertaken in 2001 outlined that 68 per cent of drugs were not registered with NAFDAC, highlighting their counterfeit nature, but there seem to have been some remarkable improvements, as in 2004 another study found that there had been 'an 80 per cent reduction in the level of counterfeit drugs in the country' (Akunyili 2006: 96).

For more information on the role and background of NAFDAC, see its website:

www.nafdacnigeria.org.

3.3 THE PROBLEM OF COUNTERFEIT DRUGS IN EUROPE AND THE US

Counterfeit drugs are not just a problem for developing countries. Even Europe and the US are not immune: counterfeit drugs have, for example, turned up on pharmacy shelves in the Netherlands, and a booming black market for Viagra has encouraged cheap imitations.

In developed countries, counterfeits are a growing problem, but their closed and highly regulated domestic systems for pharmaceuticals have so far maintained a high level of safety. However, due to the extensive movement of drugs in and out of countries through licit and illicit importation, counterfeit drugs have become more widespread in Europe and the US nowadays (Calvert *et al.* 2007). Viagra and Cialis, both erectile dysfunction treatments, are two of the most popular fake drugs distributed in the West. The pills are smuggled into Europe and the US in suitcases which can contain as many as 100,000 fake tablets each and are declared as vitamin tablets at airport customs checks (ibid.). Tests by Pfizer, the real manufacturer of Viagra, have found that some of the fake Viagra drugs contain three times the maximum dose of the active ingredient, Sildenafil, which is very alarming, since just one of those tablets would have been enough to cause an overdose (ibid.).

In recent years, however, there has been a shift away from counterfeit lifestyle drugs, such as Viagra, to more life-saving drugs for cancer, heart disease and antibiotics, but also fake anti-obesity pills, antihistamines, vitamins or infertility drugs (WHO 2006).

Seizures of counterfeit drugs across Europe rose from 500,000 fake tablets in 2005 to 2.5 million in 2006 (Clark 2008). In 2005, 2,523 packs of fake Lipitor, an anti-cholesterol drug, were sold in Britain, but only 359 of those packs were eventually recovered. Only a year later, a similar case involving the same drug made headlines when it was discovered that, out of 1,867 fake Lipitor packs, only seven were recovered; the large remainder reached the supply chain. 'One of the problems appears to be Britain's reliance on drugs bought through parallel trade – the system in which drugs are bought and sold several times because prices vary between different European countries' (Calvert *et al.* 2007).

In two other more recent cases, British customs officials confiscated more than half a million counterfeit tablets destined for the NHS and high-street chemists in 2008 (Townsend 2009). And in 2007, two counterfeit drug types, antipsychotic pill Zyprexa and stroke medication Plavix, were even able to make their way into the legitimate NHS supply chain and reached patients before the affected drug stocks could be recalled (Clark 2008).

The UK market is attractive for various reasons: First, prices for medicines are higher than the rest of Europe, ensuring greater profits. Secondly, money strapped NHS trusts have been encouraged to buy drugs as cheap as possible (Townsend 2009; Clark 2008). And lastly, the UK is used by drug counterfeiters as staging post between producers in the Far East and consumers in the United States and Europe. With London as major transit point, illicit drugs are shipped from producing countries such as China or India to free trade zones in the Middle East, like Dubai, then onwards to the UK, from where they are stamped and mailed to US and European internet buyers to add credibility and hide any traces (Clark 2008).

The costs involved in producing fake medicines are very low, but can be sold for a large profit. In one case, 100,000 tablets costing the Chinese manufacturer only 25p each to produce were sold in the UK for up to £20 each, generating £1.6m in total (ibid.).

3.4 HOW TO COMBAT COUNTERFEIT DRUGS: THE ROLE OF PHARMACEUTICAL COMPANIES

So what are legitimate pharmaceutical companies doing about counterfeit drugs? It seems that the industry is currently still primarily worried about publicity over counterfeiting, fearing that sales will fall if customers are alarmed by the existence of counterfeit medicine. Pharmaceutical companies fear that their reputation will be damaged and sales of their well branded products will decline if the true scale of the counterfeit drugs market became publicly known, in a market that is fiercely competitive (Kramer 2006).

Pharmaceutical companies do not usually disclose discoveries of counterfeit versions of their pills. 'Most data on the epidemiology of counterfeit drugs are kept secret by the pharmaceutical industry and by government agencies' (Cockburn *et al.* 2005). However, this has not deterred campaigners and policy analysts from trying to make the public more aware of the effects and dangers of counterfeit drugs.

Fairbairn *et al.* (2007) state that it is the role of 'national agencies, together with customs agents and public prosecutors' to take primary responsibility in preventing and controlling counterfeit drugs. Cockburn *et al.* (2005) agree, by outlining that it is not just the pharmaceutical industry that needs to tackle this issue head on, but that the government needs to be involved too, as well as other health workers who can work behind the scenes to tackle the problem. However, it could be argued that the main step would be for the drug regulatory authorities of different countries to take a collaborative approach to this issue, because ultimately their first responsibility is to the consumer.

> For a critical analysis of the role of pharmaceutical companies and government in combating counterfeit drugs, read Cockburn *et al.* (2005).

In response to the need of a more collaborative approach in fighting counterfeit medicines, the WHO launched in 2006 the International Medical Products Anti-Counterfeiting Taskforce (IMPACT), which promotes cooperation between governments, NGOs and the pharmaceutical industry and jointly develops preventative strategies, regulatory infrastructure and enforcement methods.

To learn more about IMPACT, visit the Taskforce's website at:

www.who.int/impact.

OPERATION STORM

In a joint operation between WHO, Interpol and the World Customs Organization, $6.65m worth of counterfeit HIV/AIDS, malaria and tuberculosis drugs were seized in Southeast Asia in 2008. More than 16 million tablets were confiscated during operations in Cambodia, China, Laos, Myanmar, Singapore, Thailand and Vietnam and 27 arrests were made following a five months investigation involving 200 raids (*Medical News Today* 2008).

4 Corruption and HIV/AIDS

Corruption is affecting the prevention and treatment of HIV/AIDS in many developing countries. The disease is particularly vulnerable to corruption. For example, corruption can contribute directly to infection with the virus, if the use of sterile needles or screening of blood donations is ignored due to a corrupt procurement process. This can even go as far as extorting illicit payments from patients who demand sterile equipment.

On the surface, corruption that affects HIV/AIDS prevention and treatment does not look very different from corruption found in other areas of the health sector. However, there is a difference between the significance of fake HIV/AIDS drugs and the problem of other counterfeit drugs, because of the scale and nature of the HIV virus – a fatal and stigmatised disease that affects millions of people and can only be contained by expensive drugs. These factors magnify the impact of counterfeit medicines. Treatment is not available to all who need it: in Africa, Asia and the rest of the developing world, many are excluded through financial and cultural constraints or distance from health facilities. Access to HIV/AIDS medication – anti-retroviral drugs (ARVs) for all people that are infected – is still a real challenge. While demand exceeds supply, it is not surprising that bribery is rife. Therefore, faking ARVs is much more profitable than faking other drugs, due to their high demand and value.

In addition, high-value drugs such as ARVs are vulnerable in the procurement and distribution process. 'Where ARVs are provided for free or at heavily subsidised rates through donor-funded programmes, requests for "top-up payments" are common' (Taylor and Dickinson 2006: 105). There is a huge black market for ARVs (for example in Nairobi, Kenya), in which patients sell their subsidised drugs, and counterfeits and those leaked out of the healthcare system are also sold on the black market. Many patients sell their own medication because it is their only valuable commodity. This can have dangerous consequences:

> *The problem ... is that ARVs are effective only when there is rigid adherence to the treatment protocol. Buying treatment from those who know little about the appropriate combinations, side-effects or dosage, and substituting one drug for another depending upon availability, means treatment is likely to become ineffective and result in the development of resistance to ARVs (Taylor and Dickinson 2006: 106).*

Solutions could be competition from companies developing cheaper generic drugs, and different pricing between the developed and the developing world by the big pharmaceutical companies. These developments have already resulted in the lowering of prices of ARVs. However, they have also opened up a new door for fraudsters to make profits:

> *A month's supply of GlaxoSmithKline's Combivir, for example, costs around US \$610 in Britain and US \$20 in Uganda, Tanzania and Kenya. The potential profit from re-importation or smuggling is large for vendors in developing countries and drug brokers in developed countries. How much of a problem this is in reality is controversial, however, and there have been allegations that the pharmaceutical countries are exaggerating the scale of the problem in order to dampen the pressure for differential pricing (Taylor and Dickinson 2006: 106).*

List 11.1   Global HIV/AIDS statistics 2009

- 30.8 million adults and 2.5 million children were living with HIV/AIDS at the end of 2009 (UNAIDS 2010: 182).
- There are 16.6 million orphans due to AIDS (under 18 years) (UNAIDS 2010: 186).
- The overwhelming majority of people with HIV live in low- and middle-income countries. (AVERT 2010).
- Sub-Saharan Africa has just over 10 per cent of the world's population, but is home to 68 per cent of all people living with HIV and is by far the worst-affected region in the world (AVERT 2010).

While the international response to the HIV/AIDS epidemic has increased in recent years, there are pressures to spend large sums of aid money in countries with a limited capacity to oversee its correct usage. In 2004, HIV/AIDS resource flows were around \$8 billion and in 2007, around \$10 billion (Taylor and Dickinson 2006: 104; Dickinson 2006). However, scaling up aid budgets without paying more attention to anti-corruption safeguards to ensure their proper use only provides further opportunity for corruption.

There are many cases reported of misappropriation and theft by Health Ministries and National AIDS Councils of funds allocated for HIV/AIDS treatment. These institutions for coordinating and overseeing the allocation of national responses and international aid often lack transparency. For example, the Zimbabwean government collects $20 million annually through an 'AIDS levy' imposed since 2000 on all employees, whereby 3 per cent of their gross salaries go towards a fund administered by the National Aids Council. However, 'no information about how the fund is used and who benefits from it has ever been made public' (Taylor and Dickinson 2006: 107). The implications of locating National AIDS Commissions under the Office of the President, as well as the process of appointing District AIDS Committees and Coordination Units, may be open to political interference.

In the case of HIV/AIDS, increasing the transparency in health services is a vital task that can save many lives. Taylor and Dickinson (2006: 110) recommend the following steps to curb corruption in this area:

• the public needs to be made more aware of the eligibility criteria for ARVs, which should be more consistent within and across countries;

• the public needs to be aware of what they should have to pay and what they will receive;

• quantities and values of drugs should be publicised and health workers need to account for them;

• a complaint mechanism must be made available;

• rebranding and packaging of ARVs sold in developing countries by pharmaceutical companies to minimise risk of re-importing; and

• the introduction of a registration system with a barcode (for example, as introduced by the EU).

The alternative is rather bleak as fake or substandard medicines lead to more chronically ill people and drug resistances which put a strain on public health finances and are far costlier to burden than the price of the legitimate medicines (ibid.: 111).

EXAMPLE: GLAXOSMITHKLINE AND NOT-FOR-PROFIT ARVS

In 2002, pharmaceutical company GlaxoSmithKline (GSK) provided heavily reduced ARV drugs at not-for-profit prices for low income countries which high HIV/AIDS infection rates. In order to distribute the desperately needed drugs as quickly as possible, the company used its European packaging for the reduced price ARVs for over a year. This well intentioned decision however, resulted in large scale corruption in the distribution chain as it created an incentive to divert the cheap medicines back to European markets to sell them for profit (Bale 2006: 92). GSK delivered the drugs to an NGO and the procurement arm of a ministry of health for distribution to African HIV/AIDS patients, however, it later transpired that West African public officials made kickbacks from diverting the ARVs to drug traders who made a profit reselling the medicines, while suffering patients in Africa were left empty handed. In response to the abuse, GSK developed different packages for its ARVs in developing countries, so that they can be more easily distinguished from those in the US and European markets (Bale 2006: 92).

 For a detailed overview of corruption in the health sector, read Transparency International's Global Corruption Report (2006c).

5 Case Study: The Global Fight against Fake Malaria Drugs

Malaria is the world's third deadliest disease, after HIV/AIDS and tuberculosis, infecting globally around 247 million people every year and killed around 781,000 people worldwide in 2009 (WHO 2010b). The threat from malaria has been made worse by the rise in counterfeit malaria drugs, which are mainly originating from China and spreading across Southeast Asia and Africa. Africa has 85 per cent of all malaria deaths worldwide and every 45 seconds a child dies in Africa of malaria and the disease accounts for 20 per cent of all childhood deaths (ibid.). The economic impact and health costs of malaria are immense for heavily affected countries: Malaria can cost up to 40 per cent of public health expenditures and cause 30 per cent to 50 per cent of inpatient hospital admissions (ibid.).

Malaria is a mosquito-borne disease and artesunate, a vital active ingredient of anti-malaria drugs, is the most potent weapon against the malaria parasites in the blood. Artesunate originates from China and is a crucial part of the artemisinin combination therapy for malaria, which is widely used in Southeast Asia and increasingly in Africa. The wrong use of this drug could have very devastating effects on global public health, as it is currently the only drug that has never shown any resistance. However, the continued spread of counterfeit malaria drugs could lead to the emergence of a drug-resistant super-bug, which already has happened in the case of tuberculosis, where the world now has to deal with the so-called extremely multi-drug resistant variants (*East African Standard* 2008).

This danger is becoming a very real one for Southeast Asia, where it is estimated that over half of all artesunate tablets are fake. These findings were confirmed by a 2009 study by the Bill and Melinda Gates Foundation which highlighted the spread of counterfeit malaria drugs from China to Cambodia where they sparked drug resistance to genuine medicines along the Thai–Cambodian border region. While some tablets contained no active ingredient, others contained small amounts of artesunate, which were not effective enough to stop the disease, but could fuel drug resistance (Bennett 2009). Apart from Thailand and Cambodia, Vietnam, Laos and Myanmar are also strongly affected by the rise in counterfeit malaria drugs and in danger of developing resistant strains (*Medical News Today* 2008).

Due to the long exposure to the counterfeit drugs, Southeast Asia is the first region in the world to have developed drug resistance to artesunate (McNeil 2008). There is now growing global concern that this could also soon happen to artemisinin drugs. If the resistant strains spread to other parts of the world, this could have disastrous effects, for example for Africa, where 90 per cent of all malaria cases worldwide exist and which already has a counterfeit drugs problem (Bennett 2009).

Evidence suggests that fake malaria drugs have already made their way to Africa and the counterfeit malaria epidemic is no longer only confined to Southeast Asia. Samples bought in six African cities showed that 35 per cent of malaria drugs did not contain enough active ingredient (McNeil 2008). UNODC estimated in 2009 that around 45 million courses of counterfeit malaria drugs, worth $438m, are trafficked ever year from China and India to West Africa (Bennett 2010).

Research over the last decade focussing on Southeast Asia has revealed some interesting insights into the trade: surveys between 2000 and 2007 conducted in Laos, Vietnam, Myanmar and Cambodia by scientists and researchers from Bangkok and Oxford University, together with support by the Wellcome Trust, found that 30–50 per cent of malaria drugs from pharmacies in these countries were in fact counterfeit (McGivering 2007). Most of the drugs contained no artesunate, others potentially toxic or wrong ingredients such as starch or paracetamol. To pass screening tests, some of the fake drugs sampled contained only small amounts of artesunate, not enough to halt the disease in sufferers, but enough to cause drug resistance (*Medical News Today* 2008).

In 2005, a collaborative investigation, 'Operation Jupiter', coordinated by Interpol, WHO, the Wellcome Trust University and Chinese authorities started to investigate samples of real and fake atesunate (Mansell 2008). Scientists examined the pollen contamination of the tablets using forensic chemistry in order to track down the location of the manufacturer and found that the counterfeit artesunate must have originated in Southern China (ibid.). This enabled Chinese police to arrest a trader in Yunnan province who had sold 240,000 blisterpacks. Authorities were able to seize 24,000 of the packs, but the rest had reportedly already been sold on to Myanmar. Despite the success of this investigation, it is not likely to be replicated on a large scale, as the laboratory checks are very costly and can only be done in very few specialised facilities (ibid.).

It has long been suggested that criminal networks are producing the fake artesunate on an industrial scale and with high-tech know how (McGivering 2007). Experts believe that China and India are the biggest source of fake malaria tablets worldwide (Hilsum 2007). In response to the counterfeiters and worried about their reputation and profits, legitimate Chinese artesunate manufacturers have developed holograms for their blisterpacks, however, even these have already been quite successfully copied by the illicit traders (ibid.).

A different method to help people distinguish between real and fake malaria medicines has been introduced in Africa, where an innovative pilot scheme using mobile phones was started in 2010 in Nigeria and Ghana. A unique scratch code has been placed on more than 500,000 pill packages and medicine bottles to stop the rise in counterfeit medicines. The codes can be texted to a free phone number and an authentication message will be received back. Using the codes will allow people to identify pharmacies, surgeries and hospitals they can trust (BBC News 2010b). Each scratch off code can only be used once to prevent fraud and attempts to reuse them will be flagged up, making patients aware that they are being given dangerous medication. It is hoped that these customers will inform authorities and take matters up with the pharmacy, which will in return increase pressure on pharmacies to check their supplies. The scheme is advertised through posters in pharmacies, radio advertisements and text messages. Mobile phones are a technology that is widespread in Africa and that millions of people have access through (Bennett 2010). If successful, the pilot is planned to be extended to six million medicines over one year and to other countries, such as Kenya, Tanzania, Liberia, Benin and Uganda (Bennett 2010). The system has been developed by Hewlett-Packard Co. and mPedigree Network Ltd and was first trialled in 2008 with pain killing syrup for children in Ghana – all 3,000 customers sent in the scratch codes for verification (Bennett 2010). The malaria pilot will hopefully also turn out successful and could be real breakthrough for the whole region if rolled out to other countries. The World Health Organization believes that 200,000 of annual malaria deaths could be prevented if the medicines were genuine (MacKinnon 2007).

Study Questions

- In what ways does corruption affect the international health sector in both high income and low income countries? Are health systems affected differently?

- What are the implications of counterfeit drugs, in particular in respect of diseases such as HIV/AIDS, malaria and tuberculosis?

- Examine the efforts of the international community to stop the spread of counterfeit medicines. What role could the pharmaceutical industry play?

12

Key Points and Suggestions for Further Study

The premise of this text has been that the proliferation of corruption transnationally – its 'internationalisation' – poses distinct challenges for the international community. Recognition of corruption as a transnational problem is reflected in the increased attention being given to the issue by actors in the international community.

As described in Part I, analysts have recognised the need to attempt to quantify the nature and scale of the problem, and identify the causes and consequences of corruption. Correspondingly, they have sought to theorise the existence and prevalence of corruption across different institutional and political settings, and translate theses analyses into policy-relevant findings. Chapters 2 and 3 introduced some of these key themes, by summarising literature which engaged with the following questions:

- Is it possible to measure the scale of corruption globally?

- Is it possible to identify the causes of corruption?

- What is the impact of corruption?

- To what extent does corruption exist in different parts of the world?

This literature highlights the range of interpretations on the relative merits of different approaches towards conceptualising and studying corruption. Differences notwithstanding, recent years have witnessed a rising tide of counter corruption activity, both at national and international levels. The UK, for example, has witnessed the creation of a National Fraud Authority to counter public sector corruption, and a drive to push through anti-bribery legislation. Internationally, as described in Chapter 4, states operating at regional and international levels have forged links to create a broad range of legislative measures to counter corruption. Non-state actors are also driving forward counter corruption campaigns, as we saw in Chapter 5, though the relative successes of these counter measures are the subject of some debate.

In Part III we considered specific instances of corruption in the international community, from wide-ranging sectors such as politics, business, finance, transnational crime, aid and health. As the varied case studies demonstrate, corruption pervades many levels of international society. Indeed, the subject is so broad that any number of additional case studies and sectors could be considered, which are both topical and relevant. For example, we would be particularly interested to further explore corruption in environmental politics and food security, international sports, and post-conflict reconstruction and peacebuilding.

In respect of environmental sustainability, there are increasing concerns that some of the issues raised by climate change may create new opportunities for corruption. For example, a recent report by the Water Integrity Network (WIN) published findings from an expert consultation on the relationship between water, corruption and climate change (Water Integrity Network 2010). The group raised significant concerns about the future of control over water resources, the possibility for corruption in the provision of water, and how future flows of money into this sector will be managed (ibid.: 2). Similarly, as environmental challenges threaten to disrupt global food supplies, there is concern that countries without transparent and accountable social and governance systems will fail to provide food for their citizens.

In the field of international sports, football, tennis, basketball and cricket have all fallen foul of some form of corruption. Scandals in recent history abound, from vote rigging and ticket scandals in relation to FIFA (the International Federation of Football Association), to bribe-paying within the IOC (International Olympic Committee), and more recently, the banning of three Pakistani cricketers for conspiring to fix matches.

In terms of peacebuilding, corruption has been identified as a key challenge for post-conflict reconstruction efforts. Not only does it have the potential to undermine the legitimacy and effectiveness of political, economic and social institutions, but it can also potentially disrupt peacebuilding efforts through the diversion of funds away from reconstruction projects. This is a particularly pertinent issue for regions where there is conflict over natural resources vital for basic human security.

Unfortunately, it has been beyond the scope of this text to explore these issues in further detail. However, they offer interesting opportunities for further study.

One of the key themes that has emerged from the preceding chapters is that corruption should no longer be seen in narrow terms, as an economic crime with no direct victims, nor as an issue with only local relevance and impact. The human costs of corruption worldwide are identifiable and significant: in many parts of the world its prevalence has the potential to produce human rights violations, and deprive people of access to basic services. Fighting corruption and promoting human rights can therefore be seen, in many respects, as two sides of the same coin.

Bibliography

Ackerman, J. 2011. Mexico, chief casualty of America's 'war on drugs'. *The Guardian*. [Online, 18 February] Available at: http://www.guardian.co.uk/commentisfree/cifamerica/2011/feb/18/drugs-trade-drugs [accessed: 27 February 2011].

Ades, A., and Di Tella, R. 1997. National champions and corruption: some unpleasant interventionist arithmetic. *The Economic Journal*, 107, 1023–1042.

African Union. 2003. *African Union convention on preventing and combating corruption*. [Online] Available at: www.africa-union.org/Official_documents /Treaties_%20Conventions_%20Protocols/Convention%20on%20 Combating%20Corruption.pdf [accessed: 26 January 2011].

Akunyili, D. 2006. The fight against counterfeit drugs in Nigeria, in *Global Corruption Report 2006: Special Focus, Corruption and Health*, edited by Transparency International. London: Pluto Press, 96–99.

Aldrighi, D. 2009. From conflict to alignment of interests: structuring internal corporate governance to minimise corruption risks, in *Global Corruption Report 2009: Corruption and the Private Sector*, edited by Transparency International. Cambridge and New York: University Press, 88–96.

Allen, P. 2010. Rogue trader jailed for bank's collapse and told to pay £4bn. *The Evening Standard*. [Online, 5 October] Available at: http://www.thisislondon. co.uk/standard/article-23884899-rogue-trader-jailed-for-banks-collapse-and-told-to-pay-pound-41bn.do [accessed: 27 February 2011].

Aranaga, C. 2009. Central Asia countries remain major drug transit routes. *US State Department's Bureau of International Information Programs*. [Online, 2 March] Available at: http://www.america.gov/st/democracyhr-english/2009/ March/20090302151112ecaganara0.9702417.html [accessed: 27 February 2011].

Arvis, J., and Berenbeim, R. 2003. *Fighting Corruption in East Asia: Solutions From the Private Sector*. Washington, DC: World Bank.

Asian Development Bank. 1998. *Anticorruption: Our Framework, Policies and Strategies*. Manila: Asian Development Bank.

Asian Development Bank. 2008. *Anticorruption and integrity.* [Online] Available at: www.adb.org/Documents/Policies/Anticorruption/anticorrupt300.asp?p=antipubs [accessed: 25 February 2011].

Asian Development Bank and Organisation for Economic Co-operation and Development (OECD) 2004. *Anti-Corruption Policies in Asia and the Pacific. The Legal and Institutional Frameworks.* Manila: Asian Development Bank.

AVERT 2010. *Worldwide HIV & AIDS statistics.* [Online] Available at: http://www.avert.org/worldstats.htm [accessed: 27 February 2011].

Bale, H. 2006. Promoting trust and transparency in pharmaceutical companies; an industry perspective, in *Global Corruption Report 2006: Special Focus, Corruption and Health,* edited by Transparency International. London: Pluto Press, 91–93.

Barrionuevo, A. 2006. Enron's Skilling is sentenced to 24 years. *The New York Times.* [Online, 24 October] Available at: http://www.nytimes.com/2006/10/24/business/24enron.html [accessed: 27 February 2011].

Basel Institute for Governance (n.d.). *International Centre for Asset Recovery (ICAR).* [Online] Available at: http://www.assetrecovery.org/kc/node/7145c5fb-a33e-11dc-bf1b-335d0754ba85.4 [accessed: 27 January 2011].

Bass, E. 2005. Uganda is learning from its Global Fund grant suspension. *The Lancet.* [Online, 26 November] Available at: http://www.thelancet.com/journals/lancet/issue/vol366no9500/PIIS0140-6736(05)X6167-0 [accessed: 27 February 2011].

BBC News 1999. *Citibank censured over money laundering.* [Online, 9 November] Available at: http://news.bbc.co.uk/1/hi/world/americas/511951.stm [accessed: 27 February 2011].

BBC News 2000. *German sleaze: The story so far.* [Online, 17 February] Available at: http://news.bbc.co.uk/1/hi/world/europe/590558.stm [accessed: 27 February 2011].

BBC News 2001. *Kohl charges dropped.* [Online, 2 March] Available at: http://news.bbc.co.uk/1/hi/world/europe/1198301.stm [accessed: 27 February 2011].

BBC News 2002a. *Anderson guilty in Enron case.* [Online, 15 June] Available at: http://news.bbc.co.uk/1/hi/business/2047122.stm [accessed: 27 February 2011].

BBC News 2002b. *Child refugee sex scandal.* [Online, 26 February] Available at: http://news.bbc.co.uk/1/hi/world/africa/1842512.stm [accessed: 27 February 2011].

BBC News 2003. *Q and A: Eurostat scandal.* [Online, 25 September] Available at: http://news.bbc.co.uk/1/hi/world/europe/3138390.stm [accessed: 27 February 2011].

BBC News 2004. *'Pinochet' bank to be sold.* [Online, 16 July] Available at: http://news.bbc.co.uk/1/hi/business/4213757.stm [accessed: 27 February 2011].

BBC News 2005. *Timeline: Oil-for-food scandal.* [Online, 7 September] Available at: http://news.bbc.co.uk/1/hi/world/middle_east/4445609.stm [accessed: 27 February 2011].

BBC News 2006. *Court rules against French PM.* [Online, 11 July] Available at: http://news.bbc.co.uk/1/hi/world/europe/5167940.stm [accessed: 27 February 2011].

BBC News 2007a. *Q&A: The BAE–Saudi allegations.* [Online, 30 July] Available at: http://news.bbc.co.uk/go/pr/fr/-/1/hi/business/6729489.stm [accessed: 27 February 2011].

BBC News 2007b. *Saudi prince 'received arms cash'.* [Online, 7 June] Available at: http://news.bbc.co.uk/go/pr/fr/-/1/hi/business/6728773.stm [accessed: 27 February 2011].

BBC News 2007c. *Lord Woolf to head BAE's review.* [Online, 11 June] Available at: http://news.bbc.co.uk/go/pr/fr/-/1/hi/business/6739805.stm [accessed: 27 February 2011].

BBC News 2008a. *MEP fraud claims to face scrutiny.* [Online, 21 February] Available at: http://news.bbc.co.uk/1/hi/world/europe/7256045.stm [accessed: 27 February 2011].

BBC News 2008b. *MEP makes fraud report public.* [Online, 5 March] Available at: http://news.bbc.co.uk/1/hi/world/europe/7280032.stm [accessed: 27 February 2011].

BBC News 2008c. *French trader 'concealed deals'.* [Online, 28 January] Available at: http://news.bbc.co.uk/1/hi/business/7211796.stm [accessed: 27 February 2011].

BBC News 2008d. *How rogue traders lose billions.* [Online, 24 January] Available at: http://news.bbc.co.uk/1/hi/business/7206798.stm [accessed: 27 February 2011].

BBC News 2008e. *World Bank 'uncovers India fraud'.* [Online, 11 January] Available at: http://news.bbc.co.uk/1/hi/7184345.stm [accessed: 27 February 2011].

BBC News 2009a. *Unravelling the 'Madoff hustle'.* [Online, 26 June] Available at: http://news.bbc.co.uk/1/hi/8120411.stm [accessed: 27 February 2011].

BBC News 2009b. *Fraudster Madoff gets 150 years.* [Online, 29 June] Available at: http://news.bbc.co.uk/1/hi/8124838.stm [accessed: 27 February 2011].

BBC News 2009c. *Madoff accepts 150-year sentence.* [Online, 9 July] Available at: http://news.bbc.co.uk/1/hi/8142931.stm [accessed: 27 February 2011].

BBC News 2010a. *Timeline: BAE corruption probes*. [Online, 2 May] Available at: http://news.bbc.co.uk/1/hi/business/8501655.stm [accessed: 27 February 2011].

BBC News 2010b. *Scratch codes aid malaria fight*. [Online, 14 December] Available at: http://www.bbc.co.uk/news/technology-11983655 [accessed: 27 February 2011].

BBC News 2011a. *Ousted Tunisian leader Ben Ali's family 'arrested'*. [Online, 20 January] Available at: http://www.bbc.co.uk/news/world-africa-12233850 [accessed: 27 February 2011].

BBC News 2011b. *'Arms dealer' Viktor Bout's lawyer challenges US trial*. [Online, 22 January] Available at: http://www.bbc.co.uk/news/world-us-canada-12257934 [accessed at: 27 February 2011].

Beaver, W. 1994. Nuclear nightmares in the Philippines. *Journal of Business Ethics*, 13(4), 271–279.

Bennett, S. 2009. Fake malaria drug spread, breed resistance to lethal parasite. *Bloomberg*. [Online, 9 October] Available at: http://www.bloomberg.com/apps/news?pid=newsarchive&sid=aWdXQmrHzLxA [accessed: 27 February 2011].

Bennett, S. 2010. Scratch and win war on Africa's counterfeit malaria medicines gets under way. *Bloomberg*. [Online, 14 May] Available at: http://www.bloomberg.com/news/2010-05-13/scratch-win-war-on-africa-s-counterfeit-malaria-medicines-gets-under-way.html [accessed: 27 February 2011].

Bloomberg 1995. *Westinghouse pact with Philippines*. [Online, 16 October] Available at: http://query.nytimes.com/gst/fullpage.html?res=9407E7D91039F935A25753C1A963958260 [accessed: 27 February 2011].

Bogere, H. 2009. Global Fund releases billions to Uganda. *The Ugandan Observer*. [Online, 29 July] Available at: http://www.observer.ug/index.php?option=com_content&view=article&id=4479:global-fund-releases-billions-to-uganda [accessed: 27 February 2011].

Borger, J. 2008. Viktor Bout: secretive and successful 'Merchant of Death'. *The Guardian*. [Online, 22 December] Available at: http://www.guardian.co.uk/world/2008/dec/22/viktor-bout-profile [accessed: 27 February 2011].

Bowers, C. 2009. *Hawala, money laundering and terrorism financing. Micro-lending as an illicit remittance*. [Online] Available at: http://law.du.edu/documents/djilp/37No3/Hawala-Money-Laundering-Terrorism-Finance-Micro-Lending-End-Illicit-Remittance-Charles-B-Bowers.pdf [accessed: 27 February 2011].

Bracking, S. (ed.) 2007. *Corruption and Development. The Anti-Corruption Campaigns*. Basingstoke: Palgrave Macmillan.

Brademas, J. 1999. *Countering Political Corruption: Can Money in Politics be Contained?* Paper to the Conference: 9th International Anti-Corruption Conference, Durban, 10–15 October. [Online] Available at: http://www.9iacc. org/papers/day2/ws5/d2ws5_jbrademas.html [accessed: 27 February 2011].

Brady, B. 2006. Saudi bribe probe 'didn't lack evidence'. *The Scotsmen*. [Online, 17 December] Available at: http://news.scotsman.com/international. cfm?id=1872952006 [accessed: 27 February 2011].

Bräutigam, D. 2009. When China goes shopping abroad: new pressure for corporate integrity? in *Global Corruption Report 2009. Corruption and the Private Sector*, edited by Zinnbauer D., Dobson, R. and Despota, K. Cambridge and New York: Cambridge University Press, 67–69.

British Petroleum (BP) 2005. *Code of Conduct. Governments and communities.* [Online, British Petroleum] Available at: www.bp.com/liveassets/bp_ internet/globalbp/STAGING/global_assets/downloads/C/coc_en_gov_ comm.pdf [accessed: 27 February 2011].

Brown, A.J. 2006. What are we trying to measure? Reviewing the basics of corruption definition, in *Measuring Corruption*, edited by C. Sampford, A. Shacklock, C. Connors and F. Galtung. Aldershot: Ashgate, 57–79.

Brown, C. 2005. *Understanding International Relations.* 3rd edition. Basingstoke: Palgrave Macmillan.

Brown, E. and Cloke, J. 2006. The critical business of corruption. *Critical Perspectives on International Business*, 2(4), 275–298.

Budima, G. 2006. Can corruption and economic crime be controlled in developing economies, and if so, is the cost worth it? *Journal of Financial Crime*, 13(4), 408–419.

Burchill, S., Linklater, A., Richard, D., Donnelly, J., Paterson, M., Reus-Smit, C. and True, J. 2005. *Theories of International Relations.* 3rd edition. Basingstoke: Palgrave Macmillan.

Burns, J. 1998. House of graft: Tracing the Bhutto Millions – A special report: Bhutto clan leaves trial of corruption. *The New York Times.* [Online, 9 January] Available at: http://www.nytimes.com/1998/01/09/world/house-graft-tracing-bhutto-millions-special-report-bhutto-clan-leaves-trail.html [accessed: 27 February 2011].

Buscaglia, E. and van Djik 2003. Controlling organized crime in the public sector. *Forum on Crime and Society*, 3(1/2), 6–18.

Busch, R.S. 2008. *Healthcare Fraud: Auditing and Detection Guide.* New York: Wiley.

Calvert, J., Foster, H., Waite, R. and Parry, S. 2007. Factory for fake prescription drugs. *The Sunday Times.* [Online, 23 September] Available at: www.

timesonline.co.uk/tol/news/uk/health/article2511583.ece   [accessed: 27 February 2011].

Carver, J. 2004. The hunt for looted state assets: the case of Benazir Bhutto, in *Global Corruption Report 2004*, edited by Transparency International. London: Pluto Press, 102–104.

CFO Magazine. 2005. *Multinationals take anti-bribery pledge.* [Online] Available at: www.cfo.com/article.cfm/3618802?f=search [accessed: 27 February 2011].

Chaikin, D. and Sharman, J.C. 2009. *Corruption and Money Laundering: A Symbiotic Relationship.* New York and London: Palgrave Macmillan.

Chaikin, D. 2010. *U4 Brief: International anti-money laundering laws.* [Online] Available at: http://www.cmi.no/publications/file/3775-international-anti-money-laundering-laws-improving.pdf [accessed: 27 February 2011].

Charnovitz, S. 2006. Nongovernmental organisations and international law. *The American Journal of International Law,* 100(2), 348–372.

Chêne, M. 2008. *U4 Expert Answer: Organised crime and corruption.* [Online, 28 May] Available at: http://www.u4.no/helpdesk/helpdesk/query.cfm?id=171 [accessed: 27 February 2011].

Chibber, K. 2009. Madoff's road to riches ends in court. *BBC News.* [Online, 12 March] Available at: http://news.bbc.co.uk/1/hi/7939145.stm [accessed: 27 February 2011]

Chrisafis, A., Treanor, J. and Allen, K. 2008. He lost his bank £3.7 billion. So was it his fault the markets crashed? *The Guardian.* [Online, 25 January] Available at: www.guardian.co.uk/business/2008/jan/25/banking.france [acessed: 27 February 2011].

Clark, A. 2010. Goldman Sachs charged with $1bn fraud over toxic sub-prime securities. *The Guardian.* [Online, 16 April] Available at: http://www.guardian.co.uk/business/2010/apr/16/goldman-sachs-fraud-charges   [accessed: 27 February 2011].

Clark, E. 2008. Counterfeit medicines: the pill that kill. *The Telegraph* [Online, 5 April] Available at: http://www.telegraph.co.uk/health/3354135/Counterfeit-medicines-the-pills-that-kill.html [accessed: 27 February 2011].

Cockburn, R., Newton, P.N., Agyarko, E.K., Akunyili, D. and White, N.J. 2005. The global threat of counterfeit drugs: why industry and governments must communicate the dangers. *Public Library of Science.* [Online] Available at: http://medicine.plosjournals.org/perlserv/?request=get-document&doi=10.1371/journal.pmed.0020100 [accessed: 27 February 2011].

Cole, J. 2011. US ignored Tunisian corruption. *Aljazeera.* [Online, 18 January] Available at: http://english.aljazeera.net/indepth/opinion/2011/01/20111171299907176.html [accessed: 27 February 2011].

Committee of Independent Experts 1999. *Second report on reform of the commission analysis of current practice and proposals for tackling mismanagement, irregularities and fraud.* [Online] Available at: www.europarl.europa.eu/experts/default_en.htm [accessed: 27 February 2011].

Control Risks and Simmons & Simmons 2006. *International business attitudes to corruption – survey 2006.* [Online] Available at: www.crg.com/pdf/corruption _survey_2006_V3.pdf [accessed: 27 February 2011].

Council of Europe (COE). 1999a. *Criminal law convention on corruption.* [Online] Available at: http://conventions.coe.int/Treaty/EN/Treaties/Html/ 173.htm [accessed: 26 January 2011].

Council of Europe (COE). 1999b. *Civil law convention on corruption.* [Online] Available at: http://conventions.coe.int/Treaty/EN/Treaties/Html/174.htm [accessed: 26 January 2011].

Council of Europe (COE). 2005. *Council of Europe convention on laundering, search, seizure and confiscation of the proceeds from crime and on the financing of terrorism.* [Online] available at: http://conventions.coe.int/Treaty/EN/ Treaties/Html/198.htm [accessed: 27 February 2011].

Council of Europe (COE). n.d. *The fight against corruption a priority for the Council of Europe.* [Online] Available at: http://www.coe.int/t/dghl/monitoring/ greco/general/1.%20The%20Fight%20against%20Corruption%20-%20A%20 Priority%20for%20the%20CoE_en.asp [accessed: 26 January 2011].

Cremer, G. 1998. On the problem of misuse in emergency aid. *Journal of Humanitarian Assistance.* [Online, 15 June] Available at: http://jha. ac/1998/06/15/on-the-problem-of-misuse-in-emergency-aid [accessed: 27 February 2011].

Cremer, G. 2008. *Corruption and Development Aid. Confronting the Challenges.* London: Lynne Rienner.

Creswell, J. and Thomas Jr., L. 2009. The talented Mr. Madoff. *The New York Times.* [Online, 24 January] Available at: http://www.nytimes.com/2009/01/25/ business/25bernie.html [accessed: 27 February 2011].

Dahl, Matilda. 2009. States under scrutiny: TI in the Baltics, in *Governments, NGOs and Anti-Corruption: The New Integrity Warriors,* edited by L. de Sousa, B. Hindess and P. Larmour. London and New York: Routledge, 152–167.

Davies, L. 2010a. Nicolas Sarkozy denies campaign took illegal donations. *The Guardian.* [Online, 6 July] Available at: http://www.guardian.co.uk/ world/2010/jul/06/nicolas-sarkozy-denies-illegal-donation [accessed: 27 February 2011].

Davies, L . 2010b. French rogue trader Jerome Kerviel sentenced to jail and €4.9bn fine. *The Guardian.* [Online, 5 October] Available at: http://www.

guardian.co.uk/business/2010/oct/05/jerome-kerviel-jail-sentence [accessed: 27 February 2011].

Deen, T. 2000. Tokyo finds money can't buy UN's love. *The Asian Times.* [Online, 20 July] Available at: http://www.atimes.com/japan-econ/BG20Dh01.html [accessed: 27 February 2011].

DellaVigna, S. and La Ferrara, E. 2008. *Detecting Illegal Arms Trade.* NBER Working Paper. No. 13355. [Online, 18 March] Available at: http://www. nber.org/papers/w13355 [accessed: 27 February 2011].

De Sousa, L. 2009. TI in search of a consistency: the institutionalisation and franchising of the global anti-corruption doctrine, in *Governments, NGOs and Anti-Corruption: The New Integrity Warriors,* edited by L. de Sousa, B. Hindess and P. Larmour. London and New York: Routledge, 186–214.

De Sousa, L., Hindess, B. and Larmour, P. (eds.). 2009. *Governments, NGOs and Anti-Corruption: The New Integrity Warriors.* London: Routledge.

De Sousa, L., Larmour, P. and Hindess, B. 2009. Introduction, in *Governments, NGOs and Anti-Corruption: The New Integrity Warriors,* edited by L. de Sousa, B. Hindess and P. Larmour. London and New York: Routledge, 1–15.

Dickinson, C. 2006. *Note from the seminar on corruption and health.* HLSP Institute. [Online] Available at: www.transparency.org/content/download/5028/29524/ file/seminar_on_corruption_health.pdf [accessed: 27 February 2011].

Duffield, M., Jok, M., O'Reilly, F., Ryle, J. and Winter, P. 2000. *Sudan: The Unintended Consequences of Humanitarian Assistance – A Report to the European Commission Humanitarian Office* (ECHO). Dublin: Trinity College.

Dumaine, B. 1986. The $2.2 billion nuclear fiasco. *CNN Money.* [Online, 1 September] Available at: http://money.cnn.com/magazines/fortune/fortune_ archive/1986/09/01/67989/index.htm [accessed: 27 February 2011].

East African Standard 2008. *Fake malaria drugs signal catastrophe.* [Online, 1 June] Available at: http://www.fightingmalaria.org/news.aspx?id=1076 [accessed: 27 February 2011].

Eigen, P. 2003. Corruption is the enemy of development. *Corporate responsibility.* [Online] Available at: http://www.responsiblepractice.com/english/issues/ transparency/ [accessed: 27 February 2011].

Eigen, P. and Eigen-Zucchi, C. 2003. *Corruption and global public goods.* [Online: United Nations Development Programme] Available at: http://www.undp. org/globalpublicgoods/globalization/pdfs/Eigen.pdf [accessed: 27 February 2011].

Elliott, K.A. 1997. Introduction, in *Corruption and the Global Economy* edited by K.A. Elliott . Washington, DC: Institute for International Economics, 1–5.

Elliott, K.A. (ed.). 1997. *Corruption and the Global Economy.* Washington, DC: Institute for International Economics.

Ernst & Young. 2008. *10th Global fraud survey: Corruption or compliance –weighing the costs*. [Online] Available at: http://www.ey.com/Publication/vwLUAssets/ Weighing_the_costs_of_corruption_or_compliance:_10th_Global_Fraud_ Survey/$FILE/EY_10th_Global_Fraud_Survey.pdf [accessed: 4 February 2011].

Ernst & Young (2010). *11th Global fraud survey: Driving ethical growth – new markets, new challenges*. [Online] Available at http://www.ey.com/ Publication/vwLUAssets/Driving_ethical_growth_-_new_markets,_new_ challenges:_11th_Global_Fraud_Survey/$FILE/EY_11th_Global_Fraud_ Survey.pdf [accessed 4 February 2011].

Escobar, R. 2010. *Escobar: The Inside Story of Pablo Escobar, the World's Most Powerful Criminal*. London: Hodder and Stoughton.

Euromonitor 2008. *OTC healthcare in Kenya*. [Online] Available at: www. euromonitor.com/OTC_Healthcare_in_Kenya#exec [accessed: 27 February 2011].

European Anti-Fraud Office (OLAF). n.d. *European Commission: OLAF*. [Online] Available at: http://ec.europa.eu/dgs/olaf/mission/mission/index_en.html [accessed: 26 January 2011].

Evans, G. and Newman, J. 1998. *The Penguin Dictionary of International Relations*. London: Penguin.

Evans, R. and Leigh, D. 2010. Judge 'astonished' by corruption denials as he fines BAE £500,000. *The Guardian*. [Online, 21 December] Available at: http://www.guardian.co.uk/world/2010/dec/21/bae-fined-illicit-payments-middleman [accessed: 27 February 2011].

Ewins, P., Harvey, P., Savage, K. and Jacobs, A. 2006. *Mapping the Risk of Corruption in Humanitarian Action. A Report for Transparency International and the U4 Anticorruption Resource Centre*. Overseas Development Institute. [Online] Available at: http://www.odi.org.uk/HPG/papers/TIU4.pdf [accessed: 27 February 2011].

Fairbairn, D., Shum, A., Schönig, W. and Milbradt, C. 2007. *Intellectual property and the fight against counterfeit drugs*. [Online, February] Available at: www.iam-magazine.com/issues/article.ashx?g=66570cbc-8e93-48e6-9488-3c898511b73c [accessed: 27 February 2011].

Fallon, A. 2010. Viktor Bout: five passports, half a dozen languages and alleged friend to all sides. *The Guardian*. [Online, 20 August] Available at: http:// www.guardian.co.uk/world/2010/aug/20/viktor-bout-profile [accessed: 27 February 2011].

Fenner, G. 2009. Financial Institutions and the fight against corruption, in *Global Corruption Report 2009. Corruption and the Private Sector*, edited by

Transparency International. Cambridge and New York: University Press, 138–144.

Financial Action Task Force (FATF). 2008. *Terrorist financing*. [Online] Available at: www.fatf-gafi.org/dataoecd/28/43/40285899.pdf [accessed: 27 February 2011].

Financial Action Task Force (FATF) n.d. *What is FATF?* [Online] Available at: http://www.fatf-gafi.org/document/57/0,3746,en_322503 79_32235720_34432121_1_1_1_1,00.html [accessed: 27 February 2011].

Financial Industry Regulatory Authority (FINRA) n.d. *About the Financial Industry Regulatory Authority*. [Online] Available at: http://www.finra.org/AboutFINRA/ [accessed: 27 February 2011].

Financial Services Authority (FSA) n.d.a. *International and EU*. [Online] Available at: www.fsa.gov.uk/pages/About/What/International/index.shtml [accessed: 27 February 2011].

Financial Services Authority (FSA) n.d.b. *Essential facts about the Financial Services Authority*. [Online] Available at: http://www.fsa.gov.uk/pubs/other/essential_facts.pdf [accessed: 27 February 2011].

Freedom House 2009. *Freedom in the world – Italy*. [Online] Available at: http://freedomhouse.org/inc/content/pubs/fiw/inc_country_detail.cfm?year=2009&country=7631&pf [accessed: 27 February 2011].

Frey, B. 1991. The public choice view of international political economy, in *The Political Economy of International Organizations*, edited by R. Vaubel, and T.D. Willett Boulder: Westview Press, 7–26.

Frison-Roche, M.A. 2005. *The relationship between European financial regulation and national regulators*. [Online: LSE seminar abstract] Available at: www.lse.ac.uk/collections/CARR/events/previousSeminars/frisonRoche.htm [accessed: 27 February 2011].

Fritz, V. and Kolstad, I. 2008. *U4 Issue: Corruption and aid modalities*. [Online] Available at: http://www.u4.no/document/publication.cfm?3102=corruption-and-aid-modalities [accessed: 27 February 2011].

Fulgeras, A.J. 2003. To bribe or not to bribe. Dealing with the OECD Anti-bribery Convention from a business perspective, in *Controlling Corruption in Asia and the Pacific: Proceedings of the 4th Regional Anti-Corruption Conference*, edited by Asian Development Bank and Organisation for Economic Co-operation and Development Anti-Corruption Initiative for Asia-Pacific, 63–68. [Online] Available at: www.adb.org/Documents/Books/Controlling-Corruption/chapter2.pdf [accessed: 27 February 2011].

Gambetta, D. 2002. Corruption: an analytical map, in *Political Corruption in Transition: A Sceptic's Handbook*, edited by S. Kotkin and A. Sajo. New York: CEU Press, 33–45.

Gerring, J. and Thacker, S. 2004. Political institutions and corruption: the role of unitarism and parliamentarism. *British Journal of Political Science*, 34, 295–330.

Gilligan, G. and Bowman, D. 2007. Countering Corruption: An Australian Perspective, in *Terrorism, Organised Crime and Corruption: Networks and Linkages*, edited by L. Holmes. Cheltenham: Edward Elgar, 170–191.

Global Integrity n.d.a. *Global Integrity's Mission*. [Online] Available at: http://www.globalintegrity.org/about/mission [accessed: 14 November 2011].

Global Integrity n.d.b. *About us*. [Online] Available at: http://www.globalintegrity.org/about [accessed: 14 November 2011].

Global Integrity n.d.c. *Our approach*. [Online] Available at: http://www.globalintegrity.org/about/approach [accessed: 14 November 2011].

Global Integrity n.d.d. *Global Integrity Report*. [Online] Available at: http://www.globalintegrity.org/report [accessed: 14 November 2011].

Global Organisation of Parliamentarians Against Corruption (GOPAC). n.d. *About GOPAC*. [Online] Available at: http://www.gopacnetwork.org/AboutUs/about_en.htm [accessed: 27 January 2011].

Global Transparency Initiative (GTI). n.d.a. *What is the GTI?* [Online] Available at: http://www.ifitransparency.org/about.shtml [accessed 14 October 2011].

Global Transparency Initiative (GTI). n.d.b. *What does the GTI do?* [Online] Available at: http://www.ifitransparency.org/about.shtml?x=44327&als[select]=44327 [accessed: 25 February 2011].

Global Humanitarian Assistance 2011. *Aid to Sudan*. [Online] Available at: http://www.globalhumanitarianassistance.org/aid-to-sudan-1995-2009-new-gha-factsheet-2737.html [accessed: 27 February 2011].

Global Witness. 2009. *Faced with a gun, what can you do?* [Online] Available at: http://www.globalwitness.org/library/faced-gun-what-can-you-do [accessed: 2 February 2011].

Global Witness. 2010a. *Bankrolling brutality – Why European timber company DLH should be held to account for profiting from Liberian conflict timber*. [Online] Available at: http://www.globalwitness.org/library/bankrolling-brutality-why-european-timber-company-dlh-should-be-held-account-profiting [accessed: 2 February 2011].

Global Witness. 2010b. *Annual Review 2009*. [Online] Available at: http://www.globalwitness.org/sites/default/files/pdfs/2009_annual_review.pdf [accessed: 2 February 2011].

Global Witness. n.d. *About us*. [Online] Available at: www.globalwitness.org/pages/en/about_us.html [accessed: 24 January 2011].

Glynn, P., Kobrin, S.J. and Naim, M. 1997. The globalisation of corruption, in *Corruption and the Global Economy*, edited by K.A. Elliott. Washington, DC: Institute for International Economics, 7–27.

Goldfarb, Z. 2010. Goldman Sachs to pay record settlement in fraud suit, change business practices. *The Washington Post.* [Online 16 July] Available at: http://www.washingtonpost.com/wp-dyn/content/article/2010/07/15/AR2010071505111.html [accessed: 27 February 2011].

Goodley, S. 2010. Battle over Madoff fraud shifts to UK as new lawsuit names London directors. *The Guardian.* [Online, 8 December] Available at: http://www.guardian.co.uk/business/2010/dec/08/madoff-legal-battle-shifts-london-directors [accessed: 27 February 2011].

Gordon, J. 2004. UN Oil for Food 'Scandal'. *The Nation.* [Online, 18 November] Available at: http://www.thenation.com/article/un-oil-food-scandal [accessed: 27 February 2011].

Gorta, A. 2006. Corruption risk areas and corruption resistance, in *Measuring Corruption,* edited by C. Sampford, A. Shacklock, C. Connors and F. Galtung. Aldershot: Ashgate, 203–219.

Governance Assessment Portal. n.d. *Corruption.* [Online] Available at: http://gaportal.org/areas-of-governance/corruption [accessed: 10 February 2011].

Gray, C.W. and Kaufmann, D. 1998. Corruption and development. *Finance and Development,* 35, 7–10.

Greenberg, T.S., Gray, L., Schantz, D., Gardner, C. and Latham, M. 2010. *Politically Exposed Persons. Preventive Measures for the Banking Sector.* Washington, DC: The International Bank for Reconstruction and Development/The World Bank.

Griffiths, I. 2009. Where did Madoff's missing billions go? Investigators face uphill task. *The Guardian.* [Online, 30 June] Available at: http://www.guardian.co.uk/business/2009/jun/29/bernard-madoff-investigation-money [accessed: 27 February 2011].

Grix, J. 2002. Introducing students to the generic terminology of social research. *Politics,* 22(3), 175–186.

Group of States against Corruption (GRECO). n.d. *What is GRECO?* [Online] Available at: http://www.coe.int/t/dghl/monitoring/greco/general/3.%20What%20is%20GRECO_en.asp [accessed: 26 January 2011].

Gumbel, P. 2002. Tough act to follow. *Time.* [Online, 15 September] Available at: www.time.com/time/magazine/article/0,9171,351174,00.html [accessed: 27 February 2011].

Gutterman, E. 2005. *NGO Activism and State Compliance with Three anti-corruption Treaties: The role of Transparency International.* Paper to the International Studies Association Convention, Honolulu, March 2005. Available at: www.allacademic.com/meta/p_mla_apa_research_citation/0/7/0/4/2/pages70423/p70423-1.php [accessed 25 February 2011].

Halliday, F. 2004. Global governance: prospects and problems. *The Global Transformations Reader*, edited by D. Held and A. McGrew. Cambridge: Polity Press, 431–441.

Hansard, H.L. 2006. *Lord Goldsmith. BAE Systems: Al Yamamah Contract. cols. 1711–1717 at col. 1712.* [Online, 14 December] Available at: http://www.publications.parliament.uk/pa/ld200607/ldhansrd/text/61214-0014.htm#06121476000283

Harris, P. and McVeigh, K. 2011. Russian arms dealer Viktor Bout found guilty of selling weapons to Farc rebels. *The Guardian* [Online: 2 November 2011] Available at: http://www.guardian.co.uk/world/2011/nov/02/viktor-bout-arms-trade [accessed: 14 November 2011]

Harris, R. 2003. *Political Corruption. In and Beyond the Nation State.* New York: Routledge.

Hasenclever, A., Mayer, P. and Rittberger, V. 1996. Interests, power, knowledge: the study of international regimes. *Mershon International Studies Review*, 40(2), 177–228.

Hasenclever, A., Mayer, P. and Rittberger, V. 1997. *Theories of International Regimes.* Cambridge: Cambridge University Press.

Hassell, N. 2007. The unexpected face of fight to save the whales. *The Times.* [Online, 23 April] Available at: http://business.timesonline.co.uk/tol/business/industry_sectors/natural_resources/article1690260.ece [accessed: 27 February 2011].

Hayman, G. 2009. Corruption and bribery in the extractive industries, in *Global Corruption Report 2009. Corruption and the Private Sector*, edited by Zinnbauer D., Dobson, R. and Despota, K. Cambridge and New York: Cambridge University Press, 54–56.

Hawley, S. 2000. Exporting corruption: privatisation, multinationals and bribery. *Corner House Briefing 19.* [Online] Available at: www.thecornerhouse.org.uk/item.shtml?x=51975 [accessed: 27 February 2011].

Heidenheimer, A. and Johnston, M. (eds). 2001. *Political Corruption: Concepts and Contexts* (3rd edn). New Brunswick, NJ: Transaction.

Heimann, F.F. 1997. Combatting international corruption: the role of the business community, in *Corruption and the Global Economy*, edited by K.A. Elliott. Washington, DC: Institute for International Economics, 147–162.

Held, D., McGrew, A., Goldblatt, D. and Perraton, J. 2005. *Global Transformations: Politics, Economics and Culture.* Oxford: Blackwell.

Henley, J. 1999. Leaked documents reveal extent of Unesco corruption. *The Guardian.* [Online, 18 October] Available at: http://www.guardian.co.uk/world/1999/oct/18/jonhenley1 [accessed: 27 February 2011].

Henriques, D. 2009. Madoff's accountant pleads guilty in scheme. *The New York Times*. [Online, 4 November] Available at: http://www.nytimes.com/2009/11/04/business/04madoff.html [accessed: 27 February 2011].

Hibis 2003. *Sarbanes–Oxley Act: Interpretation with respect to fraud resistance.* [Online] Available at: www.hibis.com/pdf/sarbanes_oxley_and_fraud.pdf [accessed: 27 February 2011].

Hilsum, L. 2007. China's deadly trade in fake drugs. *Channel 4.* [Online, 11 July] Available at: [accessed: 27 February 2011].

Hindess, B. 2009. International anti-corruption as a programme of normalisation, in *Governments, NGOs and Anti-Corruption: The New Integrity Warriors*, edited by L. de Sousa, B. Hindess and P. Larmour. London and New York: Routledge, 19–32.

Hodess, R. 2004. Introduction, in *Transparency International Global Corruption Report 2004*, edited by Hodess, R., Inowlocki, T., Rodriguez, D. and Wolfe, T. London: Pluto Press, 11–18.

Holmes, L. 2006. *Corruption, Post-Communism and Neoliberalism*. US: Duke University Press.

Holmes, L. (ed.). 2007. *Terrorism, Organised Crime and Corruption: Networks and Linkages*. Cheltenham: Edward Elgar.

Hooper, J. 2011. Prosecutors seek Silvio Berlusconi trial over sex claims. *The Guardian*. [Online, 8 February] Available at: http://www.guardian.co.uk/world/2011/feb/08/silvio-berluscon-prosecutors-seek-trial [accessed: 27 February 2011].

Hotten, R. 2010. BAE settles bribery allegations. *BBC News*. [Online, 5 February] Available at: http://news.bbc.co.uk/1/hi/business/8500742.stm [accessed: 27 February 2011].

Houlder, V. 2008. IMF set to end offshore 'stigma'. *The Financial Times*. [Online, 14 July] Available at: http://www.ft.com/cms/s/0/66b8cb70-51ba-11dd-a97c-000077b07658.html#axzz1EXw5jMPb [accessed: 27 February 2011].

Huber-Grabenwaerter, G. and Boehm, F. 2009. Laying the foundations for sound and sustainable development: strengthening corporate integrity in weak governance zones, in *Global Corruption Report 2009*, edited by Transparency International. New York and London: Cambridge University Press, 46–53.

Huberts, L., Lasthuizen, K. and Peeters, C. 2006. Measuring corruption: exploring the iceberg, in *Measuring Corruption*, edited by C. Sampford, A. Shacklock, C. Connors and F. Galtung. Aldershot: Ashgate, 265–293.

Hunt, K. 2008. Market culture 'at root of rogue trading'. *BBC News*. [Online, 24 January] Available at: http://news.bbc.co.uk/1/hi/business/7207563.stm [accessed: 27 February 2011].

Hussman, K. 2011. *Addressing corruption in the health sector. Securing equitable access to health care for everyone.* [Online] Available at: http://www.u4.no/document/publication.cfm?3934=addressing-corruption-in-the-health-sector [accessed: 27 February 2011].

IMPACT (2008). *About us.* Retrieved 21 July 2008, from: www.who.int/impact/about/en

Inman, P. 2011. Mubarak family fortune could reach $70bn, say experts. *The Guardian.* [Online, 4 February] Available at: http://www.guardian.co.uk/world/2011/feb/04/hosni-mubarak-family-fortune [accessed: 27 February 2011].

Integrated Regional Information Networks (IRIN). 2006. *Uganda: Global Fund probe reveals massive graft.* [Online, 3 April] Available at: http://www.irinnews.org/report.aspx?reportid=58620 [accessed: 27 February 2011].

International Accounting Standards Board. 2007. *Exposure draft of a proposed IFRs for small and medium-sized entities.* Retrieved 7 April 2008, from: www.iasb.org/NR/rdonlyres/DFF3CB5E-7C89-4D0B-AB85-BC099E84470F/0/SMEProposed26095.pdf

International Association of Financial Crime Investigators (IAFCI). n.d. *About IAFCI.* [Online] Available at: http://www.iafci.org/web/AM/ContentManagerNet/Default.aspx?Section=About_IAFCI&Template=/TaggedPage/TaggedPageDisplay.cfm&TPLID=3&ContentID=3377 [accessed 27 January 2011].

International Chamber of Commerce (ICC). n.d. *Policy and business practice: anti-corruption.* [Online] Available at: www.iccwbo.org/policy/anticorruption/id863/index.html [accessed: 27 January 2011].

International Court of Justice n.d. *The Court.* [Online] Available at: http://www.icj-cij.org/court/index.php?p1=1 [accessed 14 October 2011].

International Financial Institutions Task Force (IFI Task Force) 2006. *International Financial Institutions Anti-Corruption Task Force.* [Online] Available at: http://siteresources.worldbank.org/INTDOII/Resources/FinalIFITaskForceFramework&Gdlines.pdf [accessed: 27 February 2011].

International Monetary Fund (IMF). n.d. *About the IMF.* [Online] Available at: www.imf.org/external/about.htm [accessed: 26 January 2011].

Interpol. n.d.a. *About Interpol.* [Online] Available at: www.interpol.int/public/icpo/default.asp [accessed: 26 January 2011].

Interpol. n.d.b. *Interpol and corruption.* [Online] Available at: www.interpol.int/Public/Corruption/corruption.asp [accessed 26 January 2011].

Ivanov, K.S. 2007. The limits of a global campaign against corruption, in *Corruption and Development: The Anti-Corruption Campaigns,* edited by S. Bracking. Basingstoke: Palgrave Macmillan, 28–45.

Iyer, N. and Samociuk, M. 2006. *Fraud and Corruption: Prevention and Detection*. Gower: Aldershot.

Jameson, A. 2007. Siemens paid millions of euros to bribe ministers. *The Times*. [Online, 17 November] Available at: http://business.timesonline.co.uk/tol/business/industry_sectors/engineering/article2886593.ece [accessed: 27 February 2011].

Jia, H. 2007. China's battle with fake drugs. *Chemistry World*. [Online, 18 May] Available at: www.rsc.org/chemistryworld/News/2007/May/18050701.asp [accessed: 27 February 2011].

Johnson, C. 2005. Ebbers gets 25-year sentence for role in WorldCom fraud. *The Washington Post*. [Online, 14 July] Available at: http://www.washingtonpost.com/wp-dyn/content/article/2005/07/13/AR2005071300516.html [accessed: 27 February 2011].

Johnson, C. 2007. Accounting for the future. *The Washington Post*. [Online, 9 March] Available at: www.washingtonpost.com/wp-dyn/content/article/2007/03/08/AR2007030802037.html [accessed: 27 February 2011].

Johnson, R.A. 2004. Corruption in four countries, in *The Struggle Against Corruption: A Comparative Study*, edited by R.A Johnson. Basingstoke: Palgrave Macmillan, 145–165.

Johnston, M. 1997. Public officials, private interests, and sustainable democracy: when politics and corruption meet, in *Corruption and the Global Economy*, edited by K.A. Elliott. Washington, DC: Institute for International Economics, 61–82.

Johnston, M. 2002. Fighting systemic corruption: social foundations for institutional reform, in *Corruption and Development*, edited by M. Robinson. Oxon: Frank Cass, 85–104.

Kadlec, D. 2002. Enron: who's accountable? *Time*. [Online, 13 January] Available at: www.time.com/time/business/article/0,8599,193520,00.html [accessed: 27 February 2011].

Kalnins, V. 2005. *Assessing Trends in Corruption and Impact of Anti-corruption Measures: Discussion Paper*. Paper to the Anti-Corruption Network for Transition Economies 6th General Meeting, 30–31 May 2005.

Kapstein, M. 2009. The living business code: improving corporate integrity and reducing corruption from the inside. in *Global Corruption Report 2009. Corruption and the Private Sector*, edited by D. Zinnbauer, R. Dobson and K. Despota. Cambridge and New York: Cambridge University Press, 83–87.

Karugaba, M. 2009. Uganda: Global Fund probe money disappears. *The New Vision*. [Online, 7 July] Available at: http://www.unpan.org/Regions/Africa/PublicAdministrationNews/tabid/113/mctl/ArticleView/ModuleId/1460/

articleId/19469/Uganda-Global-Fund-Probe-Money-Disappears.aspx [accessed: 27 February 2011].

Kasper, T. 2006. Accountability in a time of crisis: corruption and the Global Fund, in *Global Corruption Report 2006: Special Focus Corruption and Health*, edited by Transparency International. London: Pluto Press, 108–111.

Kaufmann, D., Kraay, A. and Mastruzzi, M. 2006. *Measuring corruption: myths and realities* (World Bank Policy Research Paper). [Online] Available at: http://siteresources.worldbank.org/INTWBIGOVANTCOR/Resources/1740479-1149112210081/2604389-1167941884942/6_Myths_Measurement.pdf [accessed: 23 February 2011].

Kerbaj, R. 2010. Ban on commercial whaling to be overturned. *The Times.* [Online, 18 April] Available at: http://www.timesonline.co.uk/tol/news/environment/article7100967.ece [accessed: 27 February 2011].

Keuleers, P. 2005. Corruption, poverty and development, in *Knowledge, Commitment, Action: Against Corruption in Asia and the Pacific*. Asian Development Bank: Organisation for Economic Co-operation and Development (OECD), 58–73. Available at: http://www.oecd.org/dataoecd/11/7/36770917.pdf [accessed 25 February 2011].

Khan, M.H. 2002. Patron–client networks and the economic effects of corruption in Asia, in *Corruption and Development*, edited by M. Robinson. Oxon: Frank Cass, 15–39.

Klitgaard, R. 1988. *Controlling Corruption*. London: University of California Press.

Kim, S. 2011. Egypt's Mubarak likely to retain vast wealth. *ABC News.* [Online, 2 February] Available at: http://abcnews.go.com/Business/egypt-mubarak-family-accumulated-wealth-days-military/story?id=12821073 [accessed: 27 February 2011].

Knutsen, T.L. 1997. *A History of International Relations Theory.* Manchester: Manchester University Press.

Kollewe, J. 2011. Bernard Madoff's payroll manager pleads guilty to part in Ponzi fraud. *The Guardian.* [Online, 7 June] Available at: http://www.guardian.co.uk/business/2011/jun/07/bernard-madoff-payroll-manager-pleads-guilty [accessed: 14 November 2011].

Kramer, A. 2006. Drug piracy: a wave of counterfeit medicines washes over Russia. *The New York Times.* [Online, 5 September] Available at: www.nytimes.com/2006/09/05/business/worldbusiness/05fake.html [accessed: 27 February 2011].

Kramer, W.M. 2007. *U4 Brief: Corruption and fraud in international aid projects.* [Online] Available at: http://www.u4.no/document/publication.

cfm?2752=corruption-and-fraud-in-international-aid-projects [accessed: 27 February 2011].

Lambsdorff, J. 2006a. Measuring corruption – the validity and precision of subjective indicators (CPI), in *Measuring Corruption*, edited by C. Sampford, A. Shacklock, C. Connors and F. Galtung. Aldershot: Ashgate, 81–99.

Lambsdorff, J. 2006b. Causes and consequences of corruption: what do we know from a cross-section of countries? In *International Handbook of the Economics of Corruption*, edited by S. Rose Ackermen. Cheltenham: Edward Elgar, 3–51.

Lambsdorff, J. 2007. *The Institutional Economics of Corruption and Reform: Theory Evidence and Policy*. Cambridge: Cambridge University Press.

Landesman, P. 2003. Arms and the man. *The New York Times*. [Online, 17 August] Available at: http://www.nytimes.com/2003/08/17/magazine/arms-and-the-man.html [accessed: 27 February 2011].

Langseth, P. (2006). Measuring corruption. In *Measuring Corruption*, edited by C. Sampford, A. Shacklock, C. Connors and F. Galtung. Aldershot: Ashgate, 7–44.

Leigh, D. 2007. Diplomatic clash looms with US over BAE arms sale investigation. *The Guardian*. [Online, 16 July] Available at: www.guardian. co.uk/armstrade/story/0,,2127192,00.html [accessed: 27 February 2011].

Leigh, D. 2011. British firms face bribery blacklist, warns corruption watchdog. *The Guardian*. [Online, 31 January] Available at: http://www.guardian. co.uk/business/2011/jan/31/british-firms-face-bribery-blacklist [accessed: 27 February 2011].

Leigh, D. and Evans, R. 2010a. Perseverance and bluff – how the legal deal was done that sees BAE pay £285m fines. *The Guardian*. [Online, 5 February] Available at: http://www.guardian.co.uk/world/2010/feb/05/bae-legal-fine-arms-deal [accessed: 27 February 2011].

Leigh, D. and Evans, R. 2010b. BAE admits guilt over corrupt arms deals. *The Guardian*. [Online, 6 February] Available at: http://www.guardian.co.uk/ world/2010/feb/05/bae-systems-arms-deal-corruption [accessed: 27 February 2011].

Leith, L. 2002. How to lose a billion. *The Guardian* [Online, 26 October] Available at: http://www.guardian.co.uk/business/2002/oct/26/weekend magazine [accessed: 27 February 2011].

Levi, M., Dakolias, M. and Greenberg, T.S. 2007. Money laundering and corruption, in *The Many Faces of Corruption: Tackling the Vulnerabilities at Sector Level* 3, edited by J. Campos and S. Pradhan, Washington, DC: World Bank, 389–426.

LeVine, V. 1999. Transnational aspects of political corruption, in *Political Corruption. A Handbook,* edited by A. Heidenheimer, M. Johnston and V. LeVine. New Brunswick and London: Transaction Publishers, 685–700.

Lewis, A. 2011. Tracking down the Ben Ali and Trabelsi fortune. *BBC News* [Online, 31 January] Available at: http://www.bbc.co.uk/news/world-africa-12302659 [accessed: 27 February 2011].

Lichtblau, E. and Dougherty, C. 2008. Siemens to pay $1.34 billion in fines. *The New York Times.* [Online, 15 December] Available at: http://www.nytimes. com/2008/12/16/business/worldbusiness/16siemens.html [accessed: 27 February 2011].

Lindelow, M., Kushnarova, I. and Kaiser, K. 2006. Measuring corruption in the health sector: what we can learn from public expenditure tracking and service delivery surveys in developing countries, in *Global Corruption Report 2006: Special Focus Corruption and Health,* edited by Transparency International. London: Pluto Press, 29–36.

Lugar, R.G. 2005. Loan corruption control. *The Washington Times.* [Online, 1 July] Available at: http://www.washingtontimes.com/news/2005/jun/30/20050630-085634-1439r/ [accessed: 27 February 2011].

Lynch, C. 2007. Former U.N. oil-for-food chief indicted. *The Washington Post* [Online, 17 January] Available at: http://www.washingtonpost.com/wp-dyn/ content/article/2007/01/16/AR2007011600706.html [accessed: 27 February 2011].

MacIntyre, B. 2007. Whale hunting: a saga of cheating, bribery and greed. *The Times.* [Online, 10 May] Available at: http://www.timesonline.co.uk/ tol/comment/columnists/ben_macintyre/article1769304.ece [accessed: 27 February 2011].

MacKinnon, I. 2007. South-east Asia awash with fake drugs. *The Guardian.* [Online, 22 February] Available at: http://www.guardian.co.uk/world/2007/ feb/22/health.healthandwellbeing [accessed: 27 February 2011].

MacKinnon, I. 2008. Former Thai PM Thaksin found guilty of corruption. *The Guardian.* [Online, 21 October] Available at: http://www.guardian.co.uk/ world/2008/oct/21/thaksin-thailand-corruption [accessed: 27 February 2011].

Mamudi, S. 2008. Lehman folds with record $613bn debt. *MarketWatch* [Online, 15 September] Available at: http://www.marketwatch.com/story/lehman-folds-with-record-613-billion-debt?siteid=rss [accessed: 27 February 2011].

Mansell, P. 2008. Operation Jupiter rains on fake antimalarials. *In-Pharmatechnologist.* [Online, 28 February] Available at: http://www.in-pharmatechnologist.com/Industry-Drivers/Operation-Jupiter-rains-on-fake-antimalarials [accessed: 27 February 2011].

Marquette, H. 2003. *Corruption, Politics and Development: The Role of the World Bank.* Basingstoke: Palgrave Macmillan.

Maslyukivska, O.P. 1999. *Role of nongovernmental organisations in development cooperation.* [Online] Available at: www.gonzagajil.org/pdf/volume10/ [accessed 2 February 2011].

Matussek, K. 2008. Siemens fine in bribery case quashed by German court. *Bloomberg.* [Online, 29 August] Available at: http://www.bloomberg.com/apps/news?pid=newsarchive&sid=aQjq1j8d8ftw&refer=germany [accessed: 27 February 2011].

Mauro, P. 1998. *Corruption: Causes, consequences, and agenda for further research.* International Monetary Fund, Finance & Development. [Online] Available at: https://imf.org/external/Pubs/FT/fandd/1998/03/pdf/mauro.pdf [accessed: 25 February 2011].

McCarthy, R. 2009a. Israel's former OM Olmert charged with corruption. *The Guardian.* [Online, 30 August] Available at: http://www.guardian.co.uk/world/2009/aug/30/israel-ehud-olmert-corruption-charged [accessed: 27 February 2011].

McCarthy, R. 2009b. Israeli police recommend corruption charges against Avigdor Lieberman. *The Guardian.* [Online, 2 August] Available at: http://www.guardian.co.uk/world/2009/aug/02/israel-avigdor-lieberman-police-investigation [accessed: 27 February 2011].

McGivering, J. 2007. Tracking down the fake malaria drug threat. *BBC News.* [Online, 7 June] Available at: http://news.bbc.co.uk/1/hi/6692431.stm [accessed: 27 February 2011].

McNeill, D. 2006. Revealed: Japan's whaling 'shopping list'. *The Independent* [Online, 24 June] Available at: www.independent.co.uk/news/world/asia/revealed-japans-whaling-shopping-list-405257.html [accessed 27 February 2011].

McNeil, D. 2008. Fake malaria drugs emerging in vulnerable countries in Africa. *The New York Times.* [Online, 13 May] Available at: http://www.nytimes.com/2008/05/13/health/13glob.html?_r=1&ref=science&oref=slogin [accessed: 27 February 2011].

Medical News Today 2008. *Interpol seizes $6.65m in counterfeit HIV/AIDS, malaria and TBC drugs in Southeast Asia.* [Online, 18 November] Available at: http://www.medicalnewstoday.com/articles/129767.php [accessed: 27 February 2011].

Mekay, E. 2006. Bank bars company for years-old bribery scandal. *Inter Press Service.* [Online, 8 November] Available at: http://ipsnews.net/africa/nota.asp?idnews=35409 [accessed: 27 February 2011].

Mines and Communities 2001. *Protest at the Mindoro Nickel Project.* [Online, 11 April] Available at: http://www.minesandcommunities.org/article. php?a=838 [accessed: 27 February 2011].

Montesquiou, A. 2009. Book burner snubbed as Unesco elects woman boss. *The Scotsman* [Online, 1 February] Available at: http://thescotsman.scotsman. com/latestnews/Book-burner-snubbed-as-Unesco.5670096.jp [accessed: 27 February 2011].

Moran, J. 1999. Bribery and corruption: the OECD Convention on combating the bribery of foreign public officials in international business transactions. *Business Ethics: A European Review*, 8(3), 141–150.

Morino, V. and Iyer, N. 2003. *Managing the cost and risk of fraud and corruption.* [Online, Hibis] Available at: www.hibis.com/pdf/managing_cost_and_risk. pdf [accessed: 27 February 2011].

Muller, M. 2004. Getting priorities right is a must. *Business Day.* [Online, 3 September] Available at: http://www.odiousdebts.org/odiousdebts/index. cfm?DSP=content&ContentID=11317 [accessed: 27 February 2011].

Murphy, M. and Gill, M. 2011. UBS trader in custody after fraud charge. *The Financial Times.* [Online: 16 September] Available at: http://www.ft.com/cms/ s/0/01fb8356-e03e-11e0-ba12-00144feabdc0.html#axzz1dhlcnSv5 [accessed: 14 November 2011].

Nasaw, D. 2009. Timeline: Key dates in the Bernard Madoff case. *The Guardian.* [Online, 29 June] Available at: http://www.guardian.co.uk/business/2009/ mar/12/bernard-madoff-timeline-fraud [accessed: 27 February 2011].

Nelken, D. 2003. Political corruption in the European Union, in *Corruption in Contemporary Politics,* edited by M. Bull, and J. Newell. Basingstoke: Palgrave Macmillan, 220–233.

NGO (n.d.). *Types of NGO.* [Online] Available at: http://www.ngo.in/types-of-ngos.html [accessed: 27 January 2011].

NGO Global Network. n.d. *Definition of NGOs.* [Online] Available at: www. ngo.org/ngoinfo/define.html [accessed: 3 February 2011].

NHS Counter Fraud and Security Management Service (CFSMS). 2006. *The international fraud and corruption report. A study of selected countries.* [Online] Available at: http://www.nhsbsa.nhs.uk/CounterFraud/Documents/ International_fraud_and_corruption_report.pdf [accessed: 17 February 2011].

Nordberg, C. and Vian, T. 2008. *U4 Issue: Corruption in the health sector.* [Online] Available at: http://www.u4.no/document/publication.cfm?3208=corruption-in-the-health-sector [accessed: 27 February 2011].

Nussbaum, D. 2005. A world built on corrupt foundations. *International Herald Tribune.* [Online, 19 March] Available at: http://www.odiousdebts.

org/odiousdebts/index.cfm?DSP=content&ContentID=12625 [accessed: 27 February 2010].

O'Hara, T. 2005. Allbrittons, Riggs to pay victims of Pinochet. *The Washington Post.* [Online, 26 February] Available at: http://www.washingtonpost.com/wp-dyn/articles/A53805-2005Feb25.html [accessed: 27 February 2011].

O'Hara, T. and Day, K. 2004. Riggs Bank hid assets of Pinochet, report says. *The Washington Post.* [Online, 15 July] Available at: http://www.washingtonpost.com/wp-dyn/articles/A50222-2004Jul14.html [accessed: 27 February 2011].

OLAF *see* European Anti-Fraud Office.

Organisation for Economic Co-operation and Development (OECD). 2008. *OECD Group demands rapid UK action to enact adequate anti-bribery laws.* [Online, 16 October] Available at: http://www.oecd.org/document/8/0,3343,en_2649_34855_41515464_1_1_1_1,00.html [accessed: 27 February 2011].

Organisation for Economic Co-operation and Development (OECD). n.d.a. *About the OECD.* [Online] Available at: www.oecd.org/pages/0,3417,en_36734052_36734103_1_1_1_1_1,00.html [accessed: 26 January 2011].

Organisation for Economic Co-operation and Development (OECD). n.d.b. *OECD working group on bribery in international business transactions.* [Online] Available at: www.oecd.org/document/5/0,3343,en_2649_37447_35430021_1_1_1_37447,00.html [accessed: 26 January 2011].

Organisation for Economic Co-operation and Development (OECD). n.d.c. *Paris declaration on aid effectiveness.* [Online] Available at: http://www.oecd.org/document/18/0,3746,en_2649_3236398_35401554_1_1_1_1,00.html [accessed: 27 February 2011].

Organisation of American States (OAS). n.d. *Inter-American Convention: Background.* [Online] Available at: http://www.oas.org/juridico/english/corr_bg.htm [accessed: 13 October 2011].

Osborn, A. 2003. Edith Cresson charged with fraud. *The Guardian.* [Online, 26 March] Available at: http://www.guardian.co.uk/world/2003/mar/26/eu.france [accessed: 27 February 2011].

Owen, P. and Shenker, J. 2011. Mubarak trial – the defendants and the charges. *The Guardian.* [Online, 3 August] Available at: http://www.guardian.co.uk/world/2011/aug/03/mubarak-trial-defendants-charges [accessed: 14 November 2011].

Pagano, M. 2010. Fraud charges loom for Lehman Bros. *The Independent.* [Online, 14 March] Available at: http://www.independent.co.uk/news/business/news/fraud-charges-loom-for-lehman-bros-1920944.html [accessed: 27 February 2011].

Pallister, D., Leigh, D. and Wilson, J. 1999. Aitken, the fixer and the secret multi-million pound arms deals. *The Guardian.* [Online, 5 March] Available at: www.guardian.co.uk/politics/1999/mar/05/uk.davidpallister [accessed: 27 February 2011].

Parham, H. 2006. Promoting revenue transparency in the extractive industries. In *Knowledge, Commitment, Action: Against Corruption in Asia and the Pacific.* Asian Development Bank: Organisation for Economic Co-operation and Development (OECD), 98–104. Available at: http://www.adb.org/Documents/Books/knowledge-commitment-action/foreword.pdf [accessed 25 February 2011].

Parliamentary Office of Science and Technology 2010. *Postnote: Counterfeit medicines.* [Online] Available at: http://www.alphagalileo.org/AssetViewer.aspx?AssetId=18509&CultureCode=en [accessed: 27 February 2011].

Partnership for Transparency Fund (PTF). n.d. *General information on the PTF.* [Online] Available at: http://www.partnershipfortransparency.info/About+Us.html [accessed 27 January 2011].

Peel, M. 2008. UK taken to task for laxity on bribes. *The Financial Times.* [Online, 18 October] Available at: http://www.ft.com/cms/s/0/74058afe-9cae-11dd-a42e-000077b07658.html#axzz1FGx8IhMU [accessed: 27 February 2011].

Peston, R. 2006. Security threats and economic fears. *BBC News.* [Online, 15 December] Available at: http://news.bbc.co.uk/go/pr/fr/-/1/hi/business/6182137.stm [accessed: 27 February 2011].

Pfeiffer, S. 2004. Vote-buying and its implications for democracy: evidence from Latin America, in *Transparency International Global Corruption Report 2004,* edited by Hodess, R., Inowlocki, T., Rodriguez, D. and Wolfe, T. London: Pluto Press, 76–77.

Pfeifer, S. and Power, H. 2007. I like shooting things. *Daily Telegraph.* [Online, 15 July] Available at: www.telegraph.co.uk/money/main.jhtml?xml=/money/2007/07/15/ccsfo115.xml [accessed: 27 February 2011].

PlusNews 2009. *Uganda: Justice slowly meted out in Global Fund corruption trials.* [Online, 19 August] Available at: http://www.plusnews.org/Report.aspx?ReportId=85772 [accessed: 27 February 2011].

Posadas, A. 2000. *Combating corruption under international law.* [Online] Available at: www.law.duke.edu/journals/djcil/downloads/djcil10p345.pdf [accessed 25 February 2011].

Pujas, V. 2004. Legal hurdles: immunity, extradition and the repatriation of stolen wealth, in *Transparency International Global Corruption Report 2004,* edited by Hodess, R., Inowlocki, T., Rodriguez, D. and Wolfe, T. London: Pluto Press, 89–92.

Pujas, V. 2009. Immunity and extradition: obstacles to justice, in *Global Corruption Report 2004,* edited by Transparency International. London: Pluto Press, 89–93

Putnam, R. 1993. *Making Democracy Work: Civic Traditions in Modern Italy.* Princeton: Princeton University Press.

Raustiala, K. and Slaughter, A. 2002. International law, international relations and compliance. *Princeton Law & Public Affairs,* 2(2), 538–558.

Reed, Q. and Fontana, A. 2011. *U4 Issue: Corruption and illicit financial flows.* [Online] Available at: http://www.u4.no/document/publication. cfm?3935=corruption-and-illicit-financial-flows [accessed: 27 February 2011].

Reinikka, R. and Smith, N. n.d. *Public expenditure tracking surveys in education.* [Online: International Institute for Educational Planning] Available at: https://cms.eldis.org/go/topics/resource-guides/education/key-issues/ education-financing-and-pem/monitoring-and-evaluation&id=16749&type =Document [accessed: 27 February 2011].

Reinikka, R. and Svensson, J. 2004. The power of information: evidence from public expenditure tracking surveys, in *Transparency International Global Corruption Report 2004,* edited by Hodess, R., Inowlocki, T., Rodriguez, D. and Wolfe, T. London: Pluto Press, 326–329.

Reisen, H. 2009. *The multilateral donor non-system: Towards accountability and efficient role assignment.* OECD Discussion Paper. [Online, 5 March] Available at: www.oecd.org/dataoecd/13/43/42306585.pdf [accessed: 27 February 2011].

Reuben, A. 2008. Suharto's battle with corruption charges. *BBC News.* [Online, 27 January] Available at: http://news.bbc.co.uk/1/hi/business/7193517.stm [accessed: 27 February 2011].

Riding, A. 1999. Unesco's new director is envoy from Japan, its biggest donor. *The New York Times.* [Online, 21 October] Available at: http://www.nytimes. com/1999/10/21/world/unesco-s-new-director-is-envoy-from-japan-its-biggest-donor.html [accessed: 27 February 2011].

Riano, J. and Hodess, R. 2008. *Transparency International 2008 Bribes Payer Index.* [Online] Available at: http://www.transparency.org/news_room/in_ focus/2008/bpi_2008 [accessed: 27 February 2011].

Rickard, C. 2006. Top Lesotho water boss charged. *Sunday Times.* [Online, 12 February] Available at: http://www.odiousdebts.org/odiousdebts/index. cfm?DSP=content&ContentID=14857 [accessed: 27 February 2011].

Riley, S.P. 2002. The political economy of anti-corruption strategies in Africa, in *Corruption and Development,* edited by M. Robinson. London: Frank Cass, 129–155.

Roberts, A. 2010. Economist Debates: Africa and China. The moderator's opening remarks. *The Economist.* [Online, 15 February] Available at: http:// www.economist.com/debate/days/view/466 [accessed: 27 February 2011].

Robinson, M. 2002. Corruption and development: an introduction, in *Corruption and Development,* edited by M. Robinson. London: Frank Cass, 1–14.

Robinson, M. (ed.). 2002. *Corruption and Development.* London: Frank Cass.

Robinson, M. 2006. Foreword, in *Global Corruption Report 2006: Special Focus Corruption and Health,* edited by Transparency International. London: Pluto Press, xiv–xv.

Roeber, J. 2004. The political corruption in the arms trade: South Africa's arms and the Elf affair, in *Transparency International Global Corruption Report 2004,* edited by Hodess, R., Inowlocki, T., Rodriguez, D. and Wolfe, T. London: Pluto Press, 59–61.

Rose-Ackerman, S. 2004. Governance and corruption, in *Global Crisis, Global Solutions,* edited by B. Lomborg. Cambridge University Press: Cambridge, 301–362.

Rosenau, J.N. 2004. Governance in a new global order, in *The Global Transformations Reader,* edited by D. Held and D. McGrew. Oxford: Blackwell, 70–86.

Rowley, J. 2005. Riggs bank fined $16m for helping Chile's Pinochet. *Bloomberg.* [Online, 29 March] Available at: http://www.bloomberg.com/apps/news?pid=21070001&sid=aDX6Lhj3.j3I [accessed: 27 February 2011].

Rushe, D. 2010a. Mark Madoff suicide 'will not stop investigations into his role'. *The Guardian.* [Online, 13 December] Available at: http://www.guardian.co.uk/business/2010/dec/13/mark-madoff-suicide-not-stop-investigation [accessed: 27 February 2011].

Rushe, D. 2010b. Madoff friend's estate agrees to repay $7.2bn in Ponzi fraud settlement. *The Guardian.* [Online, 17 December] Available at: http://www.guardian.co.uk/business/2010/dec/17/bernard-madoff-friend-jeffry-picower-settlement [accessed: 27 February 2011].

Rushe, D. 2011. Bernard Madoff victims get first compensation cheques. *The Guardian.* [Online, 5 October] Available at: http://www.guardian.co.uk/business/2011/oct/05/bernard-madoff-victims-compensation [accessed: 14 November 2011].

Sage, A. 2009. French establishment players convicted over arms to Angola scandal. *The Times.* [Online, 28 October] Available at: http://www.timesonline.co.uk/tol/news/world/europe/article6892954.ece [accessed: 27 February 2011].

Samociuk, M., Iyer, N. and Morino, V. 2006. Tackling fraud and corruption. *Hibis.* [Online] Available at: www.hibis.com/pdf/tackling_fraud_and_corruption.pdf [accessed: 27 February 2011].

Sampford, C., Shacklock, A., Connors, C. and Galtung, F. (eds) 2006. *Measuring Corruption.* Aldershot: Ashgate.

Sandholtz, W. and Gray, M. 2003. International integration and national corruption. *International Organisation*, 57(4), 761–800.

Save the Children 2006. *Exploitation of children in Liberia.* [Online] Available at: http://www.savethechildren.net/alliance/media/newsdesk/2006-05-08a.html [accessed 27 February 2011].

Savedoff, W. and Hussmann, K. 2006. Why are health systems prone to corruption? in *Global Corruption Report 2006: Special Focus Corruption and Health,* edited by Transparency International. London: Pluto Press, 4–13.

Scanlon, C. 1997. Despatches: Seoul. *BBC News.* [Online, 20 December] Available at: http://news.bbc.co.uk/1/hi/despatches/41254.stm [accessed: 27 February 2011].

Scannell, K. 2010. Ernst & Young sued over Lehman. *The Financial Times.* [Online, 10 December] Available at: http://www.ft.com/cms/s/0/dfd9ed06-0d31-11e0-82ff-00144feabdc0.html#axzz1F7CKljbf [accessed: 27 February 2011].

Schmid, J. 2006. Switzerland's experience with transnational judicial cooperation, in *Knowledge, commitment, action: Against corruption in Asia and the Pacific.* [Online] Asian Development Bank: and Organisation for Economic Co-operation and Development (OECD), 202–214. Available at: http://www.oecd.org/dataoecd/11/12/36771017.pdf [accessed: 25 February 2011].

Scott-Joynt, J. 2002. An A-Z of money laundering. *BBC News.* [Online, 15 March] Available at: http://news.bbc.co.uk/1/hi/business/1871437.stm [accessed: 27 February 2011].

SEC *see* US Securities and Exchange Commission.

Shaw, M.N. 2003. *International Law,* 5th edition. Cambridge: Cambridge University Press.

Shaxson, N. 2004. The Elf trial: political corruption and the oil industry, in *Transparency International Global Corruption Report 2004,* edited by Hodess, R., Inowlocki, T., Rodriguez, D. and Wolfe, T. London: Pluto Press, 67–71.

Shichor, D. and Geis, G. 2007. The itching palm: the crimes of bribery and extortion, in *International Handbook of White-Collar and Corporate Crime,* edited by H.N. Pontell and G. Geis. New York: Springer, 405–423.

Shleifer, A. and Vishny, R. 1998. *The Grabbing Hand. Government Pathologies and Their Cures.* Cambridge: Harvard University Press.

Sik, E. 2002. The Bad, the Worse and the Worst: Guesstimating the Level of Corruption, in *Political Corruption in Transition: A Sceptic's Handbook,* edited by S. Kotkin and A. Sajo. Budapest and New York: CEU Press, 91–113.

Sokenu, C. 2011. Bribery Act is not perfect but brings the UK into line with OECD. *The Guardian.* [Online, 4 February] Available at: http://www.guardian.co.uk/law/2011/feb/04/bribery-act-delay [accessed: 27 February 2011].

Spencer, R. 2011. Tunisia riots: Reform or be overthrown, US tells Arab states amid fresh riots. *The Telegraph.* [Online, 13 January] Available at: http://www. telegraph.co.uk/news/worldnews/africaandindianocean/tunisia/8258077/ Tunisia-riots-Reform-or-be-overthrown-US-tells-Arab-states-amid-fresh-riots.html [accessed: 14 November 2011].

Sprague, O. 2006. *UN arms embargoes: An overview of the last ten years. Control Arms Briefing Note.* [Online, 16 March] Available at: http://www.controlarms. org/en/documents%20and%20files/reports/english-reports/un-arms-embargoes-an-overview-of-the-last-ten/view [accessed: 27 February 2011].

Stability Pact for South Eastern Europe (SPAI). n.d. *Objectives.* [Online] Available at: http://www.stabilitypact.org/anticorruption/default.asp [accessed: 26 January 2011].

Stewart, H. 2009. Darling wins Brussels battle over financial super-regulator. *The Guardian.* [Online, 10 June] Available at: http://www.guardian.co.uk/ business/2009/jun/10/alistair-darling-european-finance-regulator [accessed: 27 February 2011].

Stiglitz, J. 2002. Comment: corporate corruption. *The Guardian.* [Online, 4 July] Available at: www.guardian.co.uk/world/2002/jul/04/globalisation. comment

Stohl, R. and Grillot, S. 2009. *The International Arms Trade.* Cambridge: Polity Press.

Sydney Morning Herald 2011. *Swiss freeze Mubarak's bank account.* [Online, 12 February] Available at: http://www.smh.com.au/world/swiss-freeze-mubaraks-bank-accounts-20110212-1aqx7.html?from=smh_sb [accessed: 27 February 2011].

SwissInfo 2009. *Ex-dictator's assets set to help Haitians.* [Online, 12 February] Available at: http://www.swissinfo.ch/eng/politics/foreign_affairs/Ex-dictators_assets_set_to_help_Haitians.html?cid=986822 [accessed: 27 February 2011].

Tanzi, V. 1998. Corruption around the world: causes, consequences, scope, and cures. *International Monetary Fund Staff Papers,* 45(4), 559–594.

Taub, S. 2005. Multinationals take anti-bribery pledge. *CFO Magazine.* [Online, 28 January] Available at: www.cfo.com/article.cfm/3618802?f=search [acessed: 27 February 2011].

Taylor, L. and Dickinson, C. 2006. The link between corruption and HIV/AIDS, in *Global Corruption Report 2006: Special Focus, Corruption and Health* edited by Transparency International. London: Pluto Press, 104–111.

Teather, D. 2009. Bernard Madoff receives maximum 150 year sentence. *The Guardian.* [Online, 30 June] Available at: http://www.guardian.co.uk/ business/2009/jun/29/bernard-madoff-sentence [accessed: 27 February 2011].

Tedmanson, S. 2010. Limited commercial whale hunts proposed by IWC. *The Times*. [Online, 24 April] Available at: http://www.timesonline.co.uk/tol/news/environment/article7105896.ece [accessed: 27 February 2011].

Teggemann, S. n.d. Anticorruption – corruption and development assistance. *The World Bank*. [Online] Available at: http://go.worldbank.org/1AXCYRA5F0 [accessed: 27 February 2011].

Terrorism, Transnational Crime and Corruption Center (TraCCC) n.d. *Human trafficking*. [Online] Available at: http://policy-traccc.gmu.edu/transcrime/humantrafficking.html [accessed: 27 February 2011].

The Economist 2008. A survey of globalisation: Oil, politics and corruption. [Online, 18 September] Available at: http://www.economist.com/node/12080765 [accessed: 27 February 2011].

The Egmont Group 2011. *About us*. [Online] Available at: http://www.egmontgroup.org/about [accessed: 27 February 2011].

The Global Fund to Fight AIDS, Tuberculosis and Malaria (The Global Fund). 2005. *Questions on the suspension of grants in Uganda*. [Online] Available at: http://www.theglobalfund.org/content/pressreleases/pr_050824_faq.pdf [accessed: 27 February 2011].

The Global Fund to Fight AIDS, Tuberculosis and Malaria (The Global Fund). 2009. *Press release: Global fund reaffirms commitment to Uganda*. [Online, 31 July] Available at: http://www.theglobalfund.org/en/pressreleases/?pr=pr_090731 [accessed: 27 February 2011].

The Global Fund to Fight AIDS, Tuberculosis and Malaria (The Global Fund). 2011. *Who we are*. [Online] Available at: http://www.theglobalfund.org/en/about/ [accessed: 27 February 2011].

The Guardian 2002. *Aid workers in food for child sex scandal*. [Online, 27 February] Available at: www.guardian.co.uk/world/2002/feb/27/immigration.uk [accessed: 27 February 2011].

The Guardian 2011. *Avigdor Lieberman set to face Israeli corruption charges*. [Online, 13 April] Available at: http://www.guardian.co.uk/world/2011/apr/13/avigdor-lieberman-israel-corruption-charges [accessed: 14 November 2011]

The Independent 2006. *Aid workers 'using under-age African girls for sex'*. [Online, 8 May] Available at: www.independent.co.uk/news/world/africa/aid-workers-using-underage-african-girls-for-sex-477355.html [accessed: 27 February 2011].

The New York Times 1997. *Ex-Premier of India indicted on criminal bribery charges*. [Online, 7 May] Available at: http://query.nytimes.com/gst/fullpage.html?res=9B01E4DD1130F934A35756C0A961958260 [accessed: 27 February 2011].

The New York Times 2003. *Chasing the Kleptocrats*. [Online, 29 September] Available at: http://select.nytimes.com/gst/abstract.html?res=F40B1FF73B590C7A8

EDDA00894DB404482&scp=1&sq=chasing%20the%20kleptocrats&st=cse [accessed: 27 February 2011].

The Sunday Times 2010a. *Scandal of Japan's bribes over whaling.* [Online, 12 June] Available at: http://www.timesonline.co.uk/tol/comment/leading_article/ article7149142.ece [accessed: 27 February 2011].

The Sunday Times 2010b. *Flights, girls and cash buy Japan whaling votes.* [Online, 13 June] Available at: http://www.timesonline.co.uk/tol/news/uk/ article7149086.ece [accessed: 27 February 2011].

The Times 2008. *Widespread child sex abuse by UN peace troops and aid staff, says charity.* [Online, 27 May] Available at: www.timesonline.co.uk/tol/news/ world/article4012013.ece [accessed: 27 February 2011].

The White House 2010. *Presidential Memorandum – major illicit drug transit or major illicit drug producing countries.* [Online, 15 September] Available at: http://www.whitehouse.gov/the-press-office/2010/09/16/presidential-memorandum-major-illicit-drug-transit-or-major-illicit-drug [accessed: 27 February 2011].

Townsend, M. 2009. Health fears grow as fake drugs flood into Britain. *The Guardian.* [Online, 4 January] Available at: http://www.guardian.co.uk/ business/2009/jan/04/fake-pharmaceuticals-drugs-china-nhs [accessed: 27 February 2011].

TRACE International. n.d. *What is TRACE?* [Online] Available at: https://secure. traceinternational.org/about/ [accessed: 27 January 2011].

Transparency International (TI) 2000. *The TI Source Book.* [Online] Available at: http://www.transparency.org/publications/sourcebook [accessed: 3 February 2011].

Transparency International (TI) 2004. *Global Corruption Report: Special Focus, Political Corruption.* Berlin: Transparency International. Available at: www. transparency.org/publications/gcr/download_gcr/download_gcr_2004 [accessed 25 February 2011].

Transparency International (TI) 2006a. *In Focus on the ODI Risk Maps: Stages of the relief project.* [Online] Available at: http://www.transparency.org/news_ room/in_focus/2006/humanitarian_relief/relief_project_cycle [accessed at: 27 February 2011].

Transparency International (TI) 2006b. *Corruption in humanitarian aid.* [Online] Available at: http://www.transparencia.org.es/TI-%20Ayuda%20 Humanitaria%20y%20Corrupci%C3%B3n.pdf [accessed: 27 February 2011].

Transparency International (TI) 2006c. *Global Corruption Report 2006: Special Focus, Corruption and Health.* London: Pluto Press.

Transparency International (TI) 2007. *Policy paper: Poverty, Aid and Corruption*. [Online] Available at: www.transparency.org/content/download/20572/285905 [accessed: 27 February 2011].

Transparency International (TI) 2011. *2011 Bribe Payers Index*. [Online] Available at: http://bpi.transparency.org/results/ [accessed 14 November 2011].

Transparency International (TI) 2009. The scale and challenge of private sector corruption, in *Global Corruption Report 2009. Corruption and the Private Sector*, edited by Transparency International. Cambridge and New York: Cambridge University Press, 3–10.

Transparency International (TI) 2010. *Corruption Perceptions Index 2010*. [Online] Available at: http://www.transparency.org/policy_research/surveys_indices/cpi/2010/results [accessed: 4 February 2011].

Transparency International (TI) n.d.a. *Corruption Perceptions Index: Frequently asked questions.*[Online] Available at: http://www.transparency.org/policy_research/surveys_indices/cpi/2007/faq [Retrieved 19 December 2011].

Transparency International (TI) n.d.b. *Surveys and indices*. Retrieved 4 February 2011, from: http://www.transparency.org/policy_research/surveys_indices/cpi/2010/in_detail [accessed: 13 October 2011].

Transparency International (TI) n.d.c. *Global Corruption Barometer*. [Online] Available at: http://www.transparency.org/policy_research/surveys_indices/gcb/2010 [accessed: 4 February 2011].

Transparency International (TI) n.d.d. *Transparency International Bribe Payers Index 2002*. [Online] Available at: www.transparency.org/policy_research/surveys_indices/bpi [accessed: 25 February 2011].

Transparency International (TI) n.d.e. *About Transparency International*. [Online] Available at: www.transparency.org/about_us [accessed: 25 February 2011].

Transparency International (TI) n.d.f. *Policy and research*. [Online] Available at: www.transparency.org/policy_research [accessed: 25 February 2011].

Transparency International (TI) n.d.g *Corruption in different forms of aid*. [Online] Available at: http://www.transparency.org./global_priorities/poverty/corruption_aid/aid_forms#project [accessed: 27 February 2011].

Transparency International (TI) Australia 2008. *Money laundering*. [Online] Available at: www.transparency.org.au/money_laundering.php [accessed: 27 February 2011].

Traynor, I. 2001. The international dealers in death. *The Guardian*. [Online, 9 July] Available at: http://www.guardian.co.uk/world/2001/jul/09/armstrade.iantraynor [accessed: 27 February 2011].

Traynor, I. 2009. European Union agrees super-regulator to head off financial crises. *The Guardian*. [Online, 2 December 2009] Available at: http://www.guardian.co.uk/business/2009/dec/02/eu-financial-regulation-deal [accessed: 27 February 2011].

Tremblay, M. 2010. *Corruption and human trafficking: Unravelling the undistinguishable for a better fight.* Long Workshop Report Form from Conference: 14th International Anti-Corruption Conference 2010, Bangkok, 11 November. [Online] Available at: http://14iacc.org/wp-content/uploads/ws1.2CamilleKarbassi_LR.pdf [accessed: 27 February 2011].

U4 Anti-Corruption Resource Centre (U4). n.d.a. *FAQs: Causes & consequences of corruption.* [Online] Available at: www.u4.no/helpdesk/faq/faqs1.cfm [accessed 25 February 2011].

U4 Anti-Corruption Resource Centre (U4). n.d.b. *Anti-corruption organisations and institutions.* [Online] Available at: http://www.u4.no/document/acorganisations.cfm#igac [accessed 25 February 2011].

U4 Anti-Corruption Resource Centre (U4). n.d.c *Corruption in the health sector – Workers and patients interaction.* [Online] Available at: http://www.u4.no/themes/health/healthworkersandpatients.cfm [accessed: 27 February 2011].

UNAIDS 2010. *Global Report. UNAIDS report on the global AIDS epidemic* [Online] Available at: http://www.unaids.org/globalreport/Global_report.htm [accessed: 27 February 2011].

Underdal, A. and Young, O.R. 2004. *Regime Consequences: Methodological Challenges and Research Strategies.* Dordrecht: Kluwer.

United Nations (UN) 1999. *International Convention for the Suppression of the Financing of Terrorism.* [Online] Available at: www.un.org/law/cod/finterr.htm [accessed: 25 February 2011].

United Nations (UN). n.d.a. *Charter of the United Nations.* [Online] Available at: http://www.un.org/en/documents/charter/chapter1.shtml [accessed 25 February 2011].

United Nations (UN). n.d.b. *International Law Commission: Introduction.* [Online] Available at: http://www.un.org/law/ilc/ [accessed 25 February 2011].

United Nations (UN) n.d.c *Facts about the UN Oil-for-Food Programme.* [Online] Available at: http://www.un.org/News/dh/iraq/oip/facts-oilforfood.htm [accessed: 27 February 2011].

United Nations (UN) Global Compact. n.d. *What is the UN Global Compact?* [Online] Available at: http://www.unglobalcompact.org/AboutTheGC/TheTenPrinciples/index.html [accessed 25 February 2011].

United Nations Office for the Coordination of Humanitarian Affairs (OCHA). 2011a. JAPAN – Earthquake and Tsunami – March 2011. Table B: Total Humanitarian Assistance per Donor. *Financial Tracking Service.* [Online, 20 October] Available at: http://fts.unocha.org/reports/daily/ocha_R24_E16043___1110200205.pdf [accessed: 20 October 2011].

United Nations Office for the Coordination of Humanitarian Affairs (OCHA). 2011b. Flash Appeal: Pakistan Floods Relief and Early Recovery Response Plan (Revised) (August 2010–July 2011) Table G: Total Funding per Donor. *Financial Tracking Service*. [Online, 20 October] Available at: http://fts.unocha. org/reports/daily/ocha_R5_A905___1110200205.pdf [accessed: 20 October 2011].

United Nations Office for the Coordination of Humanitarian Affairs (OCHA). 2011c. Flash Appeal: Haiti Humanitarian Appeal (Revised) (January–December 2010). Table G: Total Funding per Donor. *Financial Tracking Service*. [Online, 20 October] Available at: http://fts.unocha.org/reports/daily/ocha_ R5_A893___1110200205.pdf [accessed: 20 October 2011].

United Nations Office on Drugs and Crime (UNODC). 2004a. *United Nations Convention Against Corruption*. [Online] Available at: http://www.unodc. org/documents/treaties/UNCAC/Publications/Convention/08-50026_E.pdf [accessed: 6 October 2011].

United Nations Office on Drugs and Crime (UNODC). 2004b. *United Nations Convention against Transnational Organized Crime and the Protocols Thereto*. [Online] Available at: http://www.unodc.org/documents/treaties/UNTOC/ Publications/TOC%20Convention/TOCebook-e.pdf [accessed: 6 October 2011].

United Nations Office on Drugs and Crime (UNODC). 2010. *World Drug Report 2010: Drug use is shifting towards new drugs and new markets*. UNDOC press release. [Online, 23 June] Available at: http://www.unodc.org/unodc/en/ frontpage/2010/June/drug-use-is-shifting-towards-new-drugs-and-new-markets.html [accessed: 27 February 2011].

United Nations Office on Drugs and Crime (UNODC). n.d.a. *United Nations Convention against Corruption – Convention Highlights*. [Online] Available at: http://www.unodc.org/unodc/en/treaties/CAC/convention-highlights.html [accessed: 6 October 2011].

United Nations Office on Drugs and Crime (UNODC). n.d.b. *UNODC and corruption*. [Online] Available at: www.unodc.org/unodc/en/corruption/ index.html [accessed 25 February 2011].

United Nations Office on Drugs and Crime (UNODC) n.d.c. *UNDOC and organized crime*. [Online] Available at: http://www.unodc.org/unodc/en/ organized-crime/index.html [accessed: 27 February 2011].

United Nations Office on Drugs and Crime (UNODC). n.d.d. *Human Trafficking*. [Online] Available at: http://www.unodc.org/unodc/en/human-trafficking/ what-is-human-trafficking.html [accessed: 6 October 2011].

US Bureau of Public Affairs 2010. *Trafficking in persons: Ten years of partnering to combat modern slavery.* [Online, 14 June] Available at: http://www.state.gov/r/pa/scp/fs/2010/143115.htm [accessed: 27 February 2011].

US Department of State 2010. *Trafficking in Persons Report 2010.* [Online, 14 June] Available at: http://www.state.gov/g/tip/rls/tiprpt/2010/index.htm [accessed: 27 February 2011].

US Securities and Exchange Commission (SEC) 2003. *SEC Settles Enforcement Proceedings against J.P. Morgan Chase and Citigroup.* [Online, Securities and Exchange Commission] Available at: http://www.sec.gov/news/press/2003-87.htm [accessed: 27 February 2011].

Usborne, S. 2005. Dr Dora, the scrouge of Nigeria's drug fakers, is honoured. *The Independent.* [Online, 9 December] Available at: http://www.independent.co.uk/news/world/africa/dr-dora-the-scourge-of-nigerias-drug-fakers-is-honoured-518700.html [accessed: 6 October 2011].

Vian, T. 2006. Corruption in hospital administration, in *Global Corruption Report 2006: Special Focus, Corruption and Health,* edited by Transparency International. London: Pluto Press, 49–52.

Viscusi, G. and Chassany, A.-S. 2008. Société Générale Reports EU4.9 Billion Trading Loss. *Bloomberg.* [Online, 24 January] Available at: http://www.bloomberg.com/apps/news?sid=a8GBEB7UuuXc&pid=newsarchive [accessed: 27 February 2011].

Vlasic, M. V. 2011. The search for Gaddafi's assets: How Libya and the Arab Spring have renewed the global fight against corruption. *The Huffington Post.* [Online, 9 August] Available at: http://www.huffingtonpost.com/mark-v-vlasic/gaddafi-asset-recovery-libya-arab-sring_b_954126.html [accessed: 14 November 2011].

Volcker, P., Goldstone, R. and Pieth, M. 2005. *The management of the United Nations Oil-For-Food Programme.* [Online: Independent Inquiry Committee] Available at: www.iic-offp.org/story27oct05.htm [accessed: 27 February 2011].

Wagle, S. and Shah, P. 2003. *Case Study 5 – Uganda: Participatory approaches in budgeting and public expenditure management.* [Online: World Bank Social Development Notes] Available at: http://siteresources.worldbank.org/INTPCENG/Resources/sdn74.pdf [accessed: 27 February 2011].

Warner, C. 2002. Creating a common market for fraud and corruption in the European Union: an institutional accident, or a deliberate strategy? *EUI Working Paper RSC No. 31.* San Domenico: European University Institute. [Online] Available at: www.iue.it/RSCAS/WP-Texts/02_31.pdf [accessed: 27 February 2011]

Warner, C. 2007. *The Best System Money Can Buy. Corruption in the European Union.* New York: Cornell University Press.

Water Integrity Network. 2010. *Expert consultation on water, corruption and climate change.* [Online] Available at: http://ecologic.eu/download/projekte/200-249/201-78_report_win.pdf [accessed: 28 February 2011].

Wearden, G. 2008. The biggest rogue traders in history. *The Guardian.* [Online, 24 January] Available at: www.guardian.co.uk/business/2008/jan/24/europeanbanks.banking [accessed: 27 February 2011].

Webb, P. 2005. The United Nations convention against corruption: global achievement or missed opportunity? *Journal of International Economic Law,* 8(1), 191–229.

Wehrlé, F. 2005. *Taking Responsibility for World Corruption: OECD Countries' Experience in Combating Bribery and Promoting Trade and Investment World-Wide. Investment Programme Working Group Meeting 'Open and Transparent Investment Policies'.* MENE-OECD Initiative on Governance and Investment for Development. [Online, 1–2 February] Available at: http://www.oecd.org/dataoecd/38/11/34448578.pdf [accessed: 19 October 2011].

Weiner, T. 2003. Ex-leader stole $100 million from Liberia, records show, *The New York Times.* [Online, 18 September] Available at: http://query.nytimes.com/gst/fullpage.html?res=9503E5D8153AF93BA2575AC0A9659C8B63&sec=&spon=&pagewanted=2 [accessed: 27 February 2011].

Wheeler, C. 2003. Drafting and implementing whistleblower protection laws, in *Controlling Corruption in Asia and the Pacific: Proceedings of the 4th Regional Anti-Corruption Conference,* edited by Asian Development Bank and Organisation for Economic Co-operation and Development Anti-Corruption Initiative for Asia-Pacific, 127–145. [Online] Available at: http://www.adb.org/Documents/Books/Controlling-Corruption/chapter5.pdf [accessed: 27 February 2011].

Willitts-King, B. and Harvey, P. 2005. *Managing the Risk of Corruption in Humanitarian Relief Operations. A Study for the UK Department for International Development.* [Online: Overseas Development Institute] Available at: www.odi.org.uk/HPG/papers/Corruption_DFID_disclaimer_added.pdf [accessed: 27 February 2011].

Willsher, K. 2011. Leila Trabelsi: The Lady Macbeth of Tunisia. *The Guardian.* [Online, 18 January] Available at: http://www.guardian.co.uk/world/2011/jan/18/leila-trabelsi-tunisia-lady-macbeth [accessed: 27 February 2011].

Wilson, A. 2008. Bernard Madoff: What is a Ponzi scheme and how does it work? *The Telegraph.* [Online, 15 December] Available at: http://www.telegraph.co.uk/finance/financetopics/bernard-madoff/3775923/Bernard-Madoff-What-is-a-Ponzi-scheme-and-how-does-it-work.html [accessed 27 February 2011].

Winnett, R. 2004. Saddam 'brought UN allies' with oil. *The Times*. [Online, 3 October] Available at: http://www.timesonline.co.uk/tol/news/world/article489742.ece [accessed: 27 February 2011].

World Bank 2004. *World Bank sanctions Acres International Limited*. [Online, 23 July] Available at: http://web.worldbank.org/WBSITE/EXTERNAL/NEWS/0 ,,contentMDK:20229958~menuPK:34463~pagePK:64003015~piPK:64003012~ theSitePK:4607,00.html [accessed 27 February 2011].

World Bank 2006. *World Bank sanctions Lahmeyer International for corrupt activities in bank-financed projects*. [Online, 6 November] Available at: http://web. worldbank.org/WBSITE/EXTERNAL/NEWS/0,,contentMDK:21116129~pag ePK:64257043~piPK:437376~theSitePK:4607,00.html [accessed: 27 February 2011].

World Bank. n.d.a. *The World Bank: About us*. [Online] Available at: http://web. worldbank.org/WBSITE/EXTERNAL/EXTABOUTUS/0,,pagePK:50004410~ piPK:36602~theSitePK:29708,00.html [accessed 25 February 2011].

World Bank n.d.b. *World Bank listing of ineligible firms and individuals*. [Online] Available at: http://web.worldbank.org/external/default/main?theSitePK= 84266&contentMDK=64069844&menuPK=116730&pagePK=64148989&pi PK=64148984 [accessed: 27 February 2011].

World Bank n.d.c. *Public expenditure tracking surveys*. [Online] Available at: http://web.worldbank.org/WBSITE/EXTERNAL/TOPICS/EXTSOCIAL DEVELOPMENT/EXTPCENG/0,,contentMDK:20507700~pagePK:148956~pi PK:216618~theSitePK:410306,00.html [accessed: 27 February 2011].

World Economic Forum 2005. *62 companies commit to a zero-tolerance policy to combat corruption and bribery*. [Online] Available at: www.weforum.org/ en/media/Latest%20Press%20Releases/PRESSRELEASES153 [accessed: 27 February 2011].

World Economic Forum. n.d. *World Economic Forum: Issues*. [Online] Available at: http://www.weforum.org/issues [accessed 25 February 2011].

World Health Organisation (WHO) 2006. *Fact sheet: Counterfeit medicines*. [Online 14 November] Available at: http://www.who.int/medicines/services/ counterfeit/impact/ImpactF_S/en/index.html [accessed: 27 February 2011].

World Health Organisation (WHO) 2010a. *Fact sheet No 275. Medicines: Counterfeit medicines*. [Online] Available at: http://www.who.int/mediacentre/ factsheets/fs275/en/index.html [accessed: 27 February 2011].

World Health Organisation (WHO) 2010b. *Fact sheet No 94: Malaria*. [Online] Available at: http://www.who.int/mediacentre/factsheets/fs094/ en/ [accessed: 27 February 2011].

Xin, X. and Rudel, T.K. 2004. The context for political corruption: A cross-national analysis. *Social Science Quarterly*, 85(2), 294–309.

Yuksel, C. 2008. Recent developments of corporate governance on the global economy and the new Turkish commercial draft law reforms. *Journal of International Commercial Law and Technology*, 3(2), 101–111.

Zinnbauer, D., Dobson, R. and Despota, K. (eds). 2009. *Global Corruption Report 2009. Corruption and the Private Sector*. Cambridge: University Press.

Index